Serbia under the Swastika

THE HISTORY OF MILITARY OCCUPATION

Edited by John Laband and Ian F W Beckett

A list of books in the series appears at the end of this book.

Serbia under the Swastika

A World War II Occupation

ALEXANDER PRUSIN

UNIVERSITY OF ILLINOIS PRESS
Urbana, Chicago, and Springfield

Manufactured in the United States of America
C 5 4 3 2 1
♾ This book is printed on acid-free paper.

Library of Congress Cataloging-in-Publication Data
Names: Prusin, Alexander Victor, author.
Title: Serbia under the swastika: a World War II occupation / Alexander Prusin.
Description: Urbana: University of Illinois Press, 2017. | Series: The history of military occupation
Identifiers: LCCN 2016049327 (print) | LCCN 2016050450 (ebook) | ISBN 9780252041068 (hardback) | ISBN 9780252099618 (e-book) | ISBN 9780252099618 (E-book)
Subjects: LCSH: Serbia—History—1918–1945. | Yugoslavia—History—Axis occupation, 1941–1945. | World War, 1939–1945—Serbia. | World War, 1939–1945—Underground movements—Serbia. | World War, 1939–1945—Collaborationists—Serbia. | Serbia—Politics and government—1918–1945. | Serbia—Social conditions—20th century. | Nazis—Serbia—History—20th century. | BISAC: HISTORY / Military / World War II. | HISTORY / Europe / Germany. | HISTORY / Europe / General.
Classification: LCC D802.S47 P78 2017 (print) | LCC D802.S47 (ebook) | DDC 940.53/4971—dc23
LC record available at https://lccn.loc.gov/2016049327

Contents

Biographical Note on Key Personalities

Aćimović, Milan (1898–1945)—chairman of the Council of Commissars (April–August 1941) and until November 1942 commissar (minister) of interior in the Government of National Salvation. Killed by Partisans in Bosnia.

Bader, Paul (1883–1971)—commander of the Sixty-Fifth Corps, Military Commander-in-Serbia in December 1941–August 1943.

Benzler, Felix (1891–1977)—plenipotentiary of the German Foreign Ministry in Serbia.

Böhme, Franz (1885–1947)—commander of the Eighteenth Corps, Military Commander-in-Serbia in October–December 1941. Committed suicide in May 1947.

Dankelmann, Heinrich (1887–1947)—Military Commander-in-Serbia in July–October 1941. Sentenced to death by a Yugoslav military court.

Jovanović, Dragomir-Dragi (1902–1946)—mayor of Belgrade and chief of the Serbian State Security. Executed by the Yugoslav authorities.

Ljotić, Dimitrije (1891–1945)—leader of the Zbor movement. Died in a car accident.

Meyszner, August (1886–1947)—Supreme SS-and-Police Commander (HSSPF) in Serbia, February 1942–March 1944. Sentenced to death by a Yugoslav military court.

Mihailović, Dragoljub-Draža (1893–1946)—leader of the nationalist Chetnik movement in Yugoslavia and commander of the armed forces of the Yugoslav government in exile. Executed by the Yugoslav authorities.

Nedić, Milan (1877–1946)—head of the Government of National Salvation, 1941–44. Committed suicide in prison.

Pečanac (Milovanović), Kosta (1879–1944)—commander of the "legal" (collaborationist) Chetniks in Serbia. Executed by the nationalist Chetniks.

Tito (Broz), Josip (1892–1980)—secretary general of the Communist Party of Yugoslavia and leader of the communist resistance. Premier (1945–53) and president (1953–80) of Yugoslavia.

Turner, Harald (1891–1947)—chief of the German civil administration in Serbia. Executed by the Yugoslav authorities.

Serbia under the Swastika

Introduction

On March 27, 1941, two days after Yugoslavia signed the Tripartite Pact, a group of officers in Belgrade toppled the regime of Prince Paul in a bloodless coup. The Reuter agency reported that "instantly after the coup became public, mass demonstrations erupted in Belgrade. National banners were hoisted and people hailed the king. The news of the coup spread like forest fire though the land. Huge crowds gathered at the palace of the Serbian Patriarch Gavrilo. . . . Strong military details guarded the Italian and German embassies to prevent incidents. A German tourist bureau was assaulted by stones."[1] The events in Belgrade detonated a sequence of auspicious and tragic events. Enraged that the coup upset his war plans, Hitler ordered that Yugoslavia be punished with "utmost brutality," and on April 6 the Axis armies crossed its borders. Ten days later Yugoslavia collapsed and was partitioned between Germany and its allies.

The historiography of the war in the Balkans is immense, and the appearance of yet another study requires some explanation. The most studied aspect of the war in Yugoslavia has been the guerrilla warfare, which has generated a number of excellent studies.[2] This book explores the effects of the war on Serbia, which until late 1941 was the hub of the anti-German resistance. Then the gravity of fighting shifted elsewhere, and for two years Serbia seemed to be Germany's deep hinterland, an area of "relative peace and quiet," marginal for the war in the Balkans.[3]

Consequently, with a few notable exceptions, the mechanisms of German occupation and native collaboration, and the activities of the resistance in 1942–44, have received only cursory treatment.[4] To date, most scholarship on these topics remains Serbian. A frequently quoted English-language monograph by Philip Cohen has all the appearances of serious scholarship, but under close scrutiny it fails to treat the topic objectively. Against the backdrop of the Yugoslav wars of the 1990s, Cohen artificially linked wartime collaboration in Serbia to nineteenth-century nationalism, with a clear implication that Serbs were ready to participate in the genocide of Jews without prodding by the Germans.[5]

This study, therefore, combines political with social history to explore the interaction between German occupation policies, the forces of resistance and collaboration, and the population at large. In particular, it focuses on several contentious or less explored issues. First, the April 1941 war was followed by a brief "sedate" period, when the population in Serbia initially consented to some form of social contract with the occupiers, delivering food supplies and performing labor services in exchange for relatively mild treatment. The country seemed ripe for political and economic integration into Hitler's New Order, augmenting Germany's capacity to fight the war against the Allies. However, Nazi rule in Serbia (as elsewhere in German-occupied Europe) was fraught with tensions between numerous German agencies, each aspiring to create its own bureaucratic fiefdom. Despite their rivalries, these agencies were impervious to cultural and national sensibilities in the country, where resistance to foreign domination had a centuries-long tradition. Consequently, confined to the rigid framework of ideological and racial prejudices, German officials relied more on coercion and terror, rejecting more imaginative and comprehensive methods when dealing with the native population. Constant instability in Serbia, therefore, was in many ways the outcome of Nazi policies, and the Wehrmacht's designs on maintaining Serbia as a safety zone in the Balkans came to naught. Although for a large part of the war the resistance in Serbia remained a sideshow to the fighting in Bosnia-Herzegovina and Croatia, it remained a constant menace to German communication lines, industrial sites, and to local civil offices and police stations.

Second, native collaboration in Serbia was driven by a gamut of ideological agendas and of complex reactions to the war. The German objectives in Serbia were to keep the country pacified so that its economic and manpower resources could be used most effectively. To implement these goals, the Wehrmacht could deploy only a relatively small number of German officials. As a result, while the Germans abolished existing state structures, manpower shortages forced them to seek support among certain segments of the population, which was tasked with collecting harvests, managing the native local offices and police stations, and organizing the labor force.

Native collaboration with the occupiers has become one of the most painful and contested issues in the Yugoslav historiography, which is heavily politicized.

The former members and the apologists of the collaborationist administration have explained its activities by a sole desire to spare Serbia from bloodshed, accusing the communist Partisans and the nationalist Chetniks of deliberately inciting the civil war and German reprisals.[6] This trend particularly gained momentum in the postcommunist era, whereby historical revisionism affected the current political debates over the full rehabilitation of Milan Nedić, the head of the collaborationist Government of National Salvation. For example, a 2011 monograph is dedicated to the members of the collaborationist armed forces, lamenting over their "hard fate."[7] Inevitably, revisionist authors pass over in silence the role of the collaborationist administration and police in the Nazi repressive system and in the genocide of Jews.

While most scholars concur that the quasi-fascist Zbor movement and its leader Dimitrije Ljotić aspired to emulate the German National Socialist model, they tend to treat Nedić more cautiously, portraying him as either a compliant bureaucrat bereft of any ideological convictions or a tragic figure who sacrificed himself to save Serbia from destruction.[8]

Contrary to such assertions, this book suggests that, albeit driven by different priorities and motivations than the Zbor, the Serbian collaborationist administration—first, the Council of Commissars and then Nedić's Government of National Salvation—fully subordinated themselves to Nazi ideological principles and policies and combated the regime's real and imaginary enemies with considerable zeal and ferocity.

Finally, as happened in many other European countries, German occupation served as a catalyst for the civil war, which was driven in part by conflicts internal to Serbia (and entire Yugoslavia) but which also became part of the wider international struggle among the forces of communism, fascism, nationalism, and liberalism.[9] Unlike Croatia, Bosnia-Herzegovina, and Kosovo, where opposing sides frequently identified one another along ethnic and confessional lines, Serbia's relative ethnic homogeneity entailed a bitter ideological split between Serbs of opposing political orientations. Initially, this war was fought between the forces of resistance and collaboration, but eventually it mutated into a brutal conflict between the two resistance forces—Partisans and the nationalist Chetniks.

The victory of the communists in 1945 entailed the emergence of the Partisan historiography, which portrayed the Partisans as the only resistance movement. Conversely, it has presented the Chetniks as a reactionary force, irreversibly bound to the Axis powers.[10] In turn, the pro-Chetnik publications depicted Partisans as political extremists and praised the Chetnik leader Dragoljub-Draža Mihailović as a hero and martyr, sacrificed by the Allies for political goals.[11] In 2004 the National Assembly of Serbia adopted a law according the Chetniks the status of full-fledged combatants, on the par with Partisans. The recent political rehabilitation of Mihailović seemingly justified the Chetnik collaboration with the Axis powers.[12]

Meanwhile, in the case of the Chetnik movement, the fine line between resistance and collaboration often became blurred or disappeared altogether. Partisans and the Chetniks aimed at liberating the country and warily cooperated at first, but because their ultimate goals were mutually exclusive, it proved impossible for them to forge a longtime alliance—the former aspired to turn the war into a socialist revolution, while the latter fought to protect and restore the prewar order. In autumn 1941, the growth of the communist resistance and increase of German reprisals in Serbia forced Mihailović to readjust his resistance plans in order to concentrate on fighting the communists. As a result, the so-called selective or tactical collaboration with the Axis powers (this frequently used term indicated that it was only temporary and limited in scope), effectively diverted most of the Chetnik manpower and energy from the anti-Axis resistance. In the end, the lack of imaginative ideological premises, loose organization, and the poor discipline of his troops eventually cost Mihailović a broader popular base. In contrast, the communists promoted an ideological doctrine that appealed to all ethnic and social groups, eventually achieving significant popular support at the expense of their rivals.

* * *

A few words about the terms, the sources, and the structure of this study are necessary. The Serbian language can be written both in Cyrillic and Latin alphabets, and in this book all Serbian titles are transliterated into the latter. The spelling of personal and geographical names is retained except for those with commonly recognized English spellings—for example, Belgrade instead of Beograd, Chetnik instead of Četnik, Ustasha instead of Ustaše, and Peter II instead of Petar II.

Serbia's geographical borders have changed several times in modern times. An independent kingdom since 1878, it acquired most of Kosovo and Macedonia after the Balkan Wars of 1912–13. In the interwar period, Serbia did not exist as a separate administrative unit but became a part of the Kingdom of Serbs, Croats, and Slovenians (SCS), where the pre–World War I historical divisions were replaced with thirty-three administrative *oblasts* (provinces), each having the population of no more than 800,000 people.[13] Renamed the Kingdom of Yugoslavia in 1929, the country was restructured into the *banovina* system, which was based on administrative rather than ethnic criteria.

Hence, depending on the context, here the term *Serbia* denotes either the pre–World War I Serbia or Serbia proper within the SCS and Yugoslavia (map 1). After the German invasion of Yugoslavia in 1941, Serbia was placed under the rule of the Military Commander-in-Serbia (Militärbefehlshaber-in-Serbien, MBS), whose jurisdiction also included the western (Serbian) Banat (map 2). The office of the Military Commander-in-Serbia changed its names several times, but since its functions remained essentially the same, the term MBS is used throughout this study.

The archival research for this book was undertaken in four institutions. The Yad Vashem Museum in Jerusalem and the National Archives in Washington, D.C., hold multiple collections pertinent to German occupation policies and to antiguerrilla warfare in Yugoslavia. The U.S. Holocaust Memorial Museum in Washington possesses files on the investigation of Nazi crimes by the Yugoslav War Crimes State Commission and a valuable collection of the documents produced by the Serbian collaborationist administration and police forces. The Historical Archive of Belgrade (Isorijski arhiv Beograda) has preserved a large number of documents pertaining to the activities of the German Security Police and the collaborationist Special Police. Vadim Altskan generously provided me with the files of the Military Historical Archive (Arhiv Vojnoistorijskog Instituta) in Belgrade, which contains records on German antiguerrilla operations and on war crimes trials held in Yugoslavia after the war. Regrettably, most microfilmed archival materials from Yugoslavia lack page numbers, and many have no titles. In such cases, I have cited them in the following order: collection name, a title corresponding to document contents, and available provenance.

Despite the fact that the communist historiography looks past some important conceptual issues, it offers a great deal of factual material on the topic. In combination with archival sources and the more recent scholarship, it renders a relatively accurate reconstruction of facts and events. Here it has been given preference over the pro-Chetnik, pro-collaborationist, or revisionist authors, who do not flinch from their outright distortion of facts.

Due to the relative paucity and the general character of existing English-language sources on wartime Serbia, the framework of this study is predominantly narrative and thematic. Chapter 1 provides a brief survey of the interwar period, highlighting specific socioeconomic and political factors that partially shaped the forces of collaboration and resistance. Chapter 2 examines the German invasion and the occupation system imposed on Serbia in April 1941. This initial phase of the war was critical because Yugoslavia collapsed almost overnight and the government fled the country, leaving the population leaderless. The situation propelled to the foreground individuals and groups who decided or were forced by circumstances to collaborate with the occupiers. Chapter 3 focuses on relations between the German military and civil offices and the collaborationist administration. The latter functioned within the narrow confines prescribed by German rule, but it eventually evolved into a coercive authoritarian regime. Accordingly, chapter 4 deals with the ethos of collaborationism, or "direct" collaboration, which involved the close replication of Nazi ideological postulates.

Chapter 5 examines the emergence, composition, and activities of the two resistance movements—the Chetniks and Partisans—and the complexity of their relationship. The Chetniks considered themselves part of the Yugoslav Royal Army and saw their primary objective in preserving the old political and social order. Equally determined, the Partisans wanted to destroy the old order and build a new one modeled after the Soviet regime in Russia. After a short period of cooperation, this divergence of interests prompted the Chetniks and Partisans to embark on a course of mutual destruction.

Chapter 6 examines German terror policies, which initially were directed against political opponents and Jews but eventually engulfed Serbian civilians. The murder of Jews was a key component of these policies, partially fulfilling reprisal quotas and simultaneously serving to implement the Final Solution in Serbia. Chapter 7 describes "quiet Serbia" in 1942–44, when the multilayered civil war further polarized Serbian society and to some extent overshadowed the war of liberation against the Germans. Due to determined leadership and internal cohesion, Partisans were able to recover after the defeat of 1941 and were prepared to seize power at the opportune moment. In contrast, the Chetniks' attempts to maintain a precarious balance between resistance and collaboration ultimately proved disastrous.

Chapter 8 centers on native collaboration in the Holocaust and popular attitudes toward the persecution of the Jews. While Germany's crusade against Judeo-Bolshevism coalesced with the ideological aspirations of the right-wing Zbor movement, the collaborationist administration utilized Nazi persecution of Jews for its own political and ideological reasons. Finally, chapter 9 attempts to explore the life of the "silent majority"—the population at large—which on a daily basis endured economic shortages, requisitions, and the constant threat of violence.

* * *

A number of individuals provided me with invaluable help. Milan Koljanin, Milan Ristović, Emil Kerenji, Alexander Korb, Jovan Byford, and Mirjam Rajner illuminated many complex issues in the history of the war and occupation in the Balkans. Slobodan Mandić, Irena Kolaj, Dragana Mitrašinović, and Snežana Lazić of the Belgrade Historical Archive patiently tolerated my limited Serbian and helped me find the most pertinent sources. Headed by Jonathan Zimmerman, the staff of the John Skin Library of New Mexico Tech obtained for me all secondary sources. Inevitably, I owe gratitude to my longtime friend and research companion, Vadim Altskan, without whose help this book would have been impossible. Also, I thank two anonymous readers of the manuscript for their helpful comments and suggestions.

1 Background, 1918–1941

On December 1, 1918, the dreams of the nineteenth-century romantic nationalists seemingly came true as the Kingdom of Serbs, Croats, and Slovenians (SCS) appeared on the map of the Balkans. The SCS brought together the Serbs, Croats, Slovenes, Montenegrins, Macedonians, the Muslims of Bosnia-Herzegovina and Kosovo, and smaller ethnic groups under the scepter of the Serbian Karadjordjević dynasty. A member of the Entente during the Great War, Serbia had lost a fifth of its population to combat, foreign occupation, hunger, and epidemics. Therefore, the Serbian political and military establishment felt that the "Serbian" outlook of the new state was fair compensation for war sacrifices, and they were apprehensive about the national ambitions of the non-Serbs, particularly the Croats and Slovenes who had fought on the side of the Central Powers. Conversely, Croatian and Slovene statesmen envisioned the SCS as a federation of equal administrative units free to exercise their cultural distinctiveness and political traditions, and they felt increasingly uneasy about the pronounced Serbian dominance in state politics. As a result of these conflicting expectations, the entire history of the SCS (renamed the Kingdom of Yugoslavia in 1929) was marred by political and ethnic dissent, compounded by serious economic problems.

Society, Economy, Politics

In 1921 on June 28, the date celebrated by the Serbs as the anniversary of the Kosovo battle, the SCS received a constitution guaranteeing basic civil rights to all citizens but providing the king with most executive powers and severely limiting the jurisdiction of the Skupština (parliament) and the regional gov-

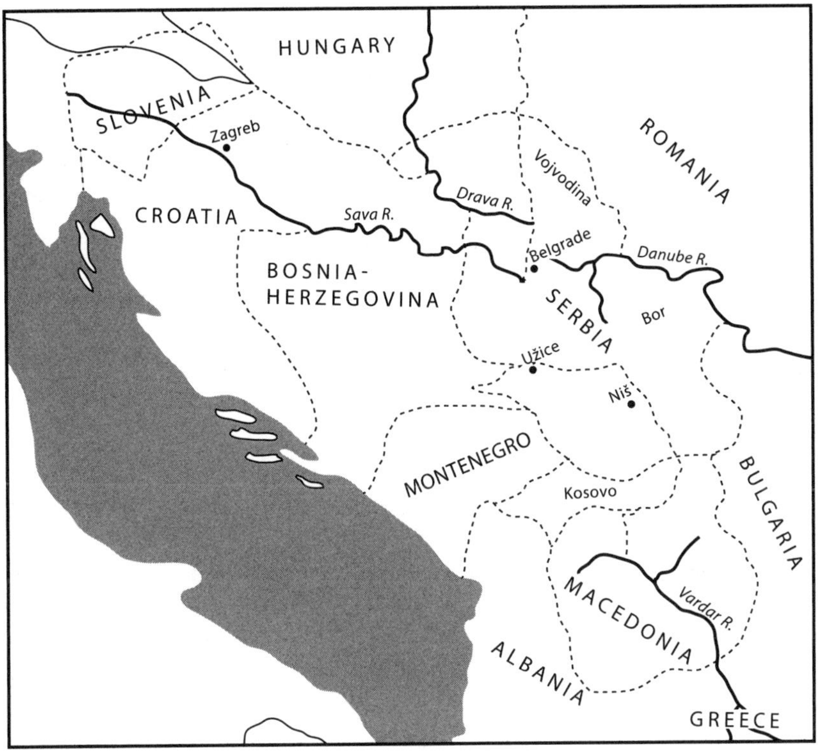

Map 1. Yugoslavia in 1939

ernments.[1] The SCS emerged as a centralized unitary state and clearly favored the Serbs albeit there were several prominent non-Serbs in government (e.g., Croat Ante Trumbić, who was the foreign minister in the SCS first government, and Slovene Anton Korošec, who held the offices of prime minister and minister of the interior and foreign affairs). Similarly, former officers of the Austro-Hungarian and Montenegrin armies were passed over by their Serbian counterparts, who dominated the SCS officer corps. Still, the real power remained in the hands of the royal court, which was backed by the army, the Serbian Orthodox Church, and monarchist organizations.[2]

This situation reflected convictions among the Serbs of various political persuasions that they deserved to dominate SCS politics as a reward for war sacrifices. In fact, the preservation of Serbian dominance assumed a form of national obsession as the Serbian administration falsified censuses, struck and broke alliances with other national groups, and intimidated voters. Bribery and corruption became inseparable from politics, and criticism of the government was effectively stifled or silenced by force. Naturally, such policies ran counter to the vision of Yugoslavism as the alliance of the South Slavs in the form of federation, aspired to by Croatian or Slovenian national activists.[3]

One of the poorest and least industrialized states in Europe, the SCS was made up of the Austro-Hungarian, Serbian, and Montenegro provinces, some of which had little or no mutual trade. Serbia's ethnic composition and economy reflected the "classic" patterns of the Eastern European landscape. While it was more homogeneous than Bosnia or Macedonia, in 1921 approximately 350,000 people (12.2 percent) of the 2,855,000 total were non-Serbs and included Romanians, Albanians, Bulgarians, and Germans. It was a smallholding peasant society—79 percent of Serbia's population in 1921 made their living by agriculture. By the late 1930s, the population grew to 4,200,000, but the region's social profile remained unchanged—in 1940, 75 percent of the labor force was engaged in agricultural work.[4] In comparison to the former Austro-Hungarian provinces, Serbia was industrializing slowly—in 1938 it had only 718 plants and factories, whereas Croatia had 1,181, Slovenia 912, and Vojvodina 818. In addition, the bulk of Serbia's industries were small. For example, each of 240 industrial enterprises in Belgrade employed a hundred workers and predominantly produced textiles and agricultural implements. Although up to 40 percent of the SCS heavy industries, such as the Bor mining region, were located in Serbia, their full development began in the second half of the 1930s and was hindered by the Great Depression.[5]

In addition, severe war damages—by 1918 the country had lost about 700,000 cattle, 70,000 horses, 3 million sheep and goats, and 800,000 pigs—undermined Serbia's economic potential, while the limited amount of arable land resulted in increased population density in the areas suitable for agriculture. Accordingly, most peasants owned plots of between 2 and 5 hectares and borrowed money at a high interest rate that further exacerbated their plight. By the late 1920s they had to give up, on average, three-quarters of their income to pay off debts. In 1924 a peasant family's annual income was 24,500 dinars; it dropped to 16,300 dinars in 1927 and to 7,125 dinars in 1933. While military and police expenditures soared, agricultural programs such as technical training received insignificant state subsidies.[6]

Given this situation, Serbia's political dominance on one hand and economic deficiency on the other hand fueled the resentment of the Croats and Slovenians, who saw the Serbs as the sole beneficiaries of the existing order. They increasingly despised the "Belgrade clique," which wielded undue power and influence while lacking necessary educational and economic prerequisites for such a task. Croat nationalism represented the key internal challenge to the government and tensions flared up in Skupština, where the leader of the Croatian Peasant Party (Hrvatska seljačka stranka, HSS) Stjepan

Radić joined forces with other disaffected political groups to counter Serbian domination. Political and national conflicts climaxed on June 28, 1928, when an extremist (the leader of a Chetnik association) shot five members of the HSS, including Radić. To fight the regime, in 1929 the right-wing Croatian nationalists formed a clandestine organization Ustasha (insurrection), whose ideology was the conflation of Roman Catholicism, exclusionary nationalism, and fascism. The Ustasha aimed at achieving Croatian independence at any cost, including terrorism and violence, and sought assistance from Italy and Hungary.[7]

In order to allow time for passions to subside, in January 1929 King Alexander suspended the constitution and dissolved the Skupština. The free press was shut down, political dissenters were arrested, and the country was renamed Yugoslavia, with the implication that the king's personal rule ushered in a time of national unity. The country was divided into nine administrative units—*banovina*—whose borders were drawn specifically to eliminate traditional historical entities and regional loyalties. Still, due to political manipulation, six *banovina* appeared to have a Serbian majority.[8] Alexander ruled directly for two years, but eventually he decided that forging a Yugoslav identity from above was an impossible proposition. In September 1931 he introduced a new constitution that established an ostensibly constitutional monarchy that looked more acceptable than his personal dictatorship. To signify a broad national consensus, Alexander called for the creation of the Yugoslav National Party (Jugoslovenska narodna stranka), which was to stand above political and ethnic disparities; a bicameral parliament was also made responsible directly to him. Although the new electoral laws made it difficult for other parties to enter the parliament, the king's authoritarian rule nevertheless restored a semblance of order and tranquility. However, on October 10, 1934, while on a state visit to France, Alexander was assassinated by a Macedonian extremist hired by the Ustasha.[9]

Alexander's death distressed most Serbs, who saw him as the guarantor of peace and stability. The strings of power passed to the king's brother, Prince Paul, who ruled as regent until the maturity of the young Peter II. Although initially Paul was determined to preserve the status quo, he realized that the country was weary of authoritarian rule and so inaugurated relaxed policies. Political parties resumed their activities, some political prisoners were amnestied, electoral process recommenced, and a new government was formed under the finance minister, Milan Stojadinović. A skillful politician, Stojadinović managed to win support of the leading Slovene and Bosnian-Muslim politicians. To mitigate the growing internal dissent, he formed the Yugoslav Radical Alliance (Jugoslovenska radicalna zajednica, JRZ), which like the Camp of National Unity (OZON) in Poland nurtured greater centralizing aspirations and acted as a single pro-government block. In 1938 the JRZ won the national elections.[10]

* * *

The interwar period produced several political currents, which would crystalize into the forces of resistance and collaboration during the Second World War. The majority of Serbs tended to hold conservative political views. Although many grew increasingly uneasy or disaffected with the kingdom of Yugoslavia, the Serbian communities in Croatia, Slovenia, Bosnia, and Kosovo were concerned that any unrest would leave them stranded among unfriendly neighbors. The monarchy, therefore, seemed to offer the only assurance of security and stability; most Serbs, particularly in the countryside, considered radical changes potentially detrimental and wished to keep things as they were. Accordingly, the majority cast their votes for the centrist-conservative National Radical Party (Narodna radicalna stranka) and the Democratic Party (Demokratska stranka). Headed by its most prominent leader, Nikola Pašić, the Radicals were considered the Great Serbian Party, promoting Serbia's dominance, the primacy of the state, and the cultural assimilation of non-Serbs. Backed by the bureaucracy, the army, and the middle class, it remained the best-organized political association of the interwar period. The Democrats promoted a single Yugoslav nation made up of the Serbs, Croats, and Slovenes, and they supported state centralism as the vehicle to eradicate differences between the three nations. Between January 1921 and December 1922, the Democrats joined the Radicals in a coalition government. The Agrarian Party (Savez zemljoradnika, later Zemljoradnička stranka) was also predominantly Serbian in its political outlook; its ideological platform combined agrarian socialism, reliance on monarchy, and corporatism.[11]

The Radicals and the Democrats provided ideological guidelines for the Chetnik associations, by far the most numerous of all monarchist groups and societies. The name *chetnik* derives from *četa* (guerrilla bands), which fought against the Ottomans and operated behind enemy lines in the Balkan Wars of 1912–13 and in World War I. The Chetnik associations functioned as a Yugoslav royalist force; the peasant activists (priests, teachers, and the rural intelligentsia) constituted the backbone of the Chetnik leadership. Priding themselves on their martial traditions and distinguished by the symbol of the white eagle in the cockades, the Chetniks were staunchly monarchist and anticommunist, and they professed to defend the existing political order. Central to the Chetnik ideological platform were two concepts—"integral Yugoslavism" and extreme Serbian nationalism—whereby the former stipulated the union of all South Slav people under the monarchy, and the latter envisioned the Great Serbia, the idea penned by the Serbian politician Ilija Garašanin in the mid-nineteenth century. In his *Načertanije* (Memorandum), Garašanin dreamed of the liberation of all South Slavs from foreign domination and their unification under Serbia's dominance. Such aspirations were acted upon during the 1912–13 Balkan Wars, when Serbia claimed "historic" rights to Macedonia and temporarily held possession of Albania's Adriatic littoral. In December 1914, after the successes of the Serbian army against Austro-Hungary, the Skupština issued the so-called Niš declaration (after the Austro-Hungarian invasion, the state institutions evacuated to Niš), which stipulated the creation of the Serbia-dominated South Slav state after the war. Similarly, a few days later, Prince Regent Alexander appealed to the Serbian army, promising that victory in the war would entail the creation of the Great Serbia.[12]

In 1937 some faculty members of Belgrade University, the Orthodox clergy, and reserve officers founded the Serbian Cultural Club, which pledged to protect Serbian national interests against the encroachment of non-Serbs and to preserve the "Serbian character" of Vojvodina, Bosnia, Kosovo, and Macedonia. Eventually, the club's leading members became the ideological spokesmen for Chetnik associations.[13]

Although political extremism in the SCS was a marginal phenomenon, the Russian revolution and the postwar economic and political instability led to the emergence of several radical organizations. In April 1919 a splinter group of the Social Democratic Party formed the Socialist Workers' Party of Yugoslavia (of Communists) (Socijalistička radnička partija Jugoslavije [komunista]). In 1920 it was renamed the Communist Party of Yugoslavia (Komunistička partija Jugoslavije, KPJ) and became the mouthpiece of the Communist International (Comintern), preaching world revolution. The party propaganda found receptive ears among the POWs returning from Russia, Austria, and Hungary and its internationalism attracted high school and university students, who joined the communist youth organization (Savez komunističke omladine Jugoslavije, SKOJ) and provided the KPJ with several prominent members. The KPJ made a particular effort to increase its popularity at Belgrade University, which evolved into a hotbed of communist agitation. At the peak of its popularity in November 1920, the KPJ claimed fifty thousand members and obtained impressive results in provincial elections, particularly in the economically underdeveloped Macedonia and Montenegro, winning fifty-nine seats (out of 419) in the Skupština.[14]

The KPJ success, however, was short-lived. Its antistate agitation and terrorist activities (its members carried out the assassination of the minister of interior, Milorad Drasković), compelled the government in August 1921 to pass the Law of the Protection of Public Security and Order, which accorded the police wide latitude in apprehending and detaining suspected subversives. The KPJ was banned, but it continued to operate clandestinely, using other leftist parties as the facade and gaining valuable experience in underground activities. Promoting the principle of self-determination and rejecting national divisions, the KPJ gained popularity in Croatia, Macedonia, and Kosovo. In Serbia, however, its propaganda found much less appeal, which the party leadership ascribed to the fact that, as a privileged national group, the Serbs were less susceptible to communist appeals. As a result, the KPJ did not establish a provincial branch in Serbia, as it had in Croatia, Macedonia, and Slovenia.[15] To make matters worse, in the late 1920s the KPJ was ripped apart by the internal struggle between the "Moscow" group, which acted on behalf of Comintern, and the "native" faction, which advocated the adjustment of the party activities to the national and confessional specifics of Yugoslavia. In addition, the police crackdown resulted in mass arrests of the party activists, and in April 1929 police agents murdered the KPJ's first secretary, Đuro Đaković.[16]

Political relaxation under the regency allowed the KPJ to reemerge from obscurity. According to the instructions of Comintern, the party stepped up a propaganda campaign against fascist Italy and Nazi Germany, which eventually mutated into vicious attacks against "imperialist" Western democracies and the "bourgeois" Yugoslav state. In fact, promoting the destruction of Yugoslavia, the communists effectively pursued the same goal as the Ustasha.[17] In August 1937, Josip Broz (Tito) was elected general secretary of the KPJ. A dedicated communist and a skillful leader, Tito realized that the main cause for the party's weakness in Serbia was its narrow social base, since most communists were workers and the urban intelligentsia. Under his leadership, the KPJ reorganized its decimated cells, began to expand into the countryside, and abandoned the idea of destroying the Yugoslav state, instead aspiring to a federalist solution to the country's national question.[18]

The KPJ was shocked by the Soviet-German nonaggression pact of August 1939, but a prominent communist, Vladimir Dedijer, recalled that the party accepted it "like disciplined communists, considering it necessary for the security of the Soviet Union."[19] Consequently, the KPJ duly ceased its propaganda against Italy and Germany, promoting instead Yugoslavia's nonintervention into the "imperialist" war in Europe. Still, the party prepared for a revolutionary situation or a crisis that would propel it to the forestage of national politics. It organized secret courses where students learned military tactics and clandestine activities, based on the experiences of the Russian and Spanish Civil Wars. In 1940 Tito proposed to the Comintern a plan to overthrow the government and to establish the "people's power" on the Soviet model. Moscow rejected the plan, but the KPJ leadership did not abandon the idea of socialist revolution, patiently waiting for an opportune moment.[20]

By the outbreak of the Soviet-German War, the KPJ had eight thousand members, augmented by 2,000 party candidates and 9,400 SKOJ members. The party's small size was compensated for by its discipline and the nucleus of highly dedicated revolutionaries, among them Tito, Alexander Ranković, Edvard Kardelj, Ivo Lola Ribar, and Milovan Djilas.[21]

As with communism, fascism found little appeal in Yugoslavia, but from the mid-1930s some small groups adopted fascist rhetoric, symbols, and ideological postulates. Like their counterparts in Romania and Bulgaria, Serbian right-wing groups blended fascism, nationalism, Christianity, and monarchism.[22] The assassination of King Alexander facilitated the fusion of these groups into a single organization. On January 6, 1935, they formed the Yugoslav National Movement (Jugoslavenski narodni pokret), Zbor (lit., assembly or rally), with Dimitrije Ljotić as chairman of its provisional committee. Born in the family of a Serbian diplomat, Ljotić was deeply religious and spent time in France as a student, where he was mesmerized by the ideology of Charles Maurras, who rejected parliamentary rule. After having fought in World War I, Ljotić entered civil service and briefly, from February to September 1931, was minister of justice. In that capacity he proposed to King Alexander that Yugoslavia be transformed into a corporatist state, in which the parliament deputies would be selected from professional, social, and cultural associations rather than from political parties. After the king rejected the proposal, Ljotić resigned—an indication that he found the royal dictatorship too liberal.[23]

Probably from that point on, Ljotić became determined that Yugoslavia's "degeneration" could be arrested only by the establishment of a regime similar to those in Germany and Italy (and, naturally, headed by the Zbor). Although Ljotić referred to the Zbor as a Yugoslav rather than as a Serbian movement, his Yugoslavism had a definite Great Serbian connotation, and he envisioned Serbia as the political core of the future corporate state. Critical of the government, Ljotić remained a dedicated monarchist, advocating absolute loyalty to the king, whom he considered the only force capable of holding Yugoslavia together.[24]

Zbor's religiosity displayed closer affinity to the Slovak Hlinka Party and the Romanian Iron Guard than to the German National Socialist Party. With the latter Ljotić shared virulent anti-Semitism, which combined religious and racial components.[25] Since religion and national identity in Serbia were deeply intertwined, Ljotić defined the nation as steeped in the "Christian spirit" and national traditions. Forces representing democracy, multiculturalism, and secularism—such as Jews, the Masons, communists, and liberals—were to be removed from the new national community. Between 1935 and 1938 the Zbor organized a touring exhibition that disseminated anticommunist and anti-Semitic messages around the country. Zbor's extremist ideology garnered little popular support but found receptive ears among nationalistically inclined university and school students, who were organized into the youth organization Young Eagles modeled on the Hitlerjugend (Hitler Youth). Importantly, some members of the Orthodox clergy, including one of its dominant personalities Bishop Nikolaj Velimirović, shared Ljotic's anticommunism and anti-Semitism; a number of officers and civil servants also tacitly backed the movement.[26]

Because of its narrow popular base—at its peak the Zbor had six thousand members—it remained on the margins of Yugoslavia's political life. In the national elections in 1935 and 1938 it received less than 1 percent of votes, which effectively ended its bid for power in the Skupština. Having decided that "going to the masses" was no longer expedient, Ljotić focused on turning the Zbor into a crack force in the fight against communism. In 1936–38 the Zbor activists trained in military tactics, organized rallies, and clashed with the communist demonstrations. Appalled at the *Sporazum* (see the next section on this 1939 agreement), Ljotić sent a memorandum to Regent Paul, advocating the abolition of Croatian autonomy and reorganizing the army along national lines, whereby the Croats and Slovenes would serve predominantly in labor units. In the atmosphere of heated international tensions, Zbor increasingly appeared as a pro-German "fifth column," and in October 1940 the government officially disbanded the organization. Ljotić was temporarily placed under house arrest.[27]

In accordance with the Minority Treaty, which the SCS government signed in 1919, all ethnic minorities of the new state were guaranteed civil and political rights. Ethnic Germans in Serbia and Banat had their own schools, publishing facilities, and numerous professional, cultural, and athletic associations. They also had their own political party—the Party of the Germans—which participated in national elections. While many Germans remained aloof to Nazi ideology, the party found a number of adherents among German youths. The Nazi office of the Hauptamt Volksdeutsche Mittelstelle (Main Welfare Office for Ethnic Germans), which supervised the activities of the ethnic-German organizations in Europe, used the Kulturbund organization in Banat as the transmitter of National Socialist ideals, and some members of the organization carried out espionage for the German intelligence services. In March 1941 the royal police arrested several leaders of Belgrade's Kulturbund and its youth organizations but released them after the German government interceded.[28]

In the Shadow of War

Notwithstanding internal tensions in Yugoslavia, it would be simplistic to ascribe its problems solely to the conflicts between the Serbs and other national groups. Indeed, the country's internal situation was intertwined with external policies, and the government was aware that ethnic conflicts could be exploited by Yugoslavia's revisionist neighbors.[29]

In the 1930s the Yugoslav government found itself in an increasingly difficult situation, threatened by Italian and German expansionism. The Yugoslav military repeatedly informed the government that in the event of military conflict, Yugoslavia stood no chance without external aid. On the background of Western appeasement policies, reliance on Great Britain and France (the latter was the architect of the Little Entente, the military-political alliance that included Czechoslovakia, Romania, and Yugoslavia) proved increasingly illusory.[30] In fact, the British prime minister Neville Chamberlain blatantly admitted that the League of Nations could not protect the "little" states from foreign aggression.[31]

Appointed finance minister in 1934 and prime minister and minister of foreign affairs in 1935, Milan Stojadinović managed to mitigate the effects of the Great Depression by expanding state financing of the industrial sector and by granting tax concessions to industrial enterprises and state credits to peasant cooperatives. Stojadinović understood that the economy and politics were closely linked and that it would be natural if Yugoslavia's economic partners were political allies, as well. The country's foreign trade and commercial relations gravitated toward the Axis powers, which relied heavily on raw materials and agricultural products from the Balkans. In 1937 Yugoslavia and Italy signed a commercial and economic treaty, although this did not mitigate Mussolini's ambitions in acquiring Dalmatia. Accordingly, closer relations with Germany seemed a potential counterbalance against the revisionist aspirations of Italy and Hungary (the latter claimed Vojvodina). In 1933 about 13 percent of Yugoslav exports and imports came from Germany, rising in 1938–39 to 50 percent.[32]

Economic ties with Germany and Italy and concerns over German and Italian territorial aspirations translated into changes of political course. When in March 1936 German troops occupied the Rhine demilitarized zone, the Yugoslav government opposed sanctions against Germany; in December

1937 the German-Yugoslav agreement stipulated the cooperation of the two countries in combating communism. On behalf of Yugoslavia, the agreement was signed by the mayor of Belgrade, Milan Aćimović, and the chief of the royal police, Dragi Jovanović (during the war, both would play crucial roles in the Serbian collaborationist administration). In a meeting in January 1938, Stojadinović promised Hitler that under no circumstances would Yugoslavia enter an anti-German alliance. In March of the same year, the Yugoslav government consented to the *Anschluss* (Germany's annexation of Austria) as a solely "German affair."[33]

By 1938 all members of the Little Entente were firmly within the German economic and political orbit. Yugoslavia's economic obligations toward Germany took precedence so that in September 1940 the Yugoslavian government caved under pressure from Berlin and canceled its deliveries to other countries. The currency exchange rate also favored Germany—in October 1940 the ratio between the German mark and the Yugoslav dinar changed from 1:14.8 to 1:17.82.[34]

Economic dependency was accompanied by political gestures, and Stojadinović adapted fascist trappings such as the so-called *Hitlergruß* (Hitler salute) and green shirts for members of the JRZ. The Italian foreign minister, Galeazzo Ciano, duly noticed Stojadinović's authoritarian style and recorded in his diary that, if not technically a fascist, Stojadinović was "certainly [one] by virtue of his conception of authority, of the state, and of life."[35] Still, Stojadinović was not a true fascist in the political sense, but rather an opportunist who tried to maneuver between the two predatory powers.

While Stojadinović's policies temporarily satisfied Hitler and Mussolini, his openly pro-Axis leanings, dictatorial inclinations, and unwillingness to find a solution for the Croatian question led to his downfall. In February 1939, Prince Paul replaced him with Dragiša Cvetković. As a result, Mussolini resumed his aggressive policies toward Yugoslavia. Yugoslav statesmen wanted Yugoslavia to remain neutral, but they could not ignore the rapidly changing international situation, desperately hoping that it would somehow dissipate without affecting their country's sovereignty. But the *Anschluss* and particularly Hitler's occupation of Czechoslovakia in March 1939 made it abundantly clear that Yugoslavia could not count on Western powers. A complete political and economic reorientation on the Axis powers appeared as the sole reasonable course, particularly as Mussolini indicated that he was willing to discuss the Italian-Yugoslav division of Albania.[36]

In this political atmosphere Prince Paul authorized Cvetković to seek accommodation with the strongest party of opposition—the HSS. In August 1939 the two sides signed the *Sporazum*, an agreement that accorded Croatia the status of autonomous *banovina* with its own parliament, taxation system, and education system. A new government was formed with Cvetković as prime minister and the HSS leader Vladko Maček as his deputy. Similar to the *Ausgleich*, which in 1867 made the Habsburg monarchy into a dual Austro-Hungarian state, the *Sporazum* was an emergency measure in the face of the imminent European conflict, generating largely negative reactions. The Serbian communities in Croatia, Slovenia, Bosnia, and Kosovo felt that the *Sporazum* endangered their status as the privileged national group, whereas Montenegrin, Macedonian, and Slovenian political activists were upset that Croatia alone received a privileged status.[37]

* * *

A week after the *Sporazum* was signed, World War II broke out. In a series of *Blitzkrieg* offensives, the Wehrmacht swept through Poland and Western Europe and in June 1940 France collapsed under German onslaught. Hopes of Yugoslav statesmen that a long war in the West would divert Hitler's attention in the east proved vain. Belgrade, therefore, was perforce to reconsider Yugoslavia's place in German-dominated Europe. Robust on paper, the Yugoslav army stood no chance against the Wehrmacht and much less against the combined Axis forces. In 1939 the government of Cvetković spent 10.5 billion dinars on armament, more than in the four previous years combined, but most Yugoslav armored cars and tanks were of old vintage. Modern antitank artillery and communication equipment were limited in numbers.[38]

Following the October 1940 Italian invasion of Greece, the Minister of War General Milan Nedić sent a memorandum to Prince Paul, admitting that the situation was critical and observing that Yugoslavia had two options: abandon neutrality and side with the Axis powers, or seek an alliance with the Soviet Union (USSR), declare mobilization, and join the Greeks. In the latter case, Yugoslavia would have to fight not just Germany and Italy but also Hungary, Romania, and Bulgaria, which since the end of World War I held territorial aspirations toward its neighbor. Similarly pessimistic was the chief of the general staff, General Petar Kosić, who predicted that, should Yugoslavia oppose the Axis powers, it would face a "new Kosovo battle and martyrdom."[39]

Meanwhile, Hitler contemplated the idea of turning Europe into a German-dominated single economic and political unit, with the Balkans as its southeastern wing. To this effect, in November 1940 Hungary, Romania, and Bulgaria and in February 1941 Slovakia joined Germany, Italy, and Japan in the Tripartite Pact. In this situation, Yugoslavia increasingly appeared to be standing alone, surrounded by hostile neighbors. Although the British were in no position to help, they tried to convince Belgrade not to bend under Berlin's pressure. Weighing all the possibilities, Regent Paul and Cvetković concluded that the only chance to avoid war was to negotiate with Hitler. Paul and his closest associates also feared that war could provoke revolutionary chaos and detonate internal ethnic conflicts. On March 25, 1941, Yugoslavia joined the Tripartite Pact. On paper, its provisions were quite generous—not only did Hitler and Mussolini promise to uphold the country's sovereignty, but, unlike Romania and Bulgaria, Yugoslavia had neither to assist the other signatories nor to consent to the passage of the Axis troops through its territory. During a meeting with Prince Paul, Hitler also implied that Yugoslavia might receive access to Thessaloniki. Still, with the sense of crisis clearly in the air, three Yugoslav cabinet ministers resigned.[40]

In retrospect, the pact accorded Yugoslavia a temporary reprieve from entering the European conflict, and the country obtained advantageous concessions without committing a single soldier. Whether Germany and Italy would honor the pact to the letter was a different matter, but on the background of traditional anti-German attitudes, the regency symbolized the country's shame and humiliation. In addition, Prince Paul did not enjoy popularity among the officer corps. He was a sybarite who seemed lukewarm to national traditions (in 1939 he did not attend the 550-year anniversary celebration of the Kosovo Battle), and average Serbs held him responsible for the *Sporazum*.[41]

Accordingly, once the pact was made public, Serbia erupted in mass protests and demonstrations. With hopes for Western help still alive, the nationalist organizations and the intellectual and economic circles felt that the pact tarnished the country's reputation in British and U.S. eyes. In Belgrade and many other places, cheering crowds took to the streets, chanting "better war than the pact," while the communist, labor, and leftist organizations demonstrated under the slogan "Long live an alliance with the Soviet Union!" blissfully ignoring the fact that the USSR and Germany were allies. The police and gendarmerie did not intervene, and Patriarch Gavrilo Dožić further fueled public emotions, announcing that the nation had but two options—"living in sanctity and freedom [or] if facing death, dying for sanctity and freedom as did the millions of the Orthodox ancestors." A young member of the Serbian Cultural Club enthusiastically called this show of national pride as the "brightest day" in his life.[42]

Accordingly, when on March 27, 1941, a group of officers led by an air force general, Dušan Simović, deposed Prince Paul and the government of Cvetković, the coup was greeted throughout Serbia as an expression of popular will. Political rivalries were temporarily forgotten as members of all political parties, with the exception of the Zbor, took part in anti-pact rallies. Gripped by emotions, most Serbs barely understood the potential implications, particularly as rumors and hopes for Western and Soviet help temporarily overrode creeping fears of war.[43]

In the meantime, desperate to avoid or at least postpone war, the plotters tried to convince Berlin that the coup was an internal affair and in no way affected Yugoslavia's obligations in foreign policy. Simović even turned to the leaders of the ethnic German community in Banat, asking them to convince Berlin that Yugoslavia would stand by its obligations as stipulated by the Tripartite Pact.[44] In the growing atmosphere of foreboding, Simović and his colleagues tried half measures, hoping not to provoke Hitler. Since Yugoslav diplomats and spies repeatedly reported of Germany's military preparations against Yugoslavia, Simović decided to put the army on alert but did not dare order general mobilization until April 3. On the same day, the government declared Belgrade, Zagreb, and Ljubljana "free cities"—a clear sign of resignation to Hitler's violent reaction.[45]

In such an atmosphere, positive signals from Moscow were received as a godsend solution for Yugoslavia's predicament. Yugoslavia did not have diplomatic relations with the USSR, and only in May 1940 had the two countries signed a trade agreement, which was followed the next month by mutual diplomatic recognition. When on March 29, 1941, the Soviet embassy in Belgrade indicated that the USSR was ready to sign an agreement with Yugoslavia and offer military assistance, Simović brushed off traditional fears of communism and grasped the Soviet proposal as the last resort to avoid confrontation with Germany. On April 5 the Soviet-Yugoslav treaty of friendship and nonaggression was signed in Moscow and implied potential Soviet aid to Yugoslavia. However, while Stalin was relying on the treaty to indicate to Berlin the Soviets' strategic interests in the Balkans, he did not want to antagonize his German ally. Hence, the Soviet military intervention in Yugoslavia was out of the question.[46]

* * *

In the creation of the post–World War I order, the SCS and its successor Yugoslavia faced a difficult task of mending and integrating regions of different economic capacities and political experiences into a centralized administrative system. In the 1930s, internal problems were exacerbated by international tensions, and the Yugoslav government desperately tried to maintain neutrality in Europe, which was now divided into two hostile camps. The Italian invasion of Albania in April 1939 and Greece in October 1940 indicated that such a policy was no longer possible. Against a background of Germany's victory over France, Yugoslav statesmen and generals realized that their state was woefully unprepared to fight the Axis. Consequently, the March 1941 coup seemed an utter blunder, based on wishful thinking and emotions rather than on a realistic appreciation of the country's limited economic and military potential. In this context, one can certainly argue that, had Yugoslavia adhered to the Tripartite Pact, it might have survived the war relatively unscathed (as did Slovakia and Bulgaria), albeit at the price of national humiliation. As it happened, the coup effectively put the country on a collision course with the most powerful military machine in Europe.

2 Invasion and Occupation

Until March 1941, Hitler considered Yugoslavia a friendly state and on occasion even expressed admiration for Serbia's tenacious resistance against Ottoman domination. Consequently, on receiving the news of the March coup, he was infuriated by Belgrade's "betrayal" and the prospect of a prolonged Balkan campaign, which could hinder his preparations for the invasion of the Soviet Union. Also, on March 26 the Japanese prime minister Yōsuke Matsuoka arrived in Berlin, and the news from Belgrade must have spoiled Hitler's festive mood. Hence, he ignored the assurances of the German council in Belgrade, Viktor von Heeren, who argued that the coup was but an internal squabble within Belgrade's political elite and any aggressive action against Yugoslavia was unnecessary. On the afternoon of March 27, Hitler ordered that as an "uncertain factor" in the impending campaign in Greece and the operation Barbarossa, Yugoslavia must be "punished with inexorable severity."[1]

The German general staff, which since January 1941 had been preparing an invasion of Greece, hastily drew up a plan for invasion, in which nineteen German divisions would play the decisive role. Twenty-two Italian divisions were concentrated to attack Slovenia and Dalmatia, whereas the Hungarian troops were to strike at Vojvodina. All in all, seven hundred thousand German, Italian, and Hungarian troops, supported by 1,500 aircraft, were poised to destroy Yugoslavia in a *Blitzkrieg* campaign.

Operation Strafgericht

Code-named Strafgericht (retribution), the invasion of Yugoslavia began on the morning of April 6, 1941. Belgrade endured a vicious bombardment as 350 German planes descended on the city in waves. The air assault continued for two days. In addition to strategic places such as the main railroad station, German planes targeted residential areas, strafing streets and houses with machine guns and killing and injuring hundreds of people. Altogether 900 tons of explosives were dropped on the capital. Human losses were estimated between 2,270 and 4,000; the numbers of wounded were much higher. More than 700 buildings and houses were destroyed and 1,588 were heavily damaged, including the main power station and the central water pump; 50 percent of the downtown was destroyed. When the National Library took a direct hit, 350,000 books, 500,000 journals, and many historical manuscripts went up in flames.[2]

Bombs also struck hospitals and schools, which caught fire or collapsed. One bomb hit the Church of Assumption, killing and maiming members of a wedding party. The effects of the bombing campaign were even more devastating because April 6 was a Sunday, when the city markets were full of people. The German military attaché in Belgrade, Colonel Rudolf Toussaint, recorded that the assault caught many residents still asleep and the "air-attack inflicted particularly heavy casualties; psychological impact was enormous. . . . People, whose homes were destroyed, ran distractedly through the streets, exacerbating panic." Masses of refugees streamed out of the city.[3]

Armed with small-caliber guns, Yugoslav antiaircraft forces proved utterly ineffective. The Royal Yugoslav Air Force could field 459 planes, most of them outdated, while the Luftwaffe alone committed almost a thousand aircraft. Stationed near Belgrade, a royal air force regiment had forty-three planes, and its pilots fought bravely, shooting down ten German aircraft, but were overwhelmed by hundreds of enemy fighters.[4] On April 11–12 the Luftwaffe subjected the capital to another severe attack. Other cities were also bombed; nine hundred people were killed and wounded in Niš.[5]

The air assault was followed by a rapid offensive by Axis land forces, fully mobilized and well-equipped German and Italian divisions. On paper, the Yugoslav army had a fair chance: it had thirty divisions and nine brigades (about 800,000 men), roughly equal to the strength of the enemy. In reality, however, it was woefully unprepared to fight a modern war; only eleven divisions were at full strength.[6]

As a result, the *Blitzkrieg* shocked everyone who remembered the fighting prowess of the Serbian army in 1914–15, when it stood up against combined German, Austro-Hungarian, and Bulgarian forces. In sharp contrast to such a heroic past, the Royal Yugoslav Army collapsed within a matter of days. While some units stood their ground, such valor only accentuated the prevailing atmosphere of panic and demoralization. The German propaganda detachments disseminated leaflets that appealed to the Croat and Slovene units to stop fighting for "Serbian chauvinism and English interests." Many soldiers dropped their weapons and went home. On April 10, 1941, in Zagreb, the nationalist Ustasha organization proclaimed the creation of the independent Croatian state (Nezavisna Država Hrvatska, NDH). The Albanian separatists in Kosovo and Metohija and ethnic Germans in Banat and northern Serbia carried out sabotage acts in the rear of the Yugoslav army and provided intelligence for advancing Italian and German troops.[7]

Exaggerated rumors of a "fifth column" led to arrests of individuals who merely looked suspicious. Even decades later, this aspect of the region's history played out in the collective memory. Directed by Aleksandar Petrović, the 1963 Yugoslav film *Three* opens with a scene of an army patrol seizing an alleged subversive at a rail station. The suspect's guilt is determined solely by the facts that he has a burr and a camera. Edged on by a scared and frenzied crowd, the patrol shoots the man and tosses his body into a ditch. In April 1941, such scenes were common, and a contemporary recalled that treason seemed to be everywhere, committed by "'fifth columnists,' Croats, ethnic Germans, and Russian émigrés."[8]

While the activities of German agents and provocateurs contributed to spreading panic, the Yugoslav high command lost control of its units as soon as the war began. Glaring signs of chaos and disorganization were everywhere. Half a million reservists were called up, but many had to travel on foot to their units, only to find that the areas had already been occupied by the enemy. Many infantrymen were registered as artillery personnel, while gunners were placed in supply details. Others were dispatched to their positions when the war was already over. Fear of the enemy overwhelmed entire regiments and divisions, which fled or surrendered. An entire army group abandoned Skopje on the second day of the war. Roads were clogged with thousands of soldiers and officers who dropped their arms, exchanged uniforms for civilian attire, and ran home.[9]

Civilians followed the example of the army, mingling with the military personnel and jamming the roads, which were bombed and strafed by Axis dive-bombers with impunity. Resentment toward the ruling elite frequently overrode all other emotions, especially as many state officials fled their posts before the enemy troops arrived. Left to its own devices, the local population broke into stores and warehouses, robbing the most precious commodities in wartime—bread, salt, fuel, and matches. In some places the Germans opened prisons and photographed or filmed inmates plundering stores and shops.[10]

Some units and town garrisons surrendered to small German motorcycle detachments or to a single German patrol without firing a shot. On April 12, the Belgrade garrison laid down arms and Mayor Ivan Miličević formally surrendered the city to the Germans. Three days later, the Yugoslav government fled the country, leaving the population to its fate, and on April 17 the army capitulated. Thousands of soldiers and civilians were killed and wounded, and three hundred thousand soldiers and officers became prisoners of war. The Wehrmacht lost fewer than two hundred men.[11]

Strafgericht, the code name of the invasion and its ferocity, reflected Hitler's intention to punish Yugoslavia, effectively setting precedence for German warfare in the Balkans. Relentless terror would soon become the trademark of the Wehrmacht's anti-insurgency operations, which entailed inflicting such a high degree of physical and psychological damage as to make any resistance impossible.

* * *

In late April, the German state secretary Ernst von Weizsäcker recorded in his diary that German policies were designed to ensure that none of the Balkan states could get along with its neighbors.[12] To achieve this goal, Hitler was determined to destroy Yugoslavia, but he had no long-term plans for it except that the entire Balkan region would constitute a unit within Germany's "continental economic space" (*Grossraumwirtschaft*). On April 12 he issued "temporary instructions" that erased the state of Yugoslavia from the map of Europe. Eager to embark on Operation Barbarossa, Hitler was content to leave most of the territorial spoils within Italy's zone of influence. Mussolini thus acquired Dalmatia, the Adriatic Islands, Montenegro, Kosovo, and western Macedonia. Slovenia was split largely between Italy and Germany, with Hungary given northern Vojvodina. The NDH emerged as an Axis satellite, divided into the Italian and German control zones and consisting of Croatia, Bosnia, and Herzegovina. Although the Ustasha claimed these territories as "historical" Croatian lands, two million Serbs constituted 30 percent of the NDH population. Hence, the Ustasha leadership was determined to create an ethnically pure Greater Croatia by forcibly removing the Serbs, Jews, and the Roma.[13] Although the NDH lost Dalmatia and much of Adriatic coast to Italy—a fact deeply resented by many Croats—it was recognized as part of the Axis alliance and received a semiformal recognition by the Vatican. The Ustasha regime enjoyed almost unlimited freedom in internal policies and could, therefore, consider its status as the first step toward full independence in German-dominated Europe.[14]

Hitler also rewarded his ally Bulgaria, which received the bulk of Macedonia and the Pirot and Vranje districts in southeastern Serbia, over which Serbia and Bulgaria had quarreled since medieval times. Bulgaria thus became the largest Balkan state.[15] Hitler's generosity, however, had its limits, for Germany retained exclusive rights to raw materials in southeastern Serbia, and Bulgaria had to refund Berlin for all financial debts accrued by this area before the war. The presence of the Bulgarian troops in Serbia also facilitated the subsequent reduction of the German forces, whose bulk was transferred to Poland.[16]

Serbia ostensibly fared the worst among the former provinces of Yugoslavia, as its status reflected Hitler's thirst for revenge against the so-called Belgrade clique. It was reduced to its 1912 borders. Along with the northern counties of the Kosovo region (Kosovska Mitrovica) and the western (Serbian) Banat, it was placed under direct rule of the Military Commander-in-Serbia (Militärbefehlshaber-in-Serbien, MBS), who exercised full legislative, executive, and judicial powers. Under closer scrutiny, however, Serbia was at least marginally better off than Slovenia and Macedonia. The Italian-occupied part of Slovenia was subjected to a forcible assimilation campaign to subsume the region into the Italian state. Similarly, marked for integration into the Third Reich, German-occupied Slovenia was to be "cleansed" of the native population. Berlin prepared plans for the mass resettlement of Slovenes to Croatia and the German administration closed Slovene schools, libraries, and associations. Most Slovene Catholic Church property was taken over by German organizations and firms, which also appropriated Slovene industrial enterprises and private businesses.[17]

Similarly, the Bulgarian government planned for the assimilation of occupied provinces into Greater Bulgaria. To this effect, Bulgarian propaganda referred to Macedonia as a "liberated territory," while southeastern Serbia was termed the "western borderlands"—an indication that its final status would be determined later. Regardless of the terminology, the Bulgarian exarchate of Sofia claimed jurisdiction over the Serbian churches in the Pirot and Vranje districts. All Serbian legal, educational, and cultural institutions were abolished, Serbian national holidays and dress were banned, and national monuments and markers were removed or destroyed.[18] The Serbian language was banned, and Serbs were forced to change their names in accordance with Bulgarian grammatical and stylistic systems. Serbian teachers were purged, and those willing to retain their positions had to take crash Bulgarian language courses. The police arrested those who refused to declare themselves "Bulgarians" and mobilized Serbian youths into the Bulgarian army and labor battalions, generating a wave of escapees to Serbia proper. Soon Bulgarian rule provoked so much resentment that in May a group of prominent Serbs appealed to the collaborationist administration in

Map 2. Serbia under occupation

Serbia to use its influence to transfer southeastern Serbia to the jurisdiction of MBS.[19]

In Banat, the situation of ethnic Serbs also deteriorated rapidly. Hitler initially contemplated turning this principal agricultural area into an autonomous German enclave and using it as a bargaining chip with Hungary and Romania, which both claimed it. In the end, Hitler subordinated Banat to the MBS office as a special administrative unit with a population of 640,000 people (including 295,000 Serbs and 120,000 Germans).[20] The Nazi ethnic hierarchy placed the Banat Germans a grade below the Reich Germans. Still, they received a privileged status, filling positions within the administration, police, and the school system. German cultural, educational, and medical facilities mushroomed, replacing Serbian ones. Serbs and Jews lost their basic rights, their property was subjected to sequestration or confiscation, and the police launched mass arrests of Serbian political activists and other individuals considered unreliable.[21]

In contrast, albeit the terms of occupation of Serbia proper were tinged with vengeance, strategic and economic considerations temporarily prevailed over Nazi ideological and racial sentiments. Yugoslavia did not feature in Hitler's plans for a "living space" (*Lebensraum*) in Eastern Europe. In contrast to Poland (and later the Soviet Union), where the mass murder of racially "inferior" groups was considered crucial for German expansion, the Serbs were not slated for physical extermination although the Nazi leadership considered them traitorous and prone to "erratic" behavior. For example, an MBS propaganda department emphasized that "the Serb is a born plotter and conspirator, infatuated with underhanded actions. The task of a future governing body is to keep the population on the short leash, for the Serb sees any expression of good will and good nature as weakness, which he would immediately use for his benefit."[22]

Similarly, in May, the Sixtieth Infantry Division reported that "brigandage is not unusual in the Balkans and could not be eradicated completely even in peacetime. After the [April] war, the bands are enhanced by adventurists, stray elements, and others, who have nothing to lose."[23]

Although many German officials and officers, especially of Austrian background, viewed Serbs as implacable foes, they nonetheless recognized them as a distinct ethnic group, so there was no attempt to "Germanize" Serbia, at least not yet. In addition, as harsh as direct military rule was intended to be, Serbia's situation was not exceptional. Hitler placed occupied Belgium and northern France under German military rule, despite those regions' closer cultural values with Germany. After the Balkan campaign, Greece was also placed under the German military administration. The German military and political leadership were predominantly interested in Serbia's strategic position as the crossroads between Austria and Greece. Preoccupied with preparing to invade the Soviet Union, Hitler considered the Balkans the supply-and-transit base for German operations in the Mediterranean and North Africa. The Zagreb-Belgrade-Salonika and the Niš-Sofia railroads and the Danube shipping lines were also crucial for transporting troops and agricultural supplies. Serbia's deposits of nonferrous metals such as zinc, lead, and copper were essential for Germany's war effort, and as the threat of the Allied invasion increased as the war continued, such considerations would take precedence over ideological ones.[24]

System of Power

A prominent scholar observes that "nowhere in German-occupied Europe was the occupation system more confusing than in Serbia."[25] Indeed, German rule in Serbia closely replicated the Nazi system of power, in which the intent to dominate frequently superseded the practicality of governance. After each conquest, Hitler ordered what he thought as the most fitting form of rule over a subjugated country, leaving practical matters to the local administration. Subsequently, Serbia became an experimental battlefield for multiple German offices, which rarely came to a uniform policy and constantly bickered over their priorities and influence. Different interests and ambitions, therefore, became the cornerstone of German occupation.[26]

The two-tier MBS structure reflected ongoing rivalries and overlapping jurisdictions of several offices. The *Kommandostab* (command staff) supervised the army units stationed in Serbia and was responsible for maintaining order, guarding communication lines, and delivering foodstuffs to Germany, whereas the *Verwaltungsstab* (administrative staff) was empowered to deal with the civilian population and to supervise all areas of public life. The *Verwaltungsstab* chief Harald Turner was an experienced administrator who had previously served in the military administration in Paris. Turner was directly subordinated to the Military Commander-in-Serbia, but as an SS-*Brigadeführer* (since September 1941 SS-*Gruppenführer*) he liaised between MBS and the SS and police forces. Since in this capacity he was answerable to Himmler, his Wehrmacht superiors viewed him as an SS upstart and regarded him with suspicion.[27]

The MBS was simultaneously answerable to the Wehrmacht High Command (Oberkommando der Wehrmacht, OKW) and from June 1941 to the Southeast Command (Wehrmachtbefehlshaber in Südosten), which oversaw the activities of all German forces in the Balkans. After the April war, the combat divisions, which participated in the invasion of Yugoslavia, were transferred to the Operation Barbarossa, and the MBS had to rely on its own units, which consisted of four territorial battalions (*Landesschützen*), the Order Police, and the Secret Field Police (GFP). To beef up MBS strength, in early June three infantry divisions subordinated to the commander of the Sixty-Fifth Corps under General Paul Bader were transferred to Serbia for garrison duties. Bader, however, was subordinated not to the MBS but to the Twelfth Army Command, stationed in Greece. As a result of this Byzantine structure, the OKW, the Southeast Command, and the Twelfth Army Command could intervene in MBS affairs or circumvent the MBS. In addition, the first three military commanders in Serbia—Helmuth Förster, Ludwig Schröder, and Heinrich Dankelmann—were the Luftwaffe generals, and consequently, the OKW and the Southeast Command viewed them as Herman Goering's proxies.[28]

For more effective control of Serbia, the *Kommandostab* preserved the old administrative system, whereby the country was divided into the three *banovinas* (Morava, Dunava, and Drina) and the city of Belgrade, all subordinated to the field-commandant offices (*Feldkommandaturen*); further down the chain of command were the *Kreiskommandaturen* in the districts and the *Ortskommandaturen* in the counties.[29] Responsible for security in their respective localities, the commandants often conflicted with the *Verwaltungsstab* officials, who supervised the taxation system and the Serbian courts. Similarly, in collecting food supplies, the commandants competed with the commanders of Bader's divisions.[30]

From the outset, the MBS authority was also challenged by several other offices, each claiming different degrees of autonomy or independence. Joachim von Ribbentrop's Ministry of Foreign Affairs set up its office in Belgrade, which dealt with Germany's quarrelsome allies—Hungary, Romania, Bulgaria, and Croatia. The office chief Felix Benzler could contact Berlin at his own discretion without informing the MBS.[31] In accordance with Hitler's decree of April 13, all economic matters in the Balkans were subordinated to Hermann Goering as the Reich plenipotentiary for the Five-Year Plan. In Belgrade, Goering was represented by Franz Neuhausen, who was considered an expert on the Balkans and assumed the title of General-Plenipotentiary for the Serbian Economy. Neuhausen had to coordinate his activities with the MBS, but as Goering's emissary he wielded almost unlimited power in his domain. In turn, the Southeast Command had its own economic office (*Wehrwirtschaftsstab Südost*) that supplied the German troops in the Balkans and could act without consulting Neuhausen.[32]

The Nazi terror apparatus was represented by three agencies; the GFP was responsible for the troops' security and screened POWs and political detainees. In cases of sabotage or political activities, it arrested and handed over the suspects to military courts-martial and imposed penalties on the civilian population through the offices of the military commandants. With more sinister reputations were the *Einsatzgruppe* Serbia and its subordinate *Einsatzkommando* Belgrade, which were hastily formed after the March coup and dispatched to Yugoslavia in the wake of the Wehrmacht. Headed respectively by Nazi Party veteran Wilhelm Fuchs and Karl Kraus, a police expert on Yugoslavia, the two units had about 120 functionaries and structurally replicated the Main Reich Security Office (RSHA), whereby the Security Service (Sicherheitsdienst, SD) and the Security Police (Sicherheitspolizei, Sipo) played the most important role in the Nazi terror system. After arriving in Belgrade, Fuchs and Kraus set up their headquarters in the building of the Serbian Ministry of Justice, where their subordinates came into possession of the archives containing the registries and data on Serbian political activists. On April 12, the Gestapo chief of the RSHA Heinrich Müller ordered the arrests of the intelligentsia who were inimical to Germany's interests. As a result, the Sipo (the population commonly called it "Gestapo") seized a number of Jews and individuals listed as "terrorists, émigrés, and saboteurs," including the patriarch of the Serbian Orthodox Church, Gavrilo Dožić.[33] Due to their small number, the Sipo and the SD heavily relied on the military intelligence (*Abwehr*), the Secret Field Police, and the native police apparatus. In Banat, the SD and Sipo functionaries supervised the ethnic German auxiliary police and its prisons. In Niš and Šabac, they collaborated with the military commandants in setting up the first concentrations camps for political activists and Jewish refugees from Germany and Hungary.[34]

* * *

According to the Hague Convention of 1907, the concept of *occupatio bellica* sanctioned military occupation as a form of governance with minimal intervention in the lives of the populace. However, the Nazi leadership had routinely ignored the international conventions and applied different ideological, racial, and economic criteria to run the German-occupied countries. In 1940 a prominent SS theoretician and a member of the German Academy of Law, Werner Best, introduced a concept of the "national arrangement of an [occupied] territory" that entailed the utilization of the economies and manpower of the subjugated territories, with minimal effort and spending on the part of Germany. To this effect, he proposed four ways of governing the occupied territories: "informal" or associative occupation such as in Denmark, where the native high- and mid-level administration functioned under control of the German foreign ministry; the "supervisory" model in the Netherlands and Belgium, where German officials ruled through the middle-level native civil services; and the so-called "ruling" occupation in the Protectorate, in which the native civil service and police were completely subordinated to the respective German offices. All these methods of governance were predicated on the employment of the native pro-German civil and police services, which enjoyed a limited degree of internal autonomy. In contrast, the so-called colonial rule was dominant in Poland and Ukraine, where the Germans made up the bulk of the bureaucratic apparatus, while the native administration and the police forces acted merely as cogs of the occupational regime.[35]

These classifications remained imprecise and changed shape or frequently overlapped in the course of the war. In Serbia, therefore, German rule appeared as the mixture of the "ruling" and colonial models. It began with the application of the *debellatio* or *debellationis* principle (neither term was used in official correspondence), which entailed the total eradication of all vestiges of Serbia's sovereignty. On April 12, 1941, the OKW chief Walther von Brauchitsch issued a proclamation defining the conditions of Serbia's occupation. The death penalty was imposed for acts of resistance and sabotage; demonstrations, strikes, lockouts, work stoppages, and public meetings were forbidden. The population had to surrender all arms and radio transmitters and was prohibited from assisting Serbian soldiers or civilians trying to evade captivity. Communicating news "injurious" to the German forces was banned, which meant that only the German-controlled press was allowed to function.[36]

After Yugoslavia's capitulation, further restrictions unequivocally relegated Serbia to an appendage within the German political-economic space in the Balkans. The royal ministries were abolished, foreign embassies and consulates were closed (exemptions were made for an Italian diplomatic attaché, the Vichy consulate, and the NDH office in the northern Belgrade suburb of Zemun), and all political parties were banned. Yugoslav citizenship was canceled, and Serbia's residents were treated merely as "state-protected subjects"—*Schutzangehörige*. German law took precedence over Yugoslav law, and Serbs became subject to German military courts before they were familiar with new legal limitations, while the introduction of the Nuremberg Laws deprived the Jews and the Roma of basic civil rights.[37] The mail, communication, and transportation systems were placed under the supervision of the appropriate German offices. Printing and mimeographing equipment was registered, strict censorship was imposed on all publications, and publishing facilities had to apply for licenses. According to a special order, even letter-carrying pigeons had to be slaughtered.[38]

The beginnings of German rule in Serbia were ominous. Although the German troops received orders to behave in a "correct manner," in several localities they robbed stores, loading themselves with photo cameras, jewelry, cloth, and groceries.[39] The military commandant of Zemun reported numerous instances of plunder, robbery, and rape committed by the military personnel.[40]

Such instances of "wild" robberies soon gave way to a more systematic and organized plunder, which became the staple of German occupation. Although article 47 of the Hague Convention (to which Germany was a signatory) forbade pillage of occupied territories, the Wehrmacht's interpretation of the convention was quite flexible, and a system of ruthless economic exploitation was set in motion to achieve the most effective utilization of Serbia's economic potential.

In accordance with the terms of the April armistice, the MBS took control over the matériel of the Yugoslav army and Serbia's main industries, which were collected as war trophies, including 14,165 metric tons of pig iron and steel, 7,020 metric tons of blister copper, 1,957 metric tons of pig lead, and 12,170 metric tons of chrome ore. The Wehrmacht claimed the exclusive use of the country's shipping industries, while the OKW economic department started dismantling more than forty industries. Between April and July, hundreds of trainloads of raw materials, textiles, and industrial plants were sent to Germany.[41] The British-owned Trepča mines were confiscated as enemy property, while the French shares in the mines were appropriated to defray the cost of occupation owed to Germany by the Vichy government.[42]

In addition to the approximately 700 million marks, which the Wehrmacht seized, Serbia had to pay for "war damages" and for the cost of occupation at inflated rates. These included troops' billeting, construction, and repair of roads and railways, and other services. Upon the devaluation of the Yugoslav dinar—from a 1939 ratio of 1:4.2 in relationship to the German mark, it fell to a 1:20 ratio in 1941—the amount to be paid increased accordingly. In April the occupation cost was estimated at 6.5 million marks monthly; in the fall it rose to 15 million marks; and in December 1943 it reached the record of 100 million marks (in 1944, 1 mark was worth 250 dinar), providing the German personnel with opportunity to buy rare commodities at far below their real value.[43] By mid-July 1942, the Serbian payments amounted to 2,670 million dinar (133 million marks). Due to ever-increasing inflation (50 percent more than in Croatia) and taxation, the cost of occupation in Serbia was six times per capita higher than levied on Croatia, by far surpassing the national revenue of Serbia.[44]

To control Serbia's finances, in June 1941 the MBS created the Serbian National Bank, which functioned as a stock company. The bank was responsible for buying and selling bonds commissioned by the Serbian administration, but the value of the bonds was dictated by Neuhausen's office.[45] The Wehrmacht also seized 467 million British and 716.2 million French stocks and bonds; the former were confiscated as enemy property, while the latter became part of the French war reparations. After Germany declared war on the United States, 294 million U.S. stocks were also confiscated.[46]

The MBS office calculated that the country's agricultural output would suffice to provide supplies to the German troops in Serbia and Greece and to maintain the population at a subsistence level. Accordingly, the MBS and the Southeast Command retained for their own use a significant amount of seized food supplies—20,121 metric tons—and in summer 1941 the Serbian administration reported the first instances of food shortages. The situation was exacerbated by the fact that in the interwar period Banat and Vojvodina were Serbia's main suppliers of agricultural products. Banat's economy, however, was used exclusively for the supplies to Germany and to German troops in the Balkans. By mid-July 1941 the Banat administration had sent to Germany 35,000 metric tons of foodstuffs. In the fall the export quotas were raised to 200,000 metric tons wheat, 100,000 metric tons corn, and up to 40,000 metric tons sunflower seeds, while all private commerce and trade between Serbia and Banat were banned.[47]

Twenty-seven private German firms arrived in Serbia to claim their share as compensation for "war damages." They were particularly zealous to take control over the Bor copper mines, which were among the largest in Europe, but also oil, metal, and timber enterprises and copper and antimony industries. In the Bulgarian-occupied zone, they supervised chrome industries. In the course of the war, Serbia's copper would supply about 16 percent of Germany's need for the metal; Serbia and Bulgaria together provided Germany with more than 50 percent of its chrome, antimony, and asbestos exports.[48]

The special commando subordinated to the head of the Nazi ideological and educational research Alfred Rosenberg swept through archives and museums, confiscating precious manuscripts and artifacts as well as diplomatic and other documents from state archives. From Belgrade University alone, the Germans sent to the Reich or destroyed 228 Cyrillic, 227 Latin, and 1,400 Turkish manuscripts.[49]

* * *

The invasion of Yugoslavia fulfilled Hitler's vision of the *Blitzkrieg*—a short, victorious conflict, after which the subjugated nation lay prostrate to augment Germany's economic capacity to fight against the Allies. In Serbia the defeat resonated most audibly and the outburst of national pride and popular enthusiasm of the March coup evaporated without trace. The ineptness of the

Yugoslav army facilitated Germany's image as an invincible military power and seemingly extinguished popular will to resistance.

The April war appeared to have vindicated German ad hoc preparations for the occupation of Yugoslavia. Other than exploiting chance opportunities, German rule in Serbia was characterized by the lack of clear vision about its future status. Obsessed with the preparation for the war against the Soviet Union, Hitler relegated Serbia to a source depot of food supplies and raw materials within the Third Reich's political-economic space. As a hinterland for the German forces in the Balkans, Serbia became a "state of emergency," whereby the system of governing was simplified to the direct chain of command from top to bottom for the purpose of fulfilling specific tasks. Within this structure, the MBS received general instructions from Hitler and the OKW, but it was free to choose any methods for carrying them out. Importantly, the German leadership hoped that such a situation could be maintained through a minimum involvement of the German armed forces. Bader's divisions were severely undermanned—each was made up of two regiments (a regular division had three regiments)—and manned by inadequately equipped and older personnel. All in all, the German forces in Serbia numbered twenty-five thousand officers and soldiers. In a country populated by four million people and known for its military traditions, such numbers were far from adequate, reflecting the conviction among the German command that the country was fully pacified.[50] But for a short time in spring 1941, such convictions seemed realistic.

3 Germans and Auxiliaries

Upon the termination of hostilities, the MBS office set out to exploit Serbia's available resources. To this end, it needed to restore communication lines and transport, to reactivate industries, and to collect food supplies. Given its limited manpower, the MBS was forced to rely on controllable native institutions, which would mediate the relationship between the occupiers and the occupied. Although the state of Yugoslavia was formally abolished, the Nazi racial and ideological considerations were temporarily sidelined in favor of administrative expedience, and German officials began looking for suitable individuals to re-create the native civil and police services.

In late April 1941, the MBS announced the creation of the so-called Council of Commissars in Belgrade. Denied any vestiges of autonomy, it was treated merely as a branch of the occupation system. Similarly, the council's successor—the Government of National Salvation—needed explicit German consent in all its activities. Both institutions obtained the support of a large portion of the former administrative and police apparatus, but the German offices constantly intervened in the functioning of the collaborationist administration. According to Benzler, rivalries between different German offices made the functioning of the Serbian administration extremely difficult.[1] Hence, in order to understand the dynamics of collaboration in Serbia, it is imperative to place it within the context of German rule.

Council of Commissars

To fulfill positions in the native administration, the MBS and the German security functionaries had considered several personalities. They would prefer Milan Stojadinović, but before the war he had been interned by the

Yugoslav government, which later handed him over to the British. Ljotić appeared to be an obvious choice, but the Zbor's political marginality and its spiritual affinity to National Socialism deprived it of meaningful popular support. In addition, Hitler was suspicious of the nationalist aspirations of European fascists, preferring personalities who enjoyed some popularity and simultaneously were pliable to German demands, such as Philipe Pétain.[2]

Several potential candidates turned down the German offer to participate in the native administration. For example, the former foreign minister Aleksandar Cincar-Marković refused on the grounds of poor health. Others, such as the last Yugoslav prime minister, Dragiša Cvetković, were suspected of Masonic connections and pro-British leanings. In addition, the Sipo agents informed their superiors that because Cvetković's ancestors were of the Roma stock, such "racial impurity" made him unacceptable.[3]

Finally, on April 27, 1941, the MBS General Förster approved the formation of the native administration, which contained no leftovers from the prewar cabinet, indicating a total break with the past. The Council of Commissars (Savet komesara) was made up of ten individuals of different political affiliations who shared a crucial common trait—all were known for anticommunist or pro-German leanings and were willing to do the Germans' bidding. Stojadinović's associate Milan Aćimović, who had a reputation of an avid Germanophile, became the council chairman and the commissar of interior. In the interwar period, Aćimović served as the deputy chief of the Belgrade city police. In that capacity, in 1936 he was appointed deputy to the Interpol chairman Reinhardt Heydrich, who was the head of the German SD, and established close contacts with Heydrich's associates, including the Gestapo chief Heinrich Müller. From August 1938 to February 1939 Aćimović also served as Yugoslavia's minister of interior.[4] A professor at Belgrade University Lazar Kostić (the ministry of transport), a former deputy minister of finance Jevrem Protić (nutrition), and a former minister Dušan Pantić (post and telegraph) were affiliated with the Radical Party, while Professor Risto Jović (education) and engineer Stanislav Josifović (construction) represented the Democratic Party.[5] Two Zbor activists Milosav Vasiljević and Stevan Ivanić headed the Council's ministries of economy and social policy, respectively; Zbor member Đorđje Perić became deputy commissar for education.[6]

The formation of the council reflected German aspirations to employ local collaborators and to reserve the limited German manpower for more important tasks. At the core of the relationship between the MBS and the council was the total subordination of the latter to the former, and the council's very name indicated its subservient status, since the title "commissar" implied temporary and far more limited functional capacities than does "minister."

The commissars were to function as managers of the former royal ministries under German control, and the fact that Aćimović was a policeman was also emblematic of the council's primary function: policing Serbia.[7]

To be sure, the native police force had been created even before the formation of the council. On April 17, Förster ordered the formation of the native police; three thousand royal policemen and gendarmes, who had proven their "Aryan" background, were selected. Suspicious of their reliability, however, the MBS refused to adequately equip and arm them. The gendarmerie oversaw the collection of taxes and food supplies and frequently administered corporal punishment to individuals who failed to fulfill their agricultural quotas. As such, the gendarmes rather than the Germans became the chief irritants for the rural population.[8]

To set up its local offices, the council called former civil servants back to their duties, and soon hundreds of royal officials filled vacancies in districts and counties. Some decided to collaborate with the occupiers for ideological reasons, others considered it practical to conduct their professional duties in the new political environment, while some served purely for steady wages. Regardless of their reasoning, they came to play a vital role in the occupation system, engaging in a wide range of activities such as resuming civil services, supervising the repair of roads and bridges, and enforcing harvesting and the labor duties.[9] At the same time, the council "cleansed" the civil service of the Jewish and the Roma employees as well as the Serbs, who were considered unreliable.[10]

While the commissars' diverse political affiliations assured that the council would not function as a united and potentially troublesome institution, the constant meddling of German offices further restricted its limited competence. One of the more flexible Nazi officials, Turner advocated a closer cooperation with the council. He aspired to turn Serbia into a German protectorate on the par with Bohemia and Moravia. In such a setting, his *Verwaltungsstab* would take over all supervisory functions, independently from the military administration. Benzler also promoted more autonomy for the council, but under the auspices of the Foreign Ministry, whereas the MBS and the *Einsatzgruppe* Serbia commander Fuchs viewed the council merely as the auxiliary executive branch and police force.[11]

Notwithstanding internal rivalries, all German officials constantly reminded the council of its subordinate place. All regulations of the council were effected only after they were approved by the respective German offices. For example, although officially the council's financial department regulated prices and wages, in reality these were dictated by Neuhausen's office.[12] In May, General Förster ordered the council to create a special commission to investigate the causes of the April war. Acting in accordance with German expectations, the commission concluded that the Yugoslav government had recklessly brushed off the "peaceful" intentions of the Third Reich and provoked the war.[13]

The MBS condescended to a few token gestures, such as allowing the council to display the Serbian national symbols, but it denied its most practical requests. For example, when Aćimović requested the release of Serbian POWs, the MBS flatly refused. In vain, Aćimović argued that the POW camps in Serbia could become the epicenters of the nationalist and communist propaganda and that the council urgently needed manpower for the labor services. Averse to release so many able-bodied men, the MBS ordered the deportation of the POWs to Germany.[14]

Despite such humiliating experiences, the commissars hoped that total obedience and effective implementation of German orders would be rewarded in the future by some sort of autonomy. This was the beginning of the so-called "shield philosophy," the claim first made by the Vichy government, whereby collaboration with the Germans allegedly protected France from German terror. To the same effect, on May 16 the council issued an appeal to the population, stressing the necessity of "genuine and loyal cooperation" with the Germany and promising that the occupiers would "not demand anything that contradicted [Serbia's] national honor and dignity."[15]

Notwithstanding the council's willingness to appease its masters, the Germans remained skeptical of its performance. Such attitudes multiplied in the summer, when an uprising broke out in Serbia. In many localities the native administrative offices and police stations collapsed overnight. Instead of looking into the inner deficiencies of the occupation system, all German offices subjected the council to withering criticism. On August 1, Benzler recorded that although the council displayed "good will," it was weak and unstable.[16] He and Turner, therefore, considered replacing the council with a more efficient body that could rally to its banners all anticommunist Serbs.[17]

To prove its worth, the council organized conferences and public rallies, which promoted full-scale collaboration with Germany as the only way to save Serbia from the horrors of civil war. The council's propaganda details favorably contrasted German rule in Serbia to the anti-Serbian terror campaigns in NDH and in the Hungarian and Bulgarian occupation zones. On July 16, addressing a conference of several political groups, Milosav Vasiljević and the deputy commissar of transport, Ranislav Avramović, stressed that in contrast to Poland, the native administration in Serbia was in the hands of the "honest [Serbian] nationalists" and that the German troops remained in the country solely for garrison duties.[18] Against a background of German reprisals, however, such arguments sounded hollow, especially as the collaborationist press tried to justify them. For example, in mid-July it admonished the population that the "correct conduct of the German troops" had its limits.[19] Similarly, when the German troops decimated the village of Skela in northern Serbia, the press slavishly justified the massacre, arguing that it was "fair in the interests of [Serbia's] future" since the village residents had assisted the Partisans.[20]

Sensing the growing displeasure of the Germans, on August 13 the council issued an appeal to the nation. Construed in a highly emotional language, it called to combat the communist resistance and entreated all Serbs to assist the council and the German administration in the process of "national regeneration." Although the Council planned to collect up to thirty thousand signatures, in the end about five hundred prominent personalities signed the appeal, including three former ministers, three bishops, and a number of statesmen, generals, professors, and lawyers; another two hundred individuals signed it a few days later. Some signatories cherished no sympathy for the Germans but hoped that the appeal would spare Serbia from more bloodshed; others signed out of fear of being branded unreliable or in order to seek social promotion through affiliation with the council. Still, several renowned personalities such as the writers Isidora Sekulić and Ivo Andrić refused to sign the appeal.[21]

By this time, however, the council's utility had run its course and General Heinrich Dankelmann (who took over MBS office on July 28) conceded to the proposal of Benzler and Turner to replace it. On August 16, Edmond Veesenmayer, who had played a key role in installing the Ustasha regime in Zagreb and was considered a Balkan expert, arrived in Belgrade. After several consultations, Veesenmayer, Turner, and Benzler concurred that General Milan Nedić possessed the qualities necessary to head the new administration.[22]

Simultaneously, the commander of the German forces in the Balkans Field Marshal Wilhelm List, who was on his way from Germany to Greece, stopped in Belgrade to confer with Dankelmann. The generals came to the same conclusion and decided to establish a new native administration, headed by a "strong personality," but pliable to German interests. On August 29 the Council of Commissars announced that since the "situation caused popular distrust in the political leadership, the council passed the rudder of the state" to General Milan Nedić. Aćimović then formally introduced Nedić to an assembly of politicians, intellectuals, and businessmen as Serbia's new leader.[23]

Enter Milan Nedić

Milan Nedić was a veteran of the Balkan Wars and during World War I had taken part in the dramatic retreat of the Serbian army through the Albanian mountains. Valued by Nikola Pašić and King Alexander, in 1923 Nedić was promoted to general and appointed the chief of the general staff. Between August 1939 and November 1940 he served as war minister under Dragiša Cvetković and Milan Stojadinović.[24]

Despite his impressive military record, Nedić seemed a strange choice to lead Serbia in the time of crisis, since he symbolized the Yugoslav army's ignominious performance in the April war. Also, although as the war minister he was pessimistic about Yugoslavia's prospects in the European war, he did not display any visible pro-German leanings. Accordingly, his supporters and apologists have maintained that he consented to head the new Serbian administration only under duress.[25]

Most likely, the Germans had considered two particular factors in their decision. First, the senior officer corps in most German-subjugated countries produced a number of prominent collaborationists, such as Philippe Pétain and J. François Darlan in France, Hendrik Seyffardt in the Netherlands, and Leon Rupnik in Slovenia.[26] Second, while seemingly apolitical, Nedić was known to have a strong aversion to communism. In November 1941, Dr. Miloš Sekulić, who worked at a Belgrade hospital and regularly sent reports from Belgrade to the royal government in exile, perceptively asserted that Nedić's appointment was a deliberate German measure—as a decorated commander of World War I and popular among the Yugoslav officer corps, he could create a "third force" capable of confronting the communist resistance and blunting the influence of the Chetniks. At the same time, his political inexperience guaranteed his malleability to German pressure.[27]

As a matter of fact, from the outset Nedić displayed either an utmost naïveté or appalling political myopia. On August 27 he informed Dankelmann that he accepted his post under several conditions. Nedić requested that the new administration become a governing body, acting in accordance with Germany's interests and on behalf of the Serbian people. He also asked for the expansion of the Serbian armed forces—the gendarmerie of ten thousand and the army of thirty thousand—which would be equipped and deployed against the communist resistance, so that the German troops were "released to their primary tasks." His other conditions included the release of Serbian POWs who were ill, old, or essential for Serbia's economy and the expansion of Serbia's borders.[28]

All his conditions ran afoul of the very nature of German occupation. The interests of the Serbian people, which Nedić solemnly pledged to uphold, contravened the Nazi ideological and racial dogmas on all points. The creation of a Serbian government entailed the strengthening of Serbian nationalism, which Hitler viewed as a main cause of trouble in the Balkans. Similarly, the formation of a Serbian army and the release of prisoners would strengthen Nedić's position and prestige—a prospect that was unacceptable to most German officials in Serbia—while any changes in border configurations infringed upon the interests of Germany's allies and satellites—Bulgaria, Hungary, Italy, and Croatia.[29]

On August 29, Nedić was inaugurated at the MBS headquarters as chairman of the new administration. He thanked Dankelmann for the "full power of authority" he had allegedly received. On behalf of the MBS, Turner expressed hope that the Serbian forces would save the country from communism. On the same day, Turner sent a circular to German civil officials, which required them to render the "highest possible degree of independence" to the new administration.[30]

The new administrative body was ambitiously named the Government of National Salvation (Vlada Narodnog Spasa, VNS). Nedić assumed the title of minister president (*ministar-predsednik*) and his cabinet members were referred to as "ministers"—an implication that the VNS enjoyed a higher status than the Council of Commissars. Among Nedić's most close associates were his friend Ognjen Kuzmanović (the ministry of construction) and the generals Josif Kostić (transport) and Panta Draškić (labor), whom Nedić knew personally. In accordance with the German scheme of power-control and despite Nedić's misgivings, Dankelmann and Turner insisted that Aćimović retain his post as minister of the interior. Zbor activists Čedomir Marjanović and Mihailo Olčan headed the ministries of justice and economy, respectively.[31]

Outwardly, the VNS appeared more resilient than its predecessor. It displayed the Serbian national colors and the coat of arms and its armed units used the royal greetings (oddly enough, such symbols were associated with the Yugoslav government in exile, officially at war with Germany). In September the Serbian district courts were empowered to administer death sentences for the activities associated with the resistance; the gendarmerie courts were to deal with nonpolitical offenses committed by the Serbs.[32]

In Hitler's plans for the Balkans, Serbia would become a self-sustaining agricultural unit, capable of supplying both the population and the occupation forces, with the latter receiving the lion's share. Hence, while all political and social organizations were banned, after the formation of the Council of Commissars, General Förster ordered the resumption of peasant cooperatives, which by the end of August 1941 were expected to begin delivering produce and livestock.[33] Although their numbers dropped from 5,284 before the war to 3,899 under German occupation, 353,219 cooperative members remained a significant economic and political force, boosting the prestige of the VNS. The latter heavily invested in the purchase of agricultural implements, and a few remaining Serbian industries functioned specifically to produce agricultural hardware.[34]

On September 1, Nedić issued his first appeal to the nation, stressing that Serbia had finally gained a "national government" under the supervision of the German military command. In the course of two weeks, Nedić issued several more appeals, pledging to form the Serbian army, to rebuild national economy, to destroy the communist resistance, and to establish peace. As the council had done, Nedić also emphasized that close cooperation with Germany was imperative for the country's regeneration and its rightful place in the new European order.[35]

All these features gave the impression that the VNS had received extensive legislative and executive prerogatives, so much so that NDH, Bulgaria, and Hungary joined diplomatic efforts to maintain their respective territorial acquisitions and to keep Serbia isolated.[36]

Germany's allies, however, worried in vain, as the VNS found itself essentially in the same situation as the Council of Commissars. Whatever Dankelmann and Turner promised, they did not give Nedić any written assurances and could renege on their promises or reinterpret them at will. Since German policies in Serbia were predicated on short-term improvisations, the MBS preferred to deal with a divided and weak collaborationist administration rather than a strong one. Although by the end of September the native police forces had grown to five thousand men, Dankelmann turned down Nedić's requests for the formation of the Serbian army. While Dankelmann promised that the Serbian gendarmerie would act independently, the German military commandants consistently used it as auxiliary units. Although the so-called legal Chetniks (see chapter 4) and the Zbor's armed units were theoretically subordinated to Nedić, they acted either independently or under German orders.[37]

The VNS had to collect the harvest, but it lacked sufficient manpower to do so, as a hundred thousand Serbian POWs and fifty thousand laborers had been sent to Germany. The separation of Banat, which before the war was a key source of agricultural supplies and now was used exclusively for the needs of Germany and the German forces in the Balkans, directly affected Serbia. As had Aćimović, Nedić requested that the MBS release some POWs to be employed in agriculture, but his request was also denied. When an important agriculture area of eastern Srijem was turned over to the NDH, the food supply situation became more pressing.[38]

In September Nedić attempted to reorganize the VNS, but he was prevented from making any significant changes. Meanwhile, the spread of resistance confined the German garrisons to cities and towns, while the collaborationist administrations in many countryside localities collapsed. Consequently, Dankelmann increasingly berated Nedić for his failures to crush the resistance but refused to grant him effective executive powers. When in the fall of 1941 thousands of Serbs perished in mass German reprisals, Nedić's promoted image as Serbia's potential savior faded away.[39] Moreover, in a letter to General Paul Bader, Turner stated that in his conversations with Nedić in August, the latter agreed that if German reprisals affected civilians, his administration would not intervene.[40]

Nedić's difficulties were compounded by a growing conflict between Turner and his immediate superiors. In a letter to Dankelmann, Turner ascribed the poor performance of the VNS forces to too much oversight by the *Kommandostab*.[41] At the same time, rivalry between the German offices fostered rifts within the VNS. Whereas Nedić and his close associates envisioned Serbia as an Axis satellite-state, similar to the NDH, the Stojadinović group (headed by Aćimović) and the Zbor faction wanted to turn Serbia into an administrative unit of the Third Reich, but they were reluctant to consider Nedić as the future leader. Both Nedić and Aćimović were suspicious of Ljotić's aspirations, while Nedić, Ljotić, and Aćimović attempted to remove the Belgrade mayor Dragi Jovanović, who enjoyed the protection of Fuchs and Kraus.[42]

Refugee Crisis

Besides coping with German pressure and the resistance, both the Council of Commissars and the VNS faced a mounting refugee crisis. Aiming to homogenize Croatia, in April the Ustasha regime launched a terror campaign against Serbs in the NDH; several hundred thousands were murdered, fled, or were forced to cross into Serbia, and Belgrade's residents watched in horror as corpses floated down the Danube and Sava Rivers. "Wild" expulsions soon gave way to more systematic population removal. In accordance with Hitler's vision, the Slovenian territory north of Ljubljana was slated for Germanization. To this end, 260,000 Slovenians were to be resettled to Serbia, but due to transportation difficulties it was eventually decided to move them to Croatia, instead.[43]

On June 7, Hitler received Pavelić and outlined to him the effectiveness of the Nazi population transfers in Europe. Reluctant to accept 260,000 Slovenians, Pavelić decided to remove an equal number of Serbs from NDH and gave appropriate orders to his subordinates. The NDH authorities began rounding up Serbs into detention camps, from which thousands were escorted on foot or transported by rail to Serbia's borders, where they were dumped without shelter.[44] At the same time, streams of refugees also poured from the areas occupied by Germany's allies. Questioned by Serbian officials, refugees recounted countless stories of horror, persecution, and murder in Bosnia-Herzegovina, Kosovo, Vojvodina, and Banat. By the end of 1941, Serbia had absorbed 165,000 refugees from NDH, 56,000 from Vojvodina, 15,000 from Slovenia, and 7,500 from the Bulgarian occupation zone.[45]

Most refugees were destitute, needing food, shelter, and medical assistance. Especially pitiful was the situation of children, who had lost their parents to the Ustasha terror—21,353 child refugees were processed by the Serbian aid agencies in 1942; by the following May the numbers were 83,225. The Council of Commissars formed a special refugee committee, which opened a number of orphanages around the country and paid allowances to the families that had taken in or adopted children. Still, about 1.5 percent of the child refugees succumbed to hunger, diseases, and exhaustion.[46] The Commissars repeatedly appealed to the MBS to intervene with Zagreb, stressing that the refugee crisis was taking a profound economic and psychological toll on Serbia, already ravaged by the civil war.[47] The Southeast Command was also concerned that the arrival of refugees caused unrest in the countryside; some refugees joined the Partisans and the Chetniks. It repeatedly requested Berlin to apply diplomatic pressure on the Ustasha to stop the expulsions. Hitler, however, remained aloof.[48]

The refugee committee (renamed the Commissariat for Refugees) appropriated empty houses, military barracks, schools, and hospitals as temporary dwellings. Soon, however, it had to appeal to the population for help, and the aid campaign became the only success story of the collaborationist administration. For the first time since the beginning of the war, the relief campaign united most Serbs regardless of political affiliation. Across the country, thousands of refugees (including Slovenians) were sheltered by Serbian families; professional associations and the Orthodox Church collected money for donations. In the summer of 1941, the Belgrade residents alone donated 7,258,000 dinars to relief efforts; the populations of Niš, Kragujevac, and Čačak collected 1,720,000 dinars.[49]

Through donations and its own funds, the Commissariat for Refugees collected and distributed cloth to the refugees; it also paid for their nourishment and shelter. The Commissariat of Transport raised prices on fares to benefit refugees, while the Commissariat of Agriculture donated 1 percent of corn and grain harvests exclusively for the same purpose. The administration set up kitchen facilities for the refugees; the revenues of soccer matches and proceeds of theatrical performances were channeled to the refugee funds.[50] Some refugees were deployed to repair roads and build dams; others worked in the countryside. Educated individuals were employed in the libraries, museums, or village schools. Still, as the numbers of refugees grew, the administration encouraged those who were able-bodied adults to enlist in labor details sent to Germany and Italy.[51]

Meanwhile, German confiscations of food supplies and the insurgent attacks on communication lines made the situation critical in several localities. In February 1942, the chief of the Niš district reported that the town starved. As the town population increased from 50,000 to 65,000 due to the increase of refugees, food supplies dwindled. Receiving, settling, provisioning, and finding employment for tens of thousands of refugees became almost impossible, and most people had to rely on black-market activities. The town had no reserve of food supplies; prices skyrocketed, corn was added to bread to stretch the wheat supply, and a daily ration was lowered from 400 to 150 grams.[52]

By mid-1942 the Commissariat for Refugees was no longer able to collect sufficient food supplies, since the MBS claimed the lion's share of agricultural output.[53] In July, Nedić had to appeal to the population to render all possible help to refugees, whose survival depended entirely on the goodwill of their co-nationals. On September 16, he described the refugee situation as critical in a letter to Bader. According to various estimates, 400,000 refugees and displaced persons made up 11 percent of Serbia's total population at that time. By the end of the year, the Commissariat for Refugees had spent more than 23 million dinars on commodities and living quarters for refugees.[54]

Loyal to the End

In December 1941 the OKW recalled the combat troops, which had helped suppress the insurgency in Serbia. The MBS forces, therefore, were again stripped to a bare minimum. According to Hitler's directive, police duties in Serbia were to be taken over by the Bulgarians, and in January 1942 a Bulgarian corps (between 20,000 and 25,000 troops) crossed over the demarcation line and occupied two-thirds of the country. The Bulgarian garrisons were stationed in large urban areas such as Vranje, Pirot, Niš, and Kragujevac, although all important industrial sites remained under MBS jurisdiction.

Officially, the Bulgarian troops were to be supplied from Bulgaria, but from the outset they lived off the land, requisitioning food and livestock daily.[55]

This was the worst setback for Nedić to date and a particularly harsh blow to the national sensibilities of many Serbs, who still remembered the harsh Bulgarian occupation of World War I. Thousands of refugees had already poured from Macedonia and southeast Serbia, and back in November 1941 a report to the Yugoslav government in exile described the situation in the Bulgarian occupation zone as a "complete chaos." The presence of the Bulgarian troops in central and western Serbia caused widespread popular resentment, and since the local native offices were forced to carry out the orders of the Bulgarian military commandants, it appeared as if the VNS had become the Bulgarian stooge.[56]

In desperation, Nedić appealed to the Romanian dictator Ion Antonescu to speak on his behalf and threatened to resign, but List and Ribbentrop brushed off his threat, warning him that in such a case, "Serbia should blame itself." Bitter and dejected, Nedić considered suicide and sullenly admitted to his associates that his regime depended entirely on the Germans' goodwill.[57] Nevertheless, he remained in his post, possibly because he realized that he had burned all bridges to the past, especially since on December 19, 1941, the Yugoslav government in exile stripped him of the rank of general for collaboration with the occupier. Possibly, Nedić also understood that, if his demands appeared too excessive, the VNS could lose any freedom of action it had in internal affairs. He therefore had no other choice but to stake his future on Germany's ultimate victory, which still seemed certain.

Meanwhile, in the winter of 1941–42 several new appointments signified a serious shift in the German power structure in Serbia. Franz Böhme, who in Berlin's view allowed Nedić too much freedom of action, was replaced by General Paul Bader. The appointment of SS-*Gruppenführer* August Meyszner as the Supreme SS-and-Police Leader (Höherer SS- und Polizeiführer, HSSPF) of all the SS, police, and security forces in Serbia indicated Himmler's intention to expand the influence of the SS in the Balkans at the expense of the Wehrmacht.[58]

An Austrian Nazi and a professional policeman, Meyszner had a reputation as a Nazi zealot and a Serb-hater, relying exclusively on terror and coercion as main policy tools. To this effect, he set out to reorganize the security and police apparatus in Serbia. The *Einsatzgruppe* Serbia was dissolved and in its place was created the stationary office of the commander in chief of the Security Police and Security Service (Befehlshaber der Sipo und des SD, BdS). Fuchs, who was criticized by Heydrich as "too mild," was replaced by SS-*Standartenführer* Emanuel Schäfer. Like Meyszner, Schäfer was a dedicated

Nazi. During the invasion of Poland, he headed an *Einsatzgruppe* that carried out mass executions of the Polish intelligentsia and Jews. Later he served as the Gestapo chief in Cologne, where he organized the deportations of Jews to Poland and Riga.[59]

All these changes affected the position of Turner, who in the eyes of the Wehrmacht and the SS often acted as Nedić's patron. Bader was less receptive than Böhme to Turner's more constructive approach to employ political, economic, and military measures to pacify the country and to use the VNS as a crucial ingredient of German power. In January 1942, Turner supported Nedić's proposal to exchange Yugoslav officers, who avoided mobilization into the Serbian administration and police forces, for more reliable ones kept in German POW camps. After Hitler forbade the exchange, Bader's chief-of-staff condescendingly reminded Turner that his *Verwaltungsstab* was but a branch of the MBS.[60] Himmler also had grown increasingly irritated about Turner's alleged "Serbophilism," meaning his support of Nedić. In early 1942, Turner objected to the resettlement of 2,900 Germans from Serbia to the Lublin province, which according to the Nazi Generalplan Ost would become a major area for the German settlement in Eastern Europe. Averse to seeing the German presence in Serbia reduced, Turner protested to Himmler. The latter, however, sharply rebuked Turner, reminding him that "no general or a chief of the military administration" could question Hitler's decisions.[61]

Turner's influence was further diminished when police matters, which were previously run by his *Verwaltungstaab*, were taken over by the HSSPF office. Both Bader and General Walther Kuntze (from July 1942 the commander of the German forces in the Balkans) considered Turner an SS man and suspected him of aspiring to transform Serbia into a civilian-run administrative unit; in such a scenario Turner could become the top civil official—*Reichskommissar*. Meyszner considered Turner to be an upstart civil functionary. In February, Bader, Meyszner, and Schäfer blocked Turner's initiative to reopen Belgrade University. Turner thought that such an opportunity would keep Serbian youths under tighter German control, but Meyszner and Schäfer considered it dangerous to accord Serbian students any opportunity to organize. Indeed, students provided a key human reservoir of the Chetnik and communist resistance, and the university walls constantly bore the signs of defiance in the forms of anti-German graffiti.[62] The university, therefore, remained closed (although students could still attend several courses).[63]

Since Bader and Meyszner considered Nedić as Turner's protégé, his position deteriorated as did his protector's. Although Bader constantly castigated

Nedić for being unable to suppress the resistance, he also turned down the latter's requests to expand the native police forces.[64] While the gendarmerie and the "legal" Chetniks theoretically remained under Nedić's command, in March the gendarmerie was reorganized into the Serbian State Guard (Srpska državna straža, SDS) and subordinated to the HSSPF office. In response to Nedić's protests, Meyszner bluntly stated that the Serbian officer corps was known for anti-German sentiments and could potentially turn the SDS into the breeding ground for the Chetniks and the Partisans.[65]

When Nedić complained, no one listened. In March, during his meeting with Turner, he grumbled that German military commandants completely disregarded the local Serbian authorities, while the enormous cost of occupation depleted the state finances and created food shortages. To pay their debts, the Serbian administration had to request German credit funds, which were to be repaid at high interest in the form of cash, natural resources, and agricultural products.[66] Nedić also blamed some members of his cabinet who allegedly tried to compromise him at every occasion. In response, Turner could only offer Nedić an assurance that he was the leading political personality in Serbia.[67]

Concomitantly with the decline of Turner, Nedić felt that whatever authority he had was slipping away as the Germans denied him even most practical concessions. In June 1942 he requested that his forces carry out an antiguerrilla operation near Niš and Zaječar. However, Bader ordered that the Serbian units be deployed as auxiliaries to the Bulgarian troops.[68] In August, Meyszner appointed Dragi Jovanović to the newly created post of the chief of the Serbian State Security (Srpska državna bezbednost), further undermining Nedić's position as Minister of Interior.[69]

In the last attempt to fortify his position, on July 7, 1942, Turner attempted to emulate Heydrich's initiatives in the Protectorate of Bohemia-Moravia by ordering the formation of the presidium of the Serbian ministerial cabinet. The creation of the presidium entailed the formation of two resorts—the ministry of defense and the ministry of foreign affairs—as the potential epigone of the Serbian national government. Bader and Meyszner were outraged, considering such a measure as the first step toward the replacement of the MBS with the civilian administration headed by Turner's *Verwaltungsstab*. In his report to the OKW, Bader stressed that Turner was seeking to concentrate all power in Serbia in his hands and requested that he be replaced by a "more suitable personality." Turner's precarious situation culminated in October, when Himmler arrived to Kraljevo to discuss the antiguerrilla operations with Meyszner, Schäfer, and Arthur Phlebs, the commander of the

SS-Division Prinz Eugen. Turner was not invited—a clear indication that he had fallen out of favor. Indeed, on November 11 he was recalled to Berlin.[70]

Turner's removal coincided with a deep crisis within the Serbian administration, compounded by the deteriorating economic situation and increasing attacks by the resistance. On September 16, 1942, Nedić described the VNS's position as catastrophic in a memorandum to Bader. He complained that stability and order were unattainable since the Serbian administration had to pay 255 million dinars monthly for war damages and the costs of occupation; the Serbian administration was also partially responsible for financing the formation of an SS division in Banat and the Russian Defense Corps (made up of the White Russian émigrés), altogether between 4 and 5 billion dinars.[71]

Nedić bitterly admitted to Bader that the VNS was but a fiction and again threatened to resign, but two days later he changed his mind and dispatched a letter to Bader, pledging to carry out his functions "until the end." Bader conceded to make a few changes in Nedić's cabinet. In November 1942, Aćimović, who was considered Turner's man and a bitter rival of Ljotić, was replaced by Tanasije Dinić (known as an inveterate enemy of the communists and the Chetniks). Nedić also fired Olčan, the chief Zbor member of the cabinet.[72]

The German occupation of Vichy France in November 1942 clearly demonstrated to Nedić the fragility of his own position. Still, he was indefatigable in his desire to demonstrate his potential usefulness and repeatedly announced that loyal cooperation with the occupying power was Serbia's only salvation. On January 1, 1943, Nedić sent Bader a memo titled "The Reconstruction of Serbia on the Basis of National Community," which stipulated the creation of an authoritarian Serbian state, based on a rigid hierarchical structure. He repeated the litany of complaints about anti-Serbian atrocities in Croatia and Kosovo, the refugee crisis, and the burden of financial and economic obligations imposed on the VNS. Nedić again proposed to transform the VNS to a national government, which would win more popular support and blunt the Chetniks' influence among the peasantry.[73]

In view of the defeat of the Africa Corps and the catastrophic situation of the German army at Stalingrad, the new commander of the German forces in the Balkans Alexander Löhr considered Nedić's proposal more carefully. Löhr admitted that a strong native collaborationist regime, supported by the population, would certainly be more beneficial to the Reich, but the final decision was Hitler's.[74] The latter instead ordered that the Bulgarian occupation zone be extended to cover what amounted to about 80 percent of Serbia's territory, and it appeared that soon the entire country would be occupied by the Bulgarian army.[75]

However, the situation on the fronts and the constant shortage of manpower compelled Bader to return to Nedić's proposal. In March his staff worked out a plan that stipulated the formation of a municipal self-government in Serbia, roughly similar to the NDH regime. But this time the OKW rejected the plan as untimely, while Hitler turned it down as entirely "inappropriate."[76] Meanwhile, Meyszner, who after Turner's fall became the leading German official in Serbia, accused Nedić of maintaining connections with the Chetniks and the Yugoslav government in exile. In 1943 Serbia was expected to send to Germany 400,000 tons of grain, and Nedić complained that these quotas were unrealistic. His appeals were ignored, and he was subjected again to harsh scolding when only three-quarters of the requested amount was delivered.[77]

In summer 1943, Germany's situation in the Mediterranean worsened considerably and the Partisans intensified their activities in Croatia and Bosnia. In July Löhr moved his headquarters from Salonika to Belgrade. On Hitler's orders, Hermann Neubacher was appointed the High Commissioner of the Foreign Ministry for the Southeast Command, effectively becoming the supervisor of the civil administration in Serbia. Like Turner, Neubacher advocated a more flexible policy—to install Nedić as president of the Great Serbian Federation, which would include Montenegro and Sandžak (a region between Serbia and Montenegro), to reopen Belgrade University, and to allow the Serbian administration to exercise more executive powers. Neubacher promised Nedić some concessions and arranged agreements between the Wehrmacht and several Chetnik commanders to coordinate their anti-Partisan operations.[78]

These seeming improvements in German attitudes toward Nedić culminated on September 18, 1943, when Nedić flew to Berlin on Benzler's recommendations. After talks with Ribbentrop and other German dignitaries, he traveled to the OKW headquarters in Eden in East Prussia to speak with Hitler. The collaborationist propaganda hailed Nedić's visit to Germany as a "historical move" toward Serbia's integration into Hitler's Europe. The press reported that Hitler and Ribbentrop "showed a deep understanding of the national interests of the [Serbian] people." In reality, Nedić's meeting with Hitler lasted twenty minutes and should have dispelled any illusions as to Serbia's place in Hitler's Europe.[79] Hitler made it clear that he was dissatisfied with the situation in Serbia, and he turned down Nedić's main requests—expansion of Serbia's borders, autonomy for the VNS, mitigation of German reprisals, and the postwar elevation of Serbia's status to Germany's ally ruled by a native political elite. Instead, Hitler only promised that the Serbian Volunteer Corps (Srpski dobrovoljački korpus) and the SDS would be resubordinated to Nedić and promised to consider the reopening of Belgrade University.[80]

In November 1943, after the capitulation of Italy, Neubacher returned to his idea of a more effective Serbian administration. He suggested to Ribbentrop that a so-called Greater Serbian Federation be formed, encompassing Serbia, Montenegro, and Sandžak, and headed by Nedić. The plan called for limited autonomy in the federation's internal affairs, the subordination of all native armed and police forces to Nedić, and the reduction of German control. Neubacher also argued that mass reprisals were ineffective and suggested that releasing Archbishop Gavrilo and Nikolaj Velimirović from German detention would facilitate popular support for the VNS. Hitler, however, refused to consider the proposal.[81]

On November 5, Nedić's administration was reshuffled for the last time. Nedić remained the VNS chairman, simultaneously assuming the post of the minister of the interior, and the SDS was resubordinated to him. Dinić became minister of social policies and health, while Jovanović lost his post as chief of the Serbian State Security but retained his positions as the chief of the Belgrade municipality and the mayor of Belgrade. It appeared as if Nedić had finally received real executive powers, but in a memo to the local police chiefs, he reminded them that Meyszner still remained the highest "supervisory" authority over all Serbian police forces.[82] Most importantly, however, all of these changes mattered little, for the Allied landing in Italy and the fall of Mussolini shifted German priorities in the Balkans.

* * *

Hitler's plans for Yugoslavia entailed an exploitation of Serbia's economic resources and labor force. A constant shortage of manpower forced the Germans to set up a collaborationist administration, which was expected to act in two capacities: to deliver necessary commodities to the Third Reich and to maintain German order through the native civil service and police. Creating a native administration entailed pragmatism and cunning: it minimized German involvement in collection of contingents and policing the country. To this effect, the Nazi leadership did not bother to develop substitute ideological concepts that could have attracted larger segments of Serbian society. Instead, to guarantee the loyalty of the collaborationist administration, it was made up of individuals of opposing affiliations and aspirations, and in accordance with the Nazi racial and ideological criteria, the Council of Commissars and the Government of National Salvation were divested of any real authority.

Often compared to Philipe Pétain, Nedić indeed appeared similar to the Old Marshal in some ways.[83] Both hailed from military backgrounds and both attempted to act as the saviors of their occupied and truncated countries at the expense of fully collaborating with the occupying power. In France and in Serbia, the hopes of the collaborationists for a mutually beneficial trade-off between them and the Germans came to nothing. While Hitler reserved to himself strategic decision making, he left to his subordinates the more immediate matters of governing. Consequently, the power of different German offices in the areas of their jurisdiction was more or less untrammeled.

Still, Pétain's Vichy government enjoyed substantial powers in internal affairs, and until November 1942 it retained some form of sovereignty. In contrast, the Council of Commissars and its more ambitious but equally anemic VNS successor were treated merely as puppet regimes and were denied any vestiges of statehood. Under closer scrutiny, the Serbian administration was more akin to the so-called Temporary Administrative Committee created by the Italians in April 1941 in Montenegro (in May replaced by the so-called Advisory Chamber), made of native conservative elements.[84]

Crucially, all German offices in Serbia were at loggerheads and accordingly fostered dissent within the collaborationist camp. The Wehrmacht and the SS eventually prevailed over the more rational approach of the civil administration; as a result, the collaborationists trimmed their expectations step by step, depending entirely on the good graces of various German offices and personalities. The latter continuously expressed displeasure with the performance of the Council of Commissars and the VNS, in all spheres, particularly in combatting the resistance. Nevertheless, counting on Germany's victory, both institutions carried out their functions to the very end, hoping that such loyalty would in the end prove beneficial, regardless of the cost.

4 Collaborationism

Zealots, Conservatives, Conformists

A prominent historian of the Balkans asserted that Nedić regarded his post merely as "caretaker" and consequently "his administration had no ideological coloration." Similarly, a former Yugoslav officer and author concluded that "except for ideologically committed anti-Communist Ljotićites, the anticommunism of the people accommodating with the Germans [in Serbia] was an accident."[1]

At first glance, such assertions appear valid. Like his ideological model, Charles Maurras, who conceived France's defeat in 1940 as beneficial for the country's regeneration, Ljotić hoped that Yugoslavia's collapse would engender a new, totalitarian Serbian state within Germany's geopolitical sphere. In contrast, Nedić's appointment looked almost like an accident since the Germans ran out of potential candidates to head the Serbian administration. Moreover, bent on exploiting Serbia's natural and human resources, all German authorities treated both the Zbor and the Government of National Salvation merely as tools of the occupation system, effectively precluding a full utilization of native collaboration.

Although the Ljotić "revolutionaries" and the Nedić "conservatives" were driven by different personal dispositions and ideological orientations, both perceived themselves as prophets of Serbia's national regeneration and attempted to eclipse the limitations German authorities imposed on them by "direct" collaboration. In contrast to "involuntary" collaboration, which entailed compliance with the orders and regulations of the enemy forces, direct collaboration—often termed collaborationism—involved not only yielding to all German demands but a close emulation of the Nazi regime. In the hope of winning concessions, the "revolutionaries" and the "conservatives" displayed substantial energy and initiative, especially in combating the forces they considered inimical to Serbia's national revival.

Collaborateurs de sentiment

So a prominent Belgian collaborationist Leon Degrelle described those individuals and political groups, which fully subscribed to the Nazi Weltanschauung.[2] Since the 1930s, German National Socialism had resonated among the fascist and right-wing parties and groups, which were particularly impressed by Hitler's victories in Europe. Although Ljotić acknowledged that the April war was humiliating, he simultaneously perceived it as a long-awaited opportunity for Serbia's integration into Germany's ideological mainstream. To this effect, he viewed German occupation through the prism of the crusade against "satanic" forces—communism, liberalism, and internationalism, primarily represented by Jews and the Masons. In a letter to King Peter II in London, he called Germany the "wall against Bolshevism" and argued that only unconditional collaboration could save Serbia, particularly since Hitler—in contrast to Bulgaria and Hungary—claimed no Serbian territories. On July 5, 1941, in his broadcast to Belgrade, Ljotić blamed the April catastrophe on the prewar Yugoslav government and emphasized that Serbia's only salvation was to join the German-led crusade against communism.[3]

Imagining himself as the spiritual leader of the new Serbia, Ljotić blended his monarchism and religiosity with the National Socialist ideology, stressing the primacy of the Orthodox Church and obedience to the leadership as the founding blocks of the new Serbian society. The Zbor's main newspaper, *Naša borba* (Our struggle), closely emulated *Mein Kampf*, accentuating the single leadership (*vođstvo*) and discipline, and the Zbor's paramilitary structure replicated the Italian "black shirts" and the German storm troopers.[4]

Due to his fanatical anticommunism, Ljotić was among very few Serbs (including Dragi Jovanović and Velibor Jonić) who enjoyed complete German trust. After Yugoslavia's capitulation, the Zbor was the only political prewar movement that was allowed to function openly and immediately proved its loyalty to the forces of occupation. Serving as agents and informers, the Zbor members actively collaborated with the Gestapo and the Special Police against the communists and the Chetniks. The Zbor's youth organization White Eagles functioned in the same capacity, informing the police about potential suspects among school and university students.[5] On August 20, 1941, Ljotić wrote a memorandum to General Dankelmann, proposing the creation of Zbor armed units. Dankelmann granted the request, and in September the first details of nationalistically inclined youngsters were organized into the Serbian Volunteer Detachments (Srpski dobrovoljački odredi, SDK; in January 1943 renamed the Serbian Volunteer Corps), which almost immediately clashed with the Partisans near Belgrade. By December the SDK units grew to 3,500 members and were fully integrated into the German police structure.[6]

Most SDK members were school and university students; many were dedicated nationalists, while some were attracted by steady wages. Some were unemployed workers and craftsmen, for whom the SDK became their only source of income. According to the German Red Cross there were eight thousand unemployed students in Belgrade, who provided a steady pool of recruits to the SDK. Enlistment provided substantial benefits—the 2,000 to 3,000 dinar monthly salary was comparable to the wages of a gendarmerie corporal or a police agent. The Ministry of Education equated a two-month service in the SDK with two university semesters and granted the Volunteers numerous privileges, such as stipends for schooling in Germany and priorities in enrollment in Belgrade University. Quick promotion was also a strong inducement—an SDK private could be promoted to lieutenant or even captain in just several weeks.[7] The SDK also found a number of willing recruits among the refugees streaming to Serbia from all over Yugoslavia. Brutalized by their experiences, they became particularly susceptible to Zbor propaganda.[8]

The SDK members effectively mirrored their main enemies—the Partisans—in that they were ideological soldiers totally devoted to Zbor and its leader. The SDK had its own political department, headed by fanatical Zbor member Ratko Parežanin, and special political officers and priests carried out ideological and religious indoctrination among the SDK rank and file. In fact, twenty-seven SDK priests died in battle.[9] Wearing the royal army uniforms and using Christian imagery, the Volunteers considered themselves modern crusaders, who fought the three targeted "forces of evil"—the Masons, Jews, and the communists. SDK members fought with suicidal courage, especially since the Partisans and the Chetniks rarely took them prisoner. They also escorted hostages to prisons and concentration camps and handed over captured guerrillas to the Germans or shot them on the spot. In October 1941 an SDK detachment took part in the gruesome Kragujevac massacre, rounding up and guarding the civilian hostages before their mass execution. In December they participated in another mass execution, this time of prisoners at the Čačak concentration camp, where SDK officers presided at the drumhead court-martial.[10]

Such extremism forged the SDK into an effective fighting force, and Meyszner even contemplated sending one SDK platoon to the eastern front as a symbol of Serbia's participation in the war against the Soviet Union. Similarly, the MBS and the German security functionaries repeatedly praised the SDK for their "irrefutable" conduct during antiguerrilla operations.[11] Although bitter that the SDK frequently acted independently or under German command, Nedić praised them as an elite unit, far superior to his own police forces.[12]

Another collaborationist unit that gained particular notoriety in Serbia was the Special Police. On April 21, 1941, the German military commandant of Belgrade appointed Dragomir-Dragi Jovanović as extraordinary commissar of the capital. In this capacity Jovanović assumed two functions: as head of the city administration and as chief of police. A law graduate of Belgrade University, Jovanović joined the royal police but was banned from the service on charges of embezzlement. Due to highly placed friends, he was reinstated and eventually was appointed as chief of the Belgrade police. In 1935–37 he and Aćimović visited Germany for the Interpol conferences, where he established contacts with Himmler, Heydrich, Heinrich Müller, and the future Gestapo chief of the *Einsatzgruppe* Serbia Hans Helm. It was Helm who particularly recommended Jovanović as an "energetic and skillful [individual] albeit prone to intrigues and financial temptations."[13]

Eager to prove his worth, Jovanović organized the Special Police to combat the communist resistance. Formed on the basis of the political department of the royal police, the new unit became a highly efficient police force, made up of skillful and dedicated professionals. Like Jovanović, most top functionaries were lawyers and jurists and had experience combating the communists or the Ustasha in the interwar period. For example, the first chief of the Special Police, Milivoje Jovanović, had sixteen years of police experience, while Ilija Paranos, who headed the unit for three years, had served in the personal guard of Prince Pavel Karađorđević and Prime Minister Stojadinović.[14] Although some Special Police functionaries were politically "flexible" opportunists, ready to serve any regime, many others were infused with right-wing or fascist ideology. Known for particular brutality, the chief of section 4 (communism), Božko Bećarević, served in a similar capacity in the Kragujevac political police before the war, apprehending communists and some Zbor activists. His colleague Sergije Golubev was an extremist White Russian émigré who had joined the royal police and participated in the crackdown on the KPJ in the late 1930s.[15]

Paranos reorganized the Special Police on the model of the *Einsatzgruppe* Serbia. Accordingly, section 4 under Bećarević became a replica of the Gestapo and the largest and the most important component of the Special Police. Bećarević maintained daily contacts with the Gestapo, whose functionaries held their Serbian counterparts in high regard.[16] Fuchs and Schäfer acknowledged the zeal and expertise of the Special Police and accorded it wide latitude in combating the communist resistance. In contrast, ever suspicious of pro-Mihailović sentiments among the Serbian collaborators, the Gestapo took on the struggle against the Chetniks. The Special Police had the right to recommend executions, imprisonment, or release of prisoners—out of 23,637 inmates in the Banjica prison camp, 6,613 were sent in by the Special Police (the regular Serbian police, the SDK, and the "legal" Chetniks sent in a total of 1,870 prisoners).[17]

The Special Police set up its branches in other localities. For example, headed by Zbor member Mirko Živanović, the Special Police functionaries in Niš brutally tortured their victims, and once cut a star (the Partisan symbol) on a young boy's forehead. The Special Police details searched the concentration camps for alleged communists and handed them over to the Sipo, participated in selection of hostages for mass executions, and took part in the shootings in Jajinci (allegedly Jovanović paid a bounty of 200 dinars for each executed guerrilla).[18]

In combatting the resistance, the Special Police achieved considerable results. It set up a large-scale network of agents around the country who repeatedly infiltrated the communist and SKOJ cells. Sometimes the Special Police deliberately released captured guerrillas to sow mutual distrust in the underground. In June 1941 the Special Police arrested Jelena Matić, a member of the KPJ regional committee, and after incarcerating her in Banjica, released her. Suspicious that Matić had become a turncoat, the committee ordered her assassination.[19] Well-versed in Marxist ideology, Bećarević ordered his subordinates to study Marxist and communist literature, and he held conferences about how to utilize their concepts in combating the resistance. He also turned several guerrillas into double agents. In the fall of 1941, the Special Police set up a pseudo-resistance radio station, which used its broadcasts to demoralize the resistance and to spread false news to affect public opinion.[20]

From its inception, the Special Police gained a reputation for extreme brutality. Captured or suspected guerrillas were brought to its headquarters, which became one of the most dreaded sites in Belgrade because of the pain and utmost suffering endured within. Poor ventilation and diet were exacerbated by constant overcrowding, whereby up to thirty inmates were crammed into small cells and allowed just ten minutes daily for washing and relieving themselves. But the real litany of horrors began in interrogation rooms, where they were subjected to the most ruthless techniques of extracting information. It started with straight questioning, suddenly interrupted by shouting and insults to catch an individual off guard. If that did not work, the police functionaries viciously beat the victims, using truncheons or rubber hoses. Women prisoners were tortured by electric shocks applied to breasts and genitals, while the tormentors played loud music or gagged their victims to suppress screams. Such practices resulted in severe physical and psychological damage; some prisoners had to be carried back to their cells. Of the ten thousand people arrested by the Special Police in Belgrade, 1,729 were sent to the city hospital for treatment.[21] No better fact illustrates the atmosphere in the Special Police dungeons than an appeal made by the inmates of the Belgrade central prison on January 5, 1943, asking to be handed over to the Gestapo. On one occasion, the Special Police mistakenly seized several ethnic Germans and mishandled them so much that even the Gestapo functionaries were shocked.[22]

Jealous of what they thought as Jovanović's special status, Nedić, Ljotić, and Aćimović repeatedly attempted to remove him from the Belgrade mayoral post, but Fuchs and Meyszner protected him as an extremely efficient policeman and an "uncompromising enemy of communism." Moreover, in August 1942 Meyszner elevated Jovanović to a newly created post of the chief of Serbian State Security. In this capacity, Jovanović supervised all Serbian police and security forces and acted as the deputy minister of the interior, encroaching on Aćimović's and Nedić's jurisdiction.[23] In September 1943, after the Gestapo arrested four Special Police functionaries suspected of collaborating with the Chetniks, Jovanović wrote to Schäfer, complaining that for "almost two-and-a half years [the Special Police] carried out its work irreproachably with inspiration and success as no other [native] police in occupied Europe. . . . The German organs could always rely on the Belgrade police, which never let them down."[24]

Similarly indispensable for the German terror system was the Department of Public Security in Banat. Created in August 1941, it was headed by Juraj Špiler, an experienced policeman. He received his doctorate in law in 1927 and served as deputy chief of the political police in Zagreb, where he combated both the Ustasha and the communists. The Department of Public Security carried out mass arrests of alleged guerrillas, and its prison cells in Petrovgrad (now Zrenjanin) were so crammed that prisoners had to stand for days and nights.[25] Špiler and his subordinates routinely tortured suspects, applying electric current to sensitive body parts or beating the soles of the feet. After such treatment, many prisoners could not walk. As a result, prisoners welcomed deportations to concentration camps as liberation from torment.[26]

Conservatives

Unlike Ljotić, Nedić was badly shaken by Yugoslavia's collapse and he was frequently troubled by his inability to mitigate the harshness of German occupation. Nedić was aware that he faced a ruthless conqueror who would not hesitate to unleash its deadly power at any moment. German reprisals convinced him that resistance would turn Serbia into another Poland, where German terror was ubiquitous. Hence he considered himself a man on a mission to save Serbia, representing *collaboration d'etat*—collaboration for reasons of state as distinguished from collaboration for reasons of ideological affinity. At the same time, Nedić was not free of ideological convictions, which informed his activities as the head of the VNS.

A professional officer, before the war Nedić was realistic or rather pessimistic about Yugoslavia's ability to fight the Axis powers, especially since he did not believe Western allies could or would help. The fall of France confirmed his apprehensions, and on November 1, 1940, Nedić warned in a memorandum to Regent Paul that a conflict with the Axis powers would be a disaster for which Serbia would pay the most horrible price.[27]

The April catastrophe strengthened his convictions that resistance was a delusion, leading to more bloodshed and the eventual destruction of Serbia. Like many French statesmen haunted by memories of World War I, Nedić dreaded the prospect of Serbia reliving the nightmare of 1914–18, when 20 percent of its population—the highest rate among all the belligerents—died in battle, starvation, and disease. Such a view reflected a profound psychological crisis of the Yugoslav officer corps, which in the aftermath of the April war faced two options: to flee the country or join the resistance. Nedić rejected both. Uncertain of the future, he declined to sign the August appeal (under the pretext that he was still a prisoner of war), but after accepting the post of *ministar-predsednik*, he proclaimed that he took upon himself the burden of saving Serbia through personal sacrifice, as had the medieval Serbian ruler Lazar, who perished in the battle against the Ottomans on the Kosovo field in 1389.[28]

At this juncture, Nedić formulated his ideological platform, emulating Philipe Pétain, who in his words "has repudiated the democratic illusion about equality and political rights, and in their place . . . put the family as the foundation of social and national life, from which naturally radiate all rights and all duties."[29] As had the "old marshal," Nedić believed that their respective countries were undermined by the ideologies of democracy and liberalism. This situation could be mended only by breaking with the past political systems through a national revolution, which would regenerate "decaying" societies by returning to traditional cultural, economic, and religious values, in so doing deploying catchwords such as labor, family, and nation.[30]

The key of Nedić's ideological premises was the so-called *zadruga*, the term that derived from a medieval socioeconomic unit, where common property was owned by an extended family. The family chief, *domaćin*, ruled *zadruga* in an authoritarian fashion, assuring a minimal subsistence to all its members and upholding the traditional Serbian values—industriousness, religiosity, and loyalty to the king and to the fatherland. A centuries-long South Slav institution, the *zadruga* was severely destabilized by the money-market economies that penetrated the Balkans in the late nineteenth century.[31] Nedić, therefore, envisioned the creation of the *zadruga*-state (*Srpska seljačka zadružna država*), headed by him as the chief *domaćin*. In keeping with this ideology, he addressed the population as his "children" to emphasize the close relationship between the state and the peasantry, the only vital national force that could rebuild Serbia. The peasant cooperatives were officially called *zadrugas* and functioned as small replicas of the future state, while the Ministry of Agriculture planned to subsidize them to make Serbia's agriculture more efficient.[32]

Such ideological precepts resembled those of the Ustasha, who also emphasized the peasantry as the embodiment of the Croatian national spirit. Importantly, before the war Nedić was sympathetic to the ideological agenda of Zbor and helped print its newspaper, and, as the head of VNS, he was influenced by his close associates and prominent Zbor activists Stanislav Krakov and Velibor Jonić.[33] Still, Nedić envisioned an ultraconservative rather than a fascist Serbian state and stood closer to Pétain than to Ante Pavelić.[34]

The official propaganda extolled the *zadruga* as the backbone of Serbia's economic life—a patriarchal, industrious, and orderly peasant community poised against the forces of capitalism, communism, and cosmopolitanism.[35] The press also propagated the cult of St. Sava—a son of the legendary Serbian prince Nemanja—who was a monk and archbishop in the early Serbian Orthodox Church and was traditionally celebrated as both the embodiment of the Serbian national spirit and the patron of education. Nedić gained support among the Serbian Orthodox Church clergy (although he failed to elicit an official declaration from Archbishop Velimirović, who doubted that the regime could generate a mass following).[36]

However, under occupation, traditional Serbian nationalism and patriotism had to be yoked to German policies and ultimately entailed the desertion of both. On one hand, Nedić attempted to function as the champion of Serbia's "natural" order, rooted in political conservatism and traditional social relations. To that end, he professed loyalty to the monarchy and his forces displayed the royal coat of arms. On the other hand, he realized that Yugoslavia's rapid collapse undermined the credibility of the monarchy, so he repeatedly dissociated himself from the prewar government. In fact, anti-Yugoslavism became one of the most palpable ideological premises of Nedić's and Ljotić's collaborationism and a key feature of the official propaganda. Viewing internal politics narrowly through a Serbian prism, Nedić ascribed the April catastrophe to the disloyalty of non-Serbs, old politicians, and the parliamentary system. In other words, it was Yugoslavia that subverted national Serbian values and it was a decadent Yugoslavia that had lost the war. For example, he grumbled that Yugoslavia "ruined us [Serbia] and brought on us all sorts of beggary."[37] On September 1, 1941, in his first appeal on Belgrade radio, Nedić bashed the "March 27 plotters" for the April war. In December, speaking to the district chiefs, he stressed that the creation of Yugoslavia was not the expression of the Serbian national will but the handiwork of the "masters from the overseas."[38]

Conversely, Nedić accepted German occupation as the painful but necessary stage before Serbia's regeneration and repeatedly emphasized that Germany would establish a new European order in which Serbia would find its rightful space, living in peace and harmony.[39] In the 1942 Christmas address, he announced that "the old world, which had destroyed our state, is over and replaced by the new one. This new world will elevate Serbia to its rightful and honorable place in the new Europe; under the new leadership [of Germany] we look courageously into the future."[40] Speaking on the occasion of the one-year anniversary of the VNS, Nedić asserted that Serbia lived "free" under German tutelage; two months later he stated that Serbia prospered under a "newly found order, labor, and peace."[41]

Ceaselessly repeating such assurances, Nedić chose to ignore that they came in the wake of mass German reprisals, in which thousands of Serbs lost their lives. Moreover, despite numerous rebuffs from his German superiors, Nedić hoped that eventually he would be rewarded by some tangible benefits. For example, in February 1942 he outlined in a memo to Bader his vision of a Great Serbia, which entailed the expansion of Serbia's borders into Bosnia-Herzegovina, Srijem, and Dalmatia and the replacement of the local population by Serbian settlers.[42]

Another key element of Nedić's ideological disposition was virulent anticommunism, which was common among the Yugoslav officer corps. On June 5, 1941, he experienced a profound personal trauma when the explosion of an ammunition warehouse in Smederevo killed and maimed about a thousand people, including his son, his daughter-in-law, and their children. Although in the atmosphere of the Soviet-German relations prior to Operation Barbarossa, the official propaganda refrained from directly blaming the communists, the loss of his relatives might have amplified Nedić's anticommunist convictions.[43]

In this context, Nedić perceived himself as a European crusader, fully determined to cooperate with Germany in the struggle against communism and "Western plutocracy." In his speeches and broadcasts, Nedić appealed to the Serbs to participate in the "crusade" against the resistance, labeling the Partisans as "aliens, robbers, outlaws, God's enemies," or the "Satanic force" to be destroyed by all possible means.[44] Such a Manichean division between the forces of good and evil conveniently posited the collaborationist regime as the only bulwark against chaos and decadence. In December 1941, Nedić declared to Bader that, in the struggle against communism, there would be no compromise, and on several occasions he petitioned the MBS to deport Serbian officers who declined to join the collaborationist armed units.[45]

Supervised by the MBS propaganda department, the Serbian press agencies were reorganized to become regime mouthpieces and carriers of the most virulent xenophobic propaganda.[46] The editor in chief of *Novo vreme*, Stanislav Krakov (a distant relative of Nedić), was a fanatical anti-Semite and Zbor activist, and among the five hundred contributors were Ljotić, Nedić, Aćimović, Jonić, Mihailo Olčan, and others known for anticommunist or anti-Semitic views.[47] *Novo vreme* and *Obnova* tried to convince their readers that the resistance replaced Serbia's traditional enemies, the Ottoman Turks, and both newspapers published photographs of captured or slain guerrillas at angles chosen to make them appear beastly and evil. Similarly, numerous authors stigmatized the resistance as headed or financed by "Jewish-Masonic" secretive cells. Special propaganda details and the district and province chiefs organized meetings and rallies that highlighted the dangers of communism and branded the Chetniks as "irresponsible elements."[48]

At the same time, veneration of the National Socialist ideological and racial values became a leitmotiv of the collaborationist propaganda. The VNS Ministry of Education authorized research on the alleged biological superiority of the Serbian people, while the doublespeak-titled Committee for the Protection of Serbian Blood (Odbor za zaštitu srpske krvi) contemplated the introduction of the law of eugenics to preserve the "purity" of Serbian blood.[49] Press-commentator Miroslav Spalajković hailed the Serbian national heroes Prince Lazar and Miloš Obilić as "ideal representatives of the [Serbian] race," and the former chairman of the "Yugoslav Action" (a precursor to Zbor) Damnjan Kovačević claimed that the VNS replicated National Socialism as a "socially fair, politically authoritarian, and economically systematic" regime.[50]

Replicating the Nazi youth and professional associations, the VNS created several organizations, which were to disseminate the regime's ideology. In November 1941 the VNS announced the formation of the youth organization Omladina, whose structure and goals closely resembled the Hitlerjugend. To the chagrin of its organizers, however, in March 1942 the MBS ordered its dissolution, fearing that Omladina could become a hotbed of Serbian nationalism.[51] Modeled after the Nazi Labor Front, several labor associations were set up to carry out public works and simultaneously to indoctrinate their members in the spirit of the new order. All these organizations had a limited effect on Serbian youths, and Meyszner and Schäfer suspected that they served as a facade for Chetnik activities.[52]

On May 25, 1941 the MBS authorized Aćimović to reopen schools, provided that instruction would be conducted along the "ideals of the Third Reich." To achieve the desired effect, the Council of Commissars and the VNS removed teachers and instructors they considered "decadent and corrupt." These included the non-Serbs, the alleged Masons, the communists, and the Jews. Reputed as a "fanatical enemy of communism, the Jewry, Marxism, and the Masonry," the minister of education Velibor Jonić initiated a comprehensive reorganization of the school system. Students became liable for labor service and special courses were set up for instructors, who were to indoctrinate students along prescribed ideological lines.[53]

Teachers proficient in German were exempted from labor duties and could not be fired without the authorization of the German authorities. About a thousand students connected to the Omladina and the Zbor received stipends from the Ministry of Education and were sent to study in Germany.[54] In December 1941 the Ministry of Education authorized the district chiefs and school directors to test the national reliability of students through the use of ideologically constructed questionnaires. Teachers and instructors who were considered insufficiently "patriotic" were fired—by April 1942, 3,958 of the 14,339 individuals employed by the Ministry of Education lost their jobs. The remaining personnel were made to swear allegiance to the VNS, which included a pledge to combat antistate activities.[55] The Ministry of Education also ordered that all sorts of "pernicious" literature be removed from schools, libraries, and museums. Jewish authors were targeted, but so were Sinclair Lewis, Thomas Mann, Maxim Gorky, and F. Scott Fitzgerald.[56]

In June, Jonić worked out a plan for the establishment of a special "reeducation facility" in Smederevska Palanka. Situated approximately fifty miles south of Belgrade, the site had previously been used as a detention camp for communists.[57] Named the Institution for the Forcible Education of Youths

(Zavod za prinudno vaspitanje omladine), the camp was designed to confine "misguided" school and university students between the ages of fourteen and twenty-five. Upon Bader's approval, Nedić ordered the forcible induction into the camp of those Serbian youths, who "did not appreciate their national obligations." The confinement lasted anywhere between six months and two years (in 1943 the maximum term was expanded to three years) and included various labor tasks.[58] The camp was guarded by Serbian gendarmes, while the overall supervision was administered by section 4 of the Special Police. The political indoctrination of the inmates was carried out by Zbor activists.[59]

In September the first group of students arrived at the camp; by the end of the year there were five hundred inmates; poor hygienic conditions in the barracks and poor diet contributed to sickness and hunger. The camp administration used harsh physical training, solitary confinement, and beating as persuasive "reeducation" tools and sent "intractable" inmates to the Banjica prison camp. The inmates endured ideological lectures of Ljotić, Jonić, Parežanin, and other personalities, whose main topics were the dangers of communism and the "Jewish-Masonic" conspiracies.[60] The Special Police reported that about 80 percent of the inmates were sufficiently "reeducated," but camp director Miodrag Popović admitted that many, particularly SKOJ members, refused to see the "light of truth" and remained opposed to the regime. When the camp closed in September 1944, 1,270 individuals had passed through it.[61]

As the war progressed, the regime's obsession with internal enemies assumed infinite proportions. The police surveillance was extended even to the White Russian émigrés, who arrived in Serbia after the Russian revolution and the civil war. According to police agents, many Russians cherished pro-Soviet sympathies. The police in Niš alleged that the Catholic missionaries in the district were agents of the Vatican, while Serbian officials responsible for the admission of refugees were authorized to select them exclusively in accordance with ethnicity and religion. Consequently, only the Serbs, the Montenegrins, and the Slovenes (the latter due to German pressure) were admitted into Serbia.[62]

* * *

The regime's propaganda campaign against the resistance was accompanied by active participation in antiguerrilla warfare. By November 1941 the collaborationist police and armed forces numbered about 13,000 men (6,260 gendarmes, 5,122 "legal" Chetniks, and 1,780 policemen and agents in the urban areas) deployed in the struggle against the Partisans and the Chetniks.[63]

The Germans considered the Serbian police highly unreliable, especially since many gendarmes sympathized with the Chetniks; some policemen were demoralized after being ordered to participate in mass reprisals, and in some instances they refused to fight or execute their fellow Serbs. Nevertheless, the native police became the most visible symbol of the collaborationist regime and the only stronghold of German power in many areas in the countryside. Moreover, its records reveal that it constituted a crucial ingredient in the German terror system. The police rounded up people for compulsory labor, participated in the forcible collection of food supplies and contingents, and guarded state offices and concentration camps. When the Soviet-German war broke out, the policemen and the gendarmes carried out mass arrests of suspected communists all over Serbia.[64]

From the outset, Aćimović and Nedić urged their subordinates to actively participate in the antiguerrilla operations. The Ministry of Interior put bounties on the guerrillas and ordered the confiscation of property of the suspected resisters and their sympathizers.[65] Despite the reluctance of some policemen, the gendarmerie took part in the arrests of suspected resisters and in the executions of hostages and captured guerrillas, albeit under German supervision. On July 5, 1941, the gendarmerie executed ten communists and three Jews as hostages for sabotage. In other instances, the gendarmes escorted victims to execution sites and provided cordons for the German firing squads. By July 23, Benzler recorded that acting under orders the gendarmerie had shot more than a hundred people. The Council of Commissars and the VNS ordered arrests of the family members of the suspected communists, including young children and the elderly. On September 16, 1941, Nedić authorized Serbian courts to mete out the death sentence to everyone "who by deed or word renders help to the communists or the anarchists." On November 26, the gendarmerie participated in the mass execution of five hundred hostages near the Rudnik mountain range.[66] In one instance, Turner, who insisted that "the Serbs [should] fight the Serbs," recorded that when armed with modern arms, the native police performed "outstandingly."[67]

After the outbreak of the Soviet-German war, the German and Serbian officials set up a prison camp for political prisoners in the vicinity of Belgrade in the barracks of the royal infantry regiment in Banjica. In early July the Gestapo and the Special Police sent to the camp suspected communists, the veterans of the Spanish Civil War, and progressive journalists. Leftist or liberal affiliations also sufficed for arrest and incarceration. For instance, Professor Dušan Đorđević was sent to Banjica because he had told the police that he neither supported nor condemned the communist resistance.[68] By fall the camp had swelled to three thousand inmates, including nine hundred members of the Serbian intelligentsia.[69]

Soon the camp gained notoriety for its brutal regimen, which was designed to break one's will and to punish the inmates for even the slightest transgressions. The Serbian commandant Svetozar Vujković, who before the war headed the anticommunist department of the Belgrade police, and his deputy Đorđe Kosmajac were reputed to be sadists who daily beat and humiliated inmates. New prisoners had to surrender all valuables; cold showers were followed by disinfection with formalin acid, which caused bad burns. The camp functionaries and guards routinely extracted bribes from prisoners' families and robbed prisoners of food packages sent by relatives. Some guards became so corrupt that the Special Police had to investigate their activities.[70]

Poor sanitary conditions quickly took their toll as sickness and hunger killed dozens of inmates. Cells only 6 square meters (about 6.5 by 10 feet) contained ten and more inmates, who often had to sleep in shifts, while 150 prisoners were crammed into barracks of 100 square meters (less than 1,100 square feet). The thick odor of unwashed bodies and buckets full of excrement was so unbearable that many lost consciousness. Inmates starved as their rations were reduced to just 200 grams of cornbread of poor quality served for breakfast. In the winter of 1942–43 when typhus epidemics broke out, the prisoners had to shave their bodies with blunt razors. In addition, inmates were subjected to capricious regulations and other dehumanizing conditions. For example, there were only a few faucets in each cell and only a few holes in the floor served as toilets; after the wake-up call the prisoners had only a few minutes to wash and to relieve themselves in front of the others.[71]

* * *

The collaborationist regime in Serbia evolved as a right-wing conservative rather than as an overtly fascist institution. While Ljotić fully embraced National Socialism, Nedić came to believe that a regeneration of Serbia could be achieved within the framework of ideological premises understood by a majority of Serbs—traditional national and family values and popular antipathy to communism. Although the MBS and the German security organs controlled the activities of the Serbian administration at every level, the latter was not totally powerless and indeed enjoyed substantial latitude in combatting the resistance. For Nedić and Ljotić, the war provided an opportunity to equate the struggle against the resistance into a holy war, analogous with national regeneration and the state-building process.

Like his French counterpart Philip Pétain, Nedić feared Germany, which was rearranging the map of Europe at will. He embraced collaborationism as a long-term project, which would eventually entail some sort of autonomy for Serbia. In contrast, Ljotić saw it as the path to Serbia's total absorption into the German geopolitical space. Although they practiced collaborationism with different intensity and conviction, the Nedić "conservatives" and the Zbor "revolutionaries" evolved as ideological warriors who displayed several common traits. In fact, prominent Zbor member Ratko Parežanin admitted that the collaboration of Nedić and Ljotić were similarly driven by "necessity, which was their cross and their burden."[72]

Nedić and Ljotić glorified Serbia's traditional patriarchic society and were united in their desire to restore Serbian society to its "original" roots—the patriarchal, industrious, and orderly peasant community, rooted in its devotion to the Church, monarchy, and God. Both envisioned the new Serbia as a reactionary and antimodernist state opposed to the "corruptible" influences of city decadence, liberalism, communism, and democracy. Despite differences in official rhetoric, Nedić and Ljotić bet on German victory, which entailed a desertion of national and traditional values such as independence and a love for freedom, and both men rationalized this as a small price to pay to achieve their objectives.

Thousands of former civil servants and policemen put themselves at the disposal of the Council of Commissars and the VNS. In Eastern European societies, joining the civil service, the army, and the police was a traditional path to social promotion, steady salary, and prestige, and there were always numerous applicants.[73] For many other individuals, the April war was also in many ways a start, a vehicle to access the positions of power, economic resources, or a tool to ingratiate oneself with the victors. Yet, joining the SDK units, the Special Police, or the Department of Public Security in Banat was a radical step since their members burned all bridges to the past and had no alternative, irreversibly linking their future to Germany's fate. The realization that Germany's defeat would entail horrible retribution drove many collaborationists to become the most ruthless and efficient participants in the German terror system in Serbia.

5 Resistance Movements

In the aftermath of the March 1941 coup, Viktor von Heeren, the German consul in Belgrade, reported to Berlin that most Serbs acknowledged Germany's military might and did not support the plotters. Concerned that a rush decision by Hitler was bound to complicate the situation in the Balkans, he warned that punitive action by the Germans could convert placid popular attitudes in Yugoslavia into the "fanatical determination of World War I."[1]

Soon after Yugoslavia's capitulation, attacks on German personnel and sabotage acts seemingly corroborated Heeren's apprehensions. On April 21, 1941, a German officer was killed and two soldiers wounded in the village of Dobrić, between Belgrade and Šabac. In the next days, shots were fired at German patrols in Belgrade. In May the German police reported that the population grew increasingly hostile to the occupiers, and the Belgrade commandant issued a warning to individuals who did not show "proper respect" to German military personnel. Familiar with the Balkans' traditions of resistance, some German officers grew apprehensive of the potential alliance between the nationalists and the communists, especially since the Yugoslav army left behind vast quantities of weapons.[2]

Nevertheless, sporadic acts of resistance seemed but a temporary nuisance, so all the more unexpected was the massive insurgency that broke out in the summer. Soon the swiftness of the April *Blitzkrieg* was overshadowed by a bitter guerrilla warfare that spread all over Yugoslavia. Initially, the two main resistance groups—the communist Partisans and the nationalist Chetniks—collaborated with each other. The Partisans had vast experience in underground activities, a centralized organization, and a determined leadership, but its "class" ideology generated limited popular support. The

Chetniks operated as the extension of the royal army, and their ideology was more comprehensible to the population. The movement's leadership, however, lacked the determination, discipline, and energy of its communist counterpart.

Chetniks

In preparation for the war, the Yugoslav military set up the central Chetnik command that included the Chetnik battalions attached to each army. After the collapse of Yugoslavia, some officers, NCOs, and soldiers took to the forests and mountains and, according to prewar instructions, organized themselves into guerrilla forces. In Šumadija (a region in central Serbia) General Ljubo Novaković organized a small Chetnik unit but failed to draw much popular following. A larger Chetnik force emerged in southern Serbia under the command of Kosta Pečanac—a popular guerrilla leader of World War I and the chairman of a prewar Chetnik association. In April, Pečanac had under his command six hundred Chetniks who operated in the Toplica valley, fighting the Albanian irregulars in the border zone between Serbia and Kosovo.[3]

Among those who refused to concede defeat was a group of officers, NCOs, and enlisted men headed by the deputy chief of staff of the Second Yugoslav Army, Colonel Dragoljub-Draža Mihailović. It retreated from northern Bosnia and by the time it reached the mountainous region in western Serbia, only thirty-one individuals remained. Mihailović set up his headquarters in the area of Ravna Gora, located between Valjevo and Čačak, which he had known since World War I and where some of his supporters came from. Consequently, Mihailović's small group became commonly known as the Ravna Gora movement, destined to become the nucleus of nationalist resistance and the military arm of the Yugoslav government in exile.[4] Mihailović realized that the royal army's abysmal performance in the April war could not generate massive popular support for him and his men. To engender a broad popular base he decided to associate his movement with the well-known Chetnik organizations and renamed it the Chetnik Units of the Yugoslav Army (Četnički odredi jugoslovenske vojske), implying a fusion of Serbia's guerilla traditions with the regular armed forces.[5]

The Ravna Gora movement was epitomized by its commander. A veteran of not just World War I but also the Balkan wars, Mihailović was an honest and brave officer who served in various capacities in the interwar period. He supported but did not directly participate in the March coup, and he fought in the April war as a staff officer. Steadfastly patriotic and loyal to the monarchy, Mihailović lacked political experience but was determined to guard and eventually restore the pre-April 1941 order. Consequently, he refused to realize that a return to the old Yugoslavia was impossible unless the country was promised some political, social, and economic reforms. An astute reporter to the Yugoslav government in exile, Dr. Miloš Sekulić duly noticed that such political myopia was a major impediment for the movement.[6] Like Nedić, Mihailović feared that Serbia would suffer horrible losses on the scale of World War I, especially since the Allies considered Yugoslavia (and other small nations) of secondary strategic value; he therefore chose a "wait-and-see" attitude as the best strategy. His conviction was further strengthened when on June 26, 1941, the BBC transmitted King Peter II's appeal for the nation to refrain from active resistance until his orders.[7]

Mihailović, therefore, concentrated on mobilizing manpower and collecting arms. The collapse of the state apparatus generated a wave of crime, and in many remote areas the Chetniks appeared to be the only force capable of maintaining order. They gathered intelligence and carried out sabotage acts, avoiding attacks on German troops and the Serbian administration. The Chetniks established contacts with some Serbian officials and gendarmes, who provided the Chetniks with information and supplied them with arms and food. Mihailović's intelligence officers regularly sent situational reports to London via the British and U.S. embassies in Istanbul.[8]

The Chetnik forces were organized as territorial units divided between reservists and the full-time, younger, and better-armed soldiers. The movement attracted the Serbian intelligentsia, merchants, teachers, clerks, and priests, who were traditionally respected in the countryside; some would become prominent Chetnik commanders. The largest reservoir of the Chetnik manpower was the peasantry, known for its political conservatism, loyalty to the monarchy, and rejection of more complex ideologies (such as communism). Some peasants flocked under Chetnik banners because it effectively made them soldiers of the king and therefore eligible for financial compensation. Entering the ranks also facilitated martial traditions and family and clan ties, cherished in Serbia as pillars of communal life, while lax discipline that characterized most Chetnik units entailed opportunities to plunder with relative immunity.[9]

The Chetniks' ethnic homogeneity translated neither into a tightly centralized organization nor political uniformity. The movement was organized loosely under semi-independent commanders—*vojvodas*—who often acted without or even in defiance of Mihailović's orders. They were unwilling to move out of their home areas, mobilized or demobilized their soldiers at will, and the fighting quality of many Chetnik units remained low. Harking back to the heroic era of the wars of independence, the bearded and long-haired

Chetniks (many vowed to shave their beards only after the final victory) wore daggers, flashed skulls and cross bones on black flags, and indeed appeared to echo the Balkan past.[10]

Most of Mihailović's supporters were monarchists, but among his followers were members of various political parties (excluding the KPJ) who opposed monarchy and strove for the democratization of Yugoslav society, and the right-wing radicals. For example, Vladimir Lenac, who arrived at Ravna Gora with Mihailović, chaired the Zbor youth organization, White Eagles. The only ideological common ground for all these elements was their "Serbism"—the strong sense of Serbian national identity. Mihailović delegated all ideological work to his close advisors: the former vice president of the Serbian Cultural Club, Dragiša Vasić, and a club member and lawyer from Bosnia, Stevan Moljević, who formulated the program of the Chetnik movement from a narrow ideological viewpoint. On June 30, 1941, Moljević penned a memorandum, titled "Homogenous Serbia," which emphasized that "the experiences of the Serbian people in the April war led them to conviction that the Serbs must be assembled in a homogenous Serbia, where they would be invested with basic rights and duties; the state would cover the whole ethnic territory, where Serbs reside." Although Moljević referred to the new state as the "carrier of Yugoslav idea and the first champion of the Balkan solidarity," he envisioned that the core of Greater Serbia would encompass up to 70 percent of the former Yugoslavia, including the so-called compact Serbian enclaves: Montenegro, Macedonia, northern Albania, Sandžak, Bosnia-Herzegovina, Dalmatia, Romanian Banat (Timišoara), Bačka, Baranja, and parts of eastern Bulgaria. Croatia was to be reduced to a rump area between Serbia and Slovenia.[11] If the concept of Great Serbia in the nineteenth and the early twentieth centuries envisioned Serbia as the nucleus of the future South Slav or Yugoslav state, where ethnic Serbs would dominate politically and culturally over Croatians, Slovenes, Muslims, and other ethnic groups, Moljević's plan entailed drastic territorial changes and the migration of all ethnic Serbs into the "core" Serbian lands, which in turn would be "cleansed" of non-Serbs. All in all, Moljević's plan entailed the forcible transfer of a million people.[12]

In August the conference of the pro-Chetnik organizations formed a Central Committee to function as the movement's advisory board, which approved the Greater Serbia project.[13] The creation of the Central Committee meant that the Chetniks had evolved into a military-political movement, as had the Partisans. Paying lip service to the idea of Yugoslavism, Mihailović issued appeals to the Croats and Slovenes to join in the fight for "King and Fatherland." In reality, however, the Chetnik movement remained a hard-core nationalist Serbian organization bent on the territorial and ethnic rearrangement of Yugoslavia. With the country divided along ethnic and confessional lines, such a narrow ideological base severely undermined the movement's military and political potential.[14]

Meanwhile, the Chetnik movement was ruptured by a split between Mihailović and Pečanac. Like Mihailović, Pečanac was a hard-core Serbian nationalist but also a sly and power-hungry individual who concluded that fighting Germany was useless and the best way to benefit from the situation was to join the victors. Throughout the summer 1941 Pečanac held secret negotiations with the commander of the *Einsatzkommando* Belgrade, Karl Kraus, and with the representatives of the Council of Commissars. On August 24–27 the talks resulted in an agreement stipulating the subordination of Pečanac and his Chetniks to German command. In turn, Pečanac received permission to police the Toplica valley, which lay in his area of operations in southern Serbia. Pečanac then appealed to the Serbs, stressing that a defeated nation had to act accordingly—submit itself fully to the will of the occupier. Pečanac pledged to fight any "irresponsible elements" who disturbed German law and order. These included not just the Partisans but also Mihailović's forces, since Pečanac ordered the dissolution of any Chetnik units not under his command. Consequently, he appointed himself the commander of *all* Chetnik forces and prohibited attacks on the German and Italian personnel as long as they "act decently toward the [Serbian] people."[15]

From this point on, German and collaborationist correspondence referred to Pečanac's units—he had a thousand men under his command—as the "legal" Chetniks, that is, those who since September had been fully engaged in the anti-Partisan operations. On September 28, Bishop Nikolaj Velimirović conveyed his blessing to Pečanac, praising his "national work" and providing him with a certain degree of legitimacy.[16]

Some of Pečanac's commanders and soldiers, however, deserted and joined Mihailović. General Novaković also refused to follow Pečanac and on September 23 issued his own directive that stipulated continuation of the struggle against the Germans and their helpers. He attempted to come to an agreement with the Partisans, but they were too suspicious of his connections with Pečanac and Mihailović. Novaković was perforce to dissolve his unit; some of his soldiers joined the Partisans, while others sided with Mihailović or merged with the "legal" Chetniks.[17]

Partisans

If haphazard action characterized the rise of the Chetniks, prior planning was essential to the emergence of their political rivals, the Partisans. Their long and tortuous journey began after the March coup, which Tito conceived as a "revolutionary situation," ready to tear apart the old social order. On March 28, 1941, Tito arrived in Belgrade from Zagreb to prepare a communist takeover. However, concerned that the coup solely benefited the British, Stalin prohibited the KPJ from instigating any action except supporting the Soviet-Yugoslav April treaty.[18]

Nevertheless, the KPJ leadership made preparations for the future struggle and the KPJ ideological guidelines encapsulated the concepts of national and social revolution, in accordance with Lenin's formula of turning an "imperialist" war into a "class" war. Utilizing its considerable experience in clandestine activities, the KPJ divided Yugoslavia into zones, each under the command of a party cell, which compiled caches of arms, set up safe houses, and learned weaponry and tactics. After the formation of the Council of Commissars, Tito accentuated that war against the Germans would be accompanied by a "no less determined struggle against the traitors to the Serbian people who have performed various functions of the [collaborationist] government." In the words of Milovan Djilas, this "new thesis" unequivocally indicated that the KPJ was determined to begin a civil war and seize power at the opportune moment.[19]

By the outbreak of the Soviet-German war, the KPJ in Serbia had two thousand members, while four hundred communists and a thousand SKOJ members were based in Belgrade, making it the largest underground cell in Yugoslavia.[20] On June 22, Tito received a radioed message from the Comintern that ordered him to "reorient" the KPJ to an immediate armed struggle. Since Stalin was concerned that a communist revolution in Yugoslavia would antagonize Western powers, the Comintern insisted that KPJ form an alliance with noncommunist groups.[21] Accordingly, on July 4 the KPJ appealed to the people of Yugoslavia to forsake political and religious differences, accentuating the Soviet-British alliance as the symbol of cooperation between the two political systems.[22] On July 12, the KPJ summoned the nation to fight side by side with the Soviet Union, and on July 25 it issued yet another appeal, calling to make Yugoslavia a "besieged land" for the occupiers. All these appeals clearly emulated Stalin's speech on July 3, whereby the Soviet leader called for mass resistance in the rear of the German army. The KPJ emphasis on the development of guerrilla tactics contained the term Partisans (the Bolshevik term for guerrillas), who were directed to attack and destroy communication lines, railroads, bridges, and munitions depots. The KPJ leadership also decided to concentrate its efforts in the countryside, where the collaborationist administration was weak.[23]

The KPJ immediately set out to implement its goals in practice. Already on June 23–24, the KPJ and SKOJ groups carried out the first acts of sabotage on the Belgrade–Zagreb railroad; in Belgrade, SKOJ groups burned newsstands selling collaborationist papers. By early July the resisters had cut several telephone lines and burned military vehicles; in the countryside, the Partisans disarmed the Serbian gendarmes, staged public meetings, propagandizing the KPJ objectives, and burned communal archives containing tax registries.[24]

On July 7 the Serbian gendarmerie tried to break up the communist-organized public meeting in the village of Bela Crkva near Krupanj in western Serbia; two gendarmes were killed in the ensuing skirmish. On July 13 the KPJ in Montenegro called for a general uprising, and by the end of the month the Partisans liberated almost the entire country. Four thousand Italian army troops were killed or wounded, and Italian garrisons were besieged in towns. In Bosnia-Herzegovina and Croatia, where the Ustasha anti-Serbian terror reached massive proportions, a mass uprising broke out in late July and the Partisans and the Chetniks liberated several districts. In Dalmatia, the Partisans seized several towns, paralyzing communication lines and sabotaging mining enterprises.[25] In contrast to the scale of resistance in these regions, the event in Bela Crkva was no more than a skirmish. Nevertheless, the communist propaganda hailed it as the beginning of the "war of liberation" because it set up the pattern of the Partisan ultimate objective: demolition of the old order.[26]

To be sure, the collaborationist administration in Serbia suffered the brunt of the Partisan assaults. By July 30 the Partisans had attacked or destroyed sixty-eight gendarmerie stations; between July and mid-September, more than two hundred gendarmes were killed or wounded.[27] On August 15 the commander of the Serbian gendarmerie Jovan Trišić sent an alarming report to Aćimović, describing the situation as catastrophic. Trišić admitted that the administration had lost its ability to act and was out of touch with the population, whereas the Partisans enjoyed popular support (which Trišić ascribed to fears of Partisan reprisals).[28]

On August 21 the MBS reported that the "bands" had increased attacks against the native administration, the gendarmerie posts, and communication lines.[29] On August 23–25, four acts of sabotage were carried out in Belgrade alone, and the communication line on the Belgrade–Niš railroad was severed. Sabotage acts increased from 220 in July to 432 in August. By the end of August the Serbian administration in many localities had collapsed. The Partisans destroyed community archives, making levying taxes impossible; mail service and transportation came to a standstill. On August 28 General Bader reported to the Southeast Command that the situation in Serbia was worsening daily as the German troops suffered casualties and the Partisan attacks on railroads made supply transportation extremely difficult.[30]

The Partisans were less successful in Banat, where predominantly flat terrain was less suitable for guerrilla activities. Crucially, the Partisans could not generate support in the ethnic-German communities, which were saturated by six thousand members of the ethnic-German auxiliary police and paramilitary forces, which engaged in antiguerrilla warfare and in the persecution of Jews. In July alone the Partisan detachment in the Petrovgrad district lost a hundred members. The Sipo also hired a number of ethnic Germans, whose language skills and knowledge of the country made them vital as interpreters and agents in the struggle against the resistance. The police tracked down and killed many of the KPJ regional leadership, including its chairman Ugleša Terzin, who died in battle.[31] Consequently, in September the KPJ regional committee ordered its remaining units to move from Banat to Srijem.[32]

From the outset, the Partisan units were organized as the KPJ armed force and, in contrast to the Chetniks, operated under a highly centralized command. By mid-August 1941 they numbered five thousand members, divided into squads, platoons, and companies. Each company (*četa*) consisted of 80 to 120 men, three or four *četa* formed a battalion, and two to four battalions made up a detachment (*odred*).[33] The veterans of the Spanish civil war (known as the Spaniards) became staff officers and political commissars. The latter were deputy commanders of every unit, responsible for ideological indoctrination. They simultaneously served as members of the territorial party committees, which had the authority to replace unit commanders. In this way, the commissars' dual authority as the military and party functionaries guaranteed a tight ideological control of Partisan forces. Discipline in Partisan units was rigorously maintained by persuasion and coercion; alcohol consumption and gambling were strictly forbidden, and desertion was punishable by death.[34]

Although Partisan propaganda in Serbia portrayed the resistance as a massive popular uprising, initially the movement was dominated by professional revolutionaries, the urban intelligentsia, students, and workers. Peasants remained lukewarm to the communist ideology, especially due to its emphasis on collectivization as crucial for modernizing the countryside.[35] A great asset of the communist resistance was its impartiality to gender and ethnicity issues. Partisan women were highly dedicated scouts, intelligence agents, and medical personnel; others fought in combat alongside their male comrades, winning their respect and admiration. As in Bosnia-Herzegovina, where the Ustasha terror filled Partisan and Chetnik ranks with thousands of the region's Serbs, initially the bulk of Partisan forces was Serbian. Gradually the movement absorbed some Croats, Slovenians, and Macedonians. Joining the Partisans also became one of very few survival avenues for Jews.

In terms of tactics, the Partisans relied on the experiences of the Russian and Spanish civil wars. Upon choosing a target, the platoon and *četa*-size units attacked it from different directions and then swiftly retreated into hills and forests, where they could rest and regroup. Hiding in the mountains, however, deprived them from contacts with the population, which supplied them with food and information. Some units operated as territorial militia, while others were not connected to any particular place and could move long distances. Although successful against the gendarmerie stations and small German detachments, Partisans lacked training in combat against large enemy forces. Scarcity of arms was the major logistical problem, and Partisan attacks were often driven by necessity to obtain rifles and ammunition. Similarly problematic was the shortage of food supplies, and although Partisans tried to pay or barter for food, they also confiscated supplies, antagonizing villagers.[36]

By the end of the summer, Partisan forces had suffered a crushing defeat in Montenegro, where too much emphasis on communist ideology backfired and the movement was almost obliterated by the combined Italian-Chetnik forces. The KPJ leadership, therefore, doubled its efforts to emphasize national sentiments over the communist revolutionary dogmas.[37] To win popular support, in the liberated territories Partisans set up kitchens for the poorest segments of the population, supplied wood for heating houses, and provided financial aid to the needy (most of the money came from attacks on the Serbian financial institutions), widely publicizing such occasions.[38]

The Partisans, however, could not resist the temptation to carry out a "socialist transformation" of the countryside. Emulating the Soviet experience of creating partisan republics, they turned liberated areas into the blueprints for the ideological and social restructuring of Yugoslavia. The Partisans proudly donned red stars, hoisted red banners, and set up communist-dominated village councils. The councils abolished the royal courts, confiscated state and church property, distributed agricultural implements to peasant communities, and burned the state archives and municipal documentation.[39] To Moscow's remonstrations, the KPJ explained that the "people's committees" replaced the old administrative system, which could not be sustained in its contemporary form, and functioned as temporary power holders until the end of the war. To corroborate this point, the committees were euphemistically named "temporary organs of power" or the "organs of national democratic power," which implied their provisional character and political diversity.[40] Terror also constituted a crucial element of Partisan rule in liberated territories—some family members of Serbian officials were taken hostage, and a prominent communist leader admitted that such individuals "were selectively" tortured.[41] Partisan courts tried looters and individuals suspected of collaboration. Death sentences were carried out either in public or under the cover of night.[42] All these features gave a clear impression that should the Partisans emerge victorious, there would be no return to the prewar political system.

Partisans' lives were extremely hard. Lack of food, medications, and sleep was exacerbated by constant maneuvering to avoid the enemy forces, and fear of ambush took a heavy psychological toll, causing lingering fatigue. However, Partisans fought alongside their comrades and could enjoy short respites when camping in mountains and forests. In contrast, the urban guerrillas could ill afford to relax, constantly threatened with arrest and vulnerable to detection by agents and provocateurs. Indeed, the invisible war in cities was particularly brutal and uncompromising, for an urban guerrilla could count only on his or her intelligence, good knowledge of terrain, and a certain degree of luck. Even those who avoided capture frequently suffered psychological damages, generated by anticipation of provocation and arrest. From May to September 1941, Tito himself faced such a nerve-wracking experience, when he lived in Belgrade under a fake identity and twice barely avoided capture.[43]

The communist urban underground had been active since the outbreak of the Soviet-German war. In June 1941 the members of the Belgrade KPJ branch cut telephone cables and damaged vehicles, disseminated propaganda leaflets, and wrote graffiti on walls, extolling the victories of the Red Army. They also pulled off several exceptionally dangerous and daring missions. On July 29, a group of the guerrillas liberated a member of the KPJ political bureau, Aleksandar Ranković, who had been arrested by the Gestapo although they did not yet know who he was. Beaten unconscious during interrogation, Ranković was transferred to a hospital, and Tito ordered that he be freed at any price. The guerrillas entered the hospital and escaped with Ranković wrapped in hospital cloths.[44] On August 3 a SKOJ member, Aleksandar Vojinović, set up explosives in the Park hotel in Niš, killing and wounding several German officers. Between September 25 and October 2, SKOJ members also assassinated three police agents.[45]

The activities of the guerrillas caused fear among the Germans and their native helpers, who ventured out at night only in groups. A German pilot from Belgrade wrote to his friend that "everywhere clatter gun-shots and our lorries burn. I can not imagine what these fanatical kids try to achieve when they burn press stands and garages or try to kill our NCOs. . . . I can hardly wait [for] when we leave, even to [go to] the East, as I have a feeling that one night I come out of the car and some Balkan fool will put a bullet in my head."[46]

The urban underground's heroic feats, however, came at an extremely high cost, for the operational activity of a single resistance cell normally lasted no more than several months. To trace and destroy the guerrillas, the Gestapo and the Special Police used various police techniques, such as the so-called *Funkspiel* (radio game) to locate guerrilla radio stations. But the most effective method was the utilization of informants, turncoats, and agents provocateurs. Once they informed their handler of a resistance cell safe house, it became a trap.

In July 1941 the Special Police agent Milutin Špartalj infiltrated a communist group, which then was destroyed by the Gestapo and the Special Police. Acting on an agent's information, in September and October the Gestapo and the Special Police decimated the KPJ Belgrade committee and the SKOJ city organization.[47] Under threats or torture, some resisters betrayed their comrades. Ratko Mitrović, an arrested member of the SKOJ Central Committee, cooperated with the Special Police to divulge the entire organizational structure of the Belgrade underground. In October the Special Police functionaries turned in an instructor of the KPJ city district committee, Lazar Dožić, who betrayed his comrades, including his brother.[48]

Arrest of a resistance member was the beginning of an excruciating experience. Brought to the headquarters of the Special Police or the Gestapo, a suspect was first subjected to hours of questioning. Interrogators began with appealing to the captive's sensibility, promising that confession would spare family members from suffering; sometimes they promised to pay for information. When persuasion did not work, other methods were brought to bear—interrogators worked in shifts, beating the victim's kidneys, soles of the feet, or stomach, breaking bones, or squeezing the head with an iron device. Often prisoners were suspended with their arms tied behind their back while their bodies were burned with cigarette butts. The torturers knew what level of pain they had to inflict for maximum effect and kept at it. If victims blacked out, they were revived only to be tortured again.[49]

Some individuals were maimed or died under torture, such as Đuro Strugar, a member of the KPJ provincial committee. After long interrogation, a secretary of the same committee, Janko Lisjak, died of his injuries in a prison hospital. Nadežda-Nada Purić was reported to have died of a "heart attack," but in reality she was tortured for eleven days and succumbed to her wounds. Others chose to take their own lives before the interrogation.[50] Some guerrillas managed to remained silent despite the torture. Headed by Bećarević, a group of Special Police agents for hours tortured a prominent SKOJ member, Josip Ščurla-Mačak, who was carried back to the cell with his body horribly mangled and the soles of his feet skinned; he died from his injuries but remained silent to the end. Vukica Mitrović refused to talk even after her brother Ratko Mitrović, who had betrayed his comrades to the Special Police, tried to persuade her to become an informant.[51]

Despite severe losses, the underground regenerated its cells repeatedly with new fighters. On October 22, 1941, the Gestapo chief Heinrich Müller issued a directive, "Combating the Communist Movement in the Former Yugoslavia," in which he admitted that the communist resistance remained well-organized and coordinated.[52]

Cooperation and Conflict

From the inception of the Chetnik movement, Mihailović was determined to avoid collisions with the German forces for fear of mass reprisals against the population, especially as the Ustasha terror in Croatia, Bosnia, and Herzegovina claimed tens of thousands of Serbian lives. His apprehensions that the Serbian population could be decimated grew after the Germans shot several hostages in reprisal for Chetnik attacks near Kragujevac; four captured Chetniks were publicly hanged in Požega. As a result, several villages sent delegations to Mihailović, begging him not to initiate any actions nearby. Such requests convinced Mihailović that his wait-and-see strategy was right, and he ordered that sabotage acts on communication lines be carried out as far away from the villages as possible.[53]

Nevertheless, a few Chetnik commanders grew impatient for action. On July 4, three days before the Partisan attack in Bela Crkva, seventy Chetniks attacked and disarmed a gendarmerie station.[54] In early August a large Chetnik unit under Captain Dragoslav Račić joined the Partisans in an assault on Maćva, where several Serbian officials and gendarmes were killed. In reprisal, the Germans shot more than a hundred people. On August 25, Racić and another Chetnik commander, Nebojša Jerković, sent a letter to Mihailović, demanding that the Chetniks join the Partisans in the anti-German struggle. A Chetnik commander in the Ibar region, Vuk Vukašinović, urged Mihailović to the same effect. In southeastern Serbia, several Chetnik commanders who had earlier left Kosta Pečanac and placed themselves under Mihailović, carried out several joint actions with the Partisans.[55]

Partisan-Chetnik cooperation had great potential as they succesfully combined guerrilla and more conventional tactics (a combination that later would bring success to Mao's and Ho Chi Minh's communist troops). While small units harassed German convoys, on September 2, 1941, 250 Partisans and 200 Chetniks stormed the town of Krupanj in western Serbia and blockaded the German garrison in their barracks. After three days of fighting, the attackers captured a large amount of arms, uniforms, ammunition, and several vehicles. Nine Germans were killed and ninety-four taken prisoner.[56] On September 23–24, a Partisan unit and 460 Chetniks under Major Dragutin Keserović (a former officer of General Novaković) attacked the town of Kruševac, a district capital. Although the attack failed, the Germans sustained heavy casualties (at least twenty-three were killed) and the city remained under siege.[57] In early October the Partisans and Chetniks besieged Kraljevo and Šabac and controlled large swaths of territory in western Serbia from the Drina River to the Bulgarian zone of occupation. In some localities, they shared power and conducted joint public meetings. The Germans and collaborationist forces increasingly found themselves confined to cities and towns.[58]

Mihailović must have realized that by avoiding battles with the Germans he could lose his soldiers' allegiance. At the same time, he was troubled that the Partisans increasingly appeared to be the dominant resistance force, while the alliance with the Chetniks provided them with national credentials understandable to the majority of the population.[59] Meanwhile, some Chetnik commanders who were known to be fanatical anticommunists had tried to establish contacts with the collaborationist administration. Mihailović did not initiate these contacts, but he did not forbid them, either, and so kept his options open for potential negotiations. Already in May 1941, Vladimir Lenac tried to convince Mihailović to declare openly for the Council of Commissars. Meetings between the Chetniks and the Serbian administration representatives continued through the summer and fall. The Germans were aware of such contacts and encouraged them.[60]

On September 9, Mihailović issued an order that the Chetniks must avoid confrontation with the Germans, Italians, and the Partisans, but he must have realized that time was running short and that remaining neutral could eventually invite assault by all three forces. He, therefore, had to make some crucial choices. On September 19–20, Mihailović met Tito to discuss potential cooperation, but he refused to commit the Chetniks in an open struggle against the Germans. In turn, although Tito spoke of the common Partisan-Chetnik struggle, he would not serve under a royal officer who represented the monarchy.[61] The meeting ended with mutual promises of maintaining peace, but apparently it solved Mihailović's potential dilemma as to who was a greater enemy, the Germans or the communists. For the time being, the latter appeared a bigger threat to the monarchy.[62]

In turn, Tito saw the Chetniks as symbolizing royal Yugoslavia and realized that conflict with Mihailović was unavoidable. Still, Tito had to obey instructions from Moscow, which insisted that the Chetniks and the Partisans put aside their differences and join forces against the Germans. On July 11,

1941, the Soviet Union and the Yugoslavian government in exile restored diplomatic relations (in April, playing up to Hitler, the Soviet government had broken diplomatic relations with Yugoslavia), and Stalin was interested in maintaining amiable relations with London, which supported Mihailović.[63]

While Tito and Mihailović tried to maintain decorum, the emergence of the so-called Užice republic detonated the simmering Chetnik-Partisan conflict into open war. In July, Tito ordered the Partisan command in Serbia to create the "liberated territories, which would serve as the launching base for the struggle for freedom," and in September the KPJ leadership organized all liberated districts in western Serbia into the Partisan heartland, which offered accessible routes to Montenegro and Bosnia-Herzegovina. On September 24, Partisans captured the town of Užice, where the labor and communist groups were particularly active before the war, and made it into the capital of the movement.[64]

Despite promises to Moscow to avoid political actions, which could alarm the British, the Užice town committee immediately set out to transform the town into a socialist republic. It announced a moratorium for all debts incurred by the "exploited classes," levied taxes on businesses, fined speculators, and regulated salaries for workers and civil servants. In an effort to expand the popular base of the resistance, the Partisan propaganda machine went to work organizing mass rallies, theatrical performances, art exhibitions, lectures, literacy courses, and the musical festivals of the national and the Soviet revolutionary songs. A prominent KPJ leader Milovan Djilas admitted that a "germ of a government" was in the making in Užice.[65]

On November 7, 1941, the KPJ leadership celebrated the twenty-fourth anniversary of the Bolshevik revolution. Tito (who arrived to Užice in late September) and other KPJ leaders stood on a podium, greeting the Partisan units in a clear imitation of parades on Moscow's Red Square. In their speeches, the communist leaders hailed the achievements of the Soviet Union as the model of a "new constitutional democracy." Edvard Kardelj later admitted that such overtly pro-Soviet gestures were "sectarian errors" that inhibited the potential propaganda impact on the population.[66]

In November, the KPJ announced the formation of the People's Main Liberation Council (Nacionalni komitet oslobođenja Jugoslavije, NKOJ), which despite its title became a thoroughly communist body. It coordinated the activities of Partisan units and supervised all political and socioeconomic measures undertaken in the liberated territories. NKOJ's two informational bulletins, *Borba* (Struggle) and *Vesti* (News), described political and social life in the Partisan-controlled areas and called for the unification of all anti-Axis forces under KPJ leadership.[67]

Mihailović was alarmed at the events in Užice, and he particularly abhorred the establishment of the NKOJ, which purported to speak on behalf of the Yugoslav people. In turn, Tito was convinced that Mihailović was playing a double game, since on September 8 the Partisans captured two Chetnik officers who carried documents from the meetings between the Chetnik and Nedić's representatives on September 2 and 4.[68] Mihailović perceived the Partisan-established councils to be the tools of political power, but Tito in a letter to Mihailović insisted that these were but temporary and "most suitable [organs] to the contemporary situation and closest to the people."[69]

The different social base of the Partisans and the Chetniks was another factor that drove the two movements apart, for the former was initially dominated by the urban intelligentsia and industrial laborers, who were not overtly concerned that German reprisals particularly affected the peasant communities. On October 26–27, the second and the last meeting between Tito and Mihailović in the village of Brajinći near Ravna Gora was conducted in a tense atmosphere. Crucially, it took place soon after the brutal German reprisals for the Partisan attacks in Kragujevac and Kraljevo (see chapter 6). For Mihailović, the massacres were the final proof that an open war with the Germans entailed the decimation of the Serbian population. In fact, he suspected that the Partisans deliberately provoked German reprisals. In addition, the arrival of a British liaison officer to Mihailović headquarters assured him of British support.[70] Hence, Mihailović flatly turned down Tito's proposal for joint operations. The two leaders merely consented to allow the free movement of their troops and transport through their respective zones. Tito also agreed to hand over to the Chetniks five hundred rifles, ammunition, five tons of grain, and 5 million dinar seized by the Partisans in Užice.[71]

Behind this show of good will, the Partisans and the Chetniks were prepared for an all-out war. On October 25 in a letter to Comintern, Tito admitted that only "because of London [i.e., British support of the Chetniks] we had to give up the total liquidation of Mihailović."[72] Conversely, on October 28, two Chetnik commanders met with an Abwehr officer to inform him that Mihailović had decided to join Nedić and the Wehrmacht in anticommunist combat. Furthermore, Mihailović promised to assume responsibility for the complete elimination of the communist resistance in exchange for the termination of German reprisals.[73]

On November 1, Mihailović repeated his request by sending a note to the German intelligence department of the 342nd Division, which operated in the Valjevo district. He pledged that if the Chetniks were supplied with arms, they alone could "solve the communist problem" and explained that the earlier Partisan-Chetnik cooperation was necessary to prevent the Partisans from appearing to be the sole resistance force. As had Pečanac, Mihailović requested that after the defeat of the communists, western Serbia be turned into a "free zone" under his control.[74]

On the same day, the Chetnik forces attacked Partisan positions at Užice. Mihailović's chief of staff, Dragoslav Pavlović, may have initiated the offensive, but it served as the signal for the assaults on Partisans at Čačak and other localities. The Partisans, however, beat off the attacks and captured the main Chetnik stronghold in Požega, located sixteen miles east of Užice. With his forces in retreat, Mihailović asked for truce. Disturbed, the Soviet government demanded that Tito call off the Partisan offensive. Under Moscow's pressure, Tito grudgingly conceded, claiming that the conflict was provoked by "irresponsible elements" among the Chetniks. The same line was maintained after the Chetniks brutally murdered Milan Blagojević, a prominent Partisan commander in Požega. The *Borba* announced that his murderers were "criminal hirelings who infiltrated the ranks of the honest Chetniks."[75]

The Partisans, however, did not leave Požega, and on November 11 Mihailović and his closest associates met several German representatives (including Turner's deputy, Georg Kiessel) in a village near Valjevo. Mihailović repeated his offer of collaboration, but the Germans accused him of surreptitious attacks on German forces. Mihailović defended himself by blaming "renegade" or "insubordinate" commanders for the Chetnik attacks. He argued that after Nedić and Pečanac openly sided with the Germans, they lost most popular support. Hence, to maintain his image as the leader of national resistance, he promised to collaborate secretly and requested arms to continue the anticommunist struggle. All his explanations, however, were in vain, for the Germans refused to supply the Chetniks and warned that should Mihailović not disarm and surrender his units, the German troops would treat them the same way they were treating the Partisans.[76]

Two days later, the Chetnik commander Jovan Škava handed 365 captured Partisans to the Germans; most of them were subsequently shot. Whether Mihailović knew of or authorized this action, the Partisans interpreted it as another proof of the Chetniks' treachery (according to Dedijer, the key culprit was Mihailović's deputy, Lieutenant Colonel Dragoslav Pavlović). Tito was further infuriated when on November 15, in his appeal to the nation, King Peter II named Mihailović as supreme commander of the "first resistance [movement] in occupied Europe."[77]

Still, bound by Moscow's instructions, Tito made the last halfhearted attempt to stop the civil war. On November 18–20 at the meeting of Partisan and Chetnik representatives, the two sides reached a tentative truce. They pledged to refrain from attacking each other, to exchange prisoners, and to establish joint commissions to investigate the causes of the fratricidal struggle. Despite the agreement, the Partisans procrastinated with the promised delivery of rifles and ammunition from Užice. Concomitantly, several Chetnik units had joined the German troops in the anti-Partisan offensive, which swept through western Serbia.[78]

* * *

In summer 1941, the communist uprising brought to an end the short "sedate" period of German rule in Yugoslavia. Serbia became the epicenter of communist and national resistance forces, which aimed at the same ultimate goal: the liberation of Yugoslavia. Together, the Chetniks and the Partisans achieved some impressive successes, but their different ideological platforms ultimately made their cooperation impossible. The Partisans envisioned the defeat of the Axis powers as a stage on the road to social revolution, stipulated by Lenin's classic concept of transforming the "imperialist" war into a civil war, while victory for the Chetniks meant the restoration of the old order.

The defeat of the Partisans (see chapter 6) warranted a certain degree of optimism among the German military and the collaborationist administration. Such a situation eventually undermined the position of the VNS: convinced of the Partisans' weakness, the Germans were determined to maintain the status quo in VNS, refusing to grant it even minor concessions. Persistently ignoring the situation in Serbia, the German command shelved the problem, believing that the occupation mode should not be changed in the midst of the war.

On December 20, Mihailović issued an instruction to his subordinates that stressed his readiness to carry out a "preventive counterrevolution."[79] In other words, he embraced a temporary accommodation with the Germans as the only possible way to save the old Yugoslavia. In this context, Mihailović eventually found common ground with Nedić. Despite mutual animosity and divergent ideological dispositions, both were horror-struck by the Ustasha massacres, and both blamed the communists for German reprisals. Such a convergence of attitudes entailed potential cooperation in the fight against their common foe. In turn, after the German defeat at Moscow in December 1941, the KPJ Central Committee ordered its forces in Serbia to disarm or destroy all non-Partisan formations, first and foremost the Chetniks, who in the words of Tito became the "main enemy of the liberation struggle."[80]

In several European countries, the Second World War unleashed a series of civil wars, between the forces of resistance and collaboration and between the communists and nationalists. Yugoslavia became a particularly vicious battlefield of conflicting ideologies, augmented by confessional and ethnic tensions. In Serbia, Partisans, Nedić's forces, and Chetniks engaged in a brutal fratricidal conflict that became inseparable from the "big" war and symbolized a profound chasm within Serbian society. A participant in these events bitterly lamented that "instead of fighting the fascist bandits, we fight our brothers; instead of shedding the enemy's blood, we shed our own."[81]

6 Repression

Referring to his experience, the commander of the French counterinsurgency forces in North Africa in the late nineteenth century General Joseph Galliéni stressed that "by combined use of politics and force, pacification of a country and its future organization will be achieved. . . . Political action is by far the most important."[1] Galliéni meant that a successful counterinsurgency campaign should amalgamate military, police, and political measures. Combating guerrillas by force alone is not only difficult, it is often counterproductive. While most theorists of counterinsurgency warfare would agree with Galliéni, governments more often rely on sheer force and terror that correspond with their ideological doctrines. In this regard, the German methods of antiguerrilla warfare in Yugoslavia (as well as elsewhere) was the very antithesis of Galliéni's precepts.

The German military and civil officials did not consider the Serbs as ideological enemies solely on the basis of race. That designation was initially reserved only for Jews and for resistance fighters, who the Germans placed outside the law. However, the outbreak of resistance elevated racial stereotypes to the forestage of occupation policies, particularly since the Germans did not have enough troops to enforce the "Carthaginian peace" they had imposed on Serbia.[2] In comparison to Poland or Ukraine, where maintaining security was the prerogative of Himmler's SS and police, his forces in Serbia were too small for such a task. As a result, the Wehrmacht assumed what were essentially police functions. The German officer corps's commitment to the Nazi ideology ensured that it perceived its task through a political prism and applied unrestricted terror as the most effective method to crush the resistance.

German Anti-Insurgency Warfare

The Wehrmacht's reactions to the uprising in Serbia were partially rooted in the imperial German concepts of antiguerrilla operations. These originated in the aftermath of the Franco-Prussian War of 1870–71, when the activities of the French militiamen threatened German communications. Looking for the most appropriate methods to fight the guerrillas, the German General Staff declared that they were illegal combatants and ordered mass reprisals as a potent psychological deterrent. Colonial wars in Africa and China further molded a set of doctrines that stipulated the uncompromising use of reprisals as imperative military necessity. During World War I, the German policing of Belgium, parts of France, and Russia's western borderlands entailed executions of potential resisters, the forcible resettlement of the population away from the fronts, and the formation of special units to combat guerrillas.[3]

Still, before the outbreak of World War II, the German army did not have a well-defined doctrine of antiguerrilla warfare. Instead, in August 1938 Hitler issued a decree that defined criminal activities, which were to be suppressed by mass reprisals. These included espionage, hostile acts committed by civilians, violations of German military regulations, and the undermining of German military power, all punishable by death. The wording of the decree gave German commanders wide latitude in interpreting what constituted hostile acts and allowed the seizure and execution of hostages. Accordingly, after the occupation of Czechoslovakia (and later Western Europe), the German commanders applied terror as a tool of intimidation, in the form of selective executions of political opponents and hostages.[4]

The invasion of Poland ushered in a new radical stage in the Nazi application of terror. On August 22, 1939, Hitler confided to a circle of German dignitaries that the war against Poland would be waged with utmost brutality. This speech effectively became the blueprint for the Nazi policies in occupied Poland, whereby terror was to accelerate German victory and the total destruction of the Polish state.[5] To this effect, mass reprisals—interchangeably called atonement measures (*Sühnenmassnahmen*) and reprisals (*Vergeltungsmassnahmen*)—were used daily to eradicate real and potential opponents of the regime. Any potential acts of resistance and sabotage were to be crushed only by overwhelming ferocity. In this context, the entire local population, regardless of whether it had anything to do with the acts of resistance, was assumed to be guilty. Concomitantly, the so-called exterminatory terror was directed against Jews, the resistance members, the intelligentsia, political activists, and the clergy. In accordance with Nazi racial ideology, Jews (defined both in ideological and in racial terms), the Roma, and individuals with mental or physical disabilities were considered unfit for Hitler's New Order and slated for murder.[6]

In Yugoslavia, the Wehrmacht and the SS initially envisioned the application of selective terror. Before the invasion, the OKW chief of staff General Franz Halder and the RSHA chief Reinhardt Heydrich compiled lists of potential enemies, which included three thousand political émigrés, "terrorists, saboteurs, Jews," and the communists, to be eliminated immediately.[7] Article 18 of the April armistice explicitly forbade Yugoslav citizens from wearing arms and military uniforms. Consequently, from the German point of view, after the Yugoslav army capitulated, any form of resistance by the citizenry became illegal. Such reasoning was contrary to The Hague International Convention of 1907, which legalized guerrillas as long as they wore recognizable uniforms and insignia. Besides the fact that this condition rendered useless the very purpose of guerrilla warfare, the convention also stipulated that residents of an occupied country were to obey the occupying force as long as the latter abode by the same convention.

The Wehrmacht, however, was beyond such nuances. Between April 11 and 20, 1941, German troops carried out initial reprisals in Banat, where 149 people were executed for possessing arms, Chetnik activities, and alleged crimes against ethnic Germans. In reprisal for the killing of a German soldier (who was murdered in a drunken brawl), on April 22 the German command in Pančevo ordered the hanging of thirty-six hostages. As yet lacking the experience to dispatch the victims quickly, the executioners botched the job so that the victims suffered before finally dying.[8] Still, in comparison to the Hungarian reign of terror in Vojvodina, where in April about 3,500 people were shot, German reprisals claimed fewer lives.[9]

Soon, however, German selective terror gave way to "kill-all" policies, which were implemented to the letter. When an officer was killed near the village of Donji Dobrić in the Toplica district, the German troops burned the village and shot its inhabitants. On April 28, Maximilian von Weichs, the commander of the Second Army, issued a directive that provided the foundation for German anti-resistance policies in Serbia. The directive stipulated that "traitorous assaults" on German military personnel necessitated the "harshest measures" and that, since the Yugoslav military personnel had no right to bear arms, anyone in Yugoslavian military uniform or with arms should be treated as an outlaw. Crucially, the directive linked the resistance to the population, which was accused of providing the insurgents with supplies and shelter or told that it "should have known" of impending guerrilla attacks. The villages where the guerrillas appeared, therefore, were slated for reprisals unless there was "undeniable proof" that they had no connection to the resistance. Finding such proof was left to the discretion of German commanders.[10]

Significantly, Weichs's directive provided for the execution of a hundred Serbs for each German killed, or fifty for one wounded. This ratio became a guiding tool for German reprisals, precipitating by three and a half months Hitler's notorious order in September. Also, Weichs referred to the guerrillas as "bandits," the term adopted by Himmler in June 1942 as the official designation for the resistance.[11]

German terror policies in Yugoslavia were further impacted by the war against the Soviet Union. One month before Operation Barbarossa, the OKW issued "Guidelines for the Behavior of the Army in Russia," which called for the "restless elimination" of active or passive resistance, while the so-called Jurisdiction Barbarossa order exonerated military personnel from crimes committed against the Soviet population. Another directive ascribed absolute value to the deterrent effect of mass reprisals. From the outset of the Soviet-German war, unrestricted terror had become the staple of the antiguerrilla warfare—dubbed *Bandenbekämpfung* (anti-bandit warfare)—and evolved into an ideological-racial category, whereby the terms *bandits*, *communists*, and *Jews* became identical. When on July 3 Stalin urged the Soviet populace to wage a merciless guerrilla war against the German invaders, Hitler told his associates that the partisan war enabled him to "exterminate everyone" who opposed the regime.[12]

On the day the German invasion of the Soviet Union began, the MBS Ludwig Schröder ordered that "preventive" measures be launched in Serbia, and by early July the *Einsatzkommando* Belgrade and the Special Police had arrested seven hundred individuals, including thirty-two Belgrade University professors.[13] These arrests seemingly deprived the resistance of potential leaders and so all the more unexpected to the Germans was the massive uprising that broke out several days later. In fact, German intelligence reports estimated the strength of the guerrillas at thirty thousand. On July 17, Schröder issued a directive ordering the death penalty and prison terms for acts of sabotage, abetting individuals sought by the authorities, and any form of resistance to German power.[14]

On July 22–23, the supreme commander of the German forces in the Balkans, Field Marshal Wilhelm List, visited Belgrade to discuss with Schröder the situation in Serbia. As a result of the talks, Schröder issued additional guidelines for reprisal policies. On one hand, these guidelines dictated that reprisals should be carried out only *after* the connection between the resistance and hostages was fully established, while on the other hand the populace was held responsible for acts of sabotage if it did not prevent the commission of such acts.[15]

These mutually exclusive conditions underscored the random nature of reprisals, which rapidly became more commonplace. On July 18, twenty-eight hostages were shot in Belgrade; among the victims were civil servants, school and university students, merchants, and workers who were randomly picked up on the streets.[16] On July 27, the troops shot eighty-one peasants who happened to be near the site where a German car was attacked. In late July, 290 alleged communists were shot in Banat; in the countryside, the troops left corpses where they fell to intimidate the population.[17]

The fate of the village of Skela in northern Serbia became paradigmatic of the Wehrmacht anti-insurgency warfare. On August 14 Partisans ambushed a car, killing an officer, two NCOs, and two soldiers near Skela. The local German command claimed that the villagers knew of the impending attack but failed to inform the authorities. In reprisal, the village was burned, all males suspected of helping the guerrillas were shot, and fifty hostages were hanged.[18]

On August 17, 1941, a lamppost in Terazijama square in downtown Belgrade was gruesomely swathed with five hanging corpses. All alleged members of the resistance, the victims had been tortured in the Gestapo headquarters, then shot, and finally their corpses hung by order of the commander of the *Einsatzkommando* Belgrade, Karl Kraus. Intended to intimidate the population, the sight certainly spread fear among the residents, but it also became a symbol of Serbia's martyrdom and thus actually fortified the resistance. The communist underground immediately disseminated leaflets calling for retribution, while an anonymous letter to General Heinrich Dankelmann (who assumed the MBS post in July, after General Schröder died from injuries in a plane crash) promised that the general would soon hang on the same spot alongside Aćimović and Ljotić.[19]

By late August the German troops reported having killed, wounded, and captured 221 armed insurgents. At the same time, they shot a thousand alleged communists and Jews.[20] The rising numbers of executions could be partially attributed to the conditions of the antiguerrilla warfare in Serbia, where the topography is particularly well-suited for guerrilla activities. Although averaging only about 2,000 meters high, forested mountains cover much of the country, and difficult terrain added to the troops' exhaustion, fatigue, and frustration at their lack of success. Indeed, the situation in Serbia resembled that of the Peninsular War in the early nineteenth century, where French troops found themselves continuously harassed by Spanish guerrillas. However, in contrast to Napoleon, who kept a large army in Spain, Dankelmann faced a much tougher situation, since all German combat troops were siphoned off by the eastern front. He had, therefore, to rely solely on his units, many of which were dispersed to guard communication lines and industrial sites. For example, a thousand officers and soldiers were garrisoned at the Bor mines alone. All in all, Dankelmann had 25,000 German troops and policemen, who faced 15,000 Partisans and the Chetniks. Even if it was impossible to achieve the much-cited ten to one soldier versus guerrilla ratio for successful anti-insurgency, the constant shortage of German manpower could have been compensated by the expansion and shrewder use of the collaborationist forces. But this was never done.

The German forces in Serbia were fighting an elusive enemy and facing a population that appeared indifferent at best and hostile at worst. Difficulties in combating the guerrillas were compounded by the overlapping command structure, whereby the OKW, the MBS, and the Southeast Command constantly worked at cross-purposes. Random roundups and blockading villages did not bring the desired results, as the guerrillas easily avoided the encirclement. In early September, eleven German companies (1,300 men) swept the countryside south of Čačak, but the Partisans managed to slip through German lines. Without reinforcements, the small hunting units (*Jagdkommandos*) that combed the mountains proved ineffective.[21]

Crucially, in the summer of 1941, the Wehrmacht in Serbia faced a massive guerrilla war for the first time since the beginning of World War II. The partisan movement in the Soviet Union had not yet reached its maturity, and resistance groups elsewhere in Europe confined their activities to sabotage acts, propaganda, and intelligence gathering. In contrast, in the last ten days of August alone, Partisans in Serbia carried out thirty attacks on railroads; between September 6 and 12, another forty-two attacks on railroads and stations were launched. In September the Partisans carried out thirty-two attacks on German troops and 552 assaults on Serbian administrative offices, gendarmerie posts, rail stations, and other installations. Between September 27 and October 3, there were 126 acts of sabotage, fifty assaults on the Serbian administration and the gendarmerie, and three on the German forces.[22]

Every German office had to be particularly concerned because attacks and sabotage acts partially or completely paralyzed Serbia's industries, threatening deliveries of zinc, fuel, pyrite, and antimony from mines in Obrenovac, Kragujevac, Kraljevo, and other localities. Serbia's economy and transportation system needed 110,000 tons of coal and 50,000 tons of lignite monthly, but in September the Partisan attacks reduced the industrial output to 25,000 and 24,000 tons, respectively. Communication lines were severely damaged, and the supplies of raw materials, crucial for Germany's war effort, dwindled with alarming speed.[23]

German rule in Serbia increasingly appeared to be on the verge of collapse. A sense of urgency and insecurity was reflected in desperate reports, particularly as the Chetniks and Partisans temporarily joined forces. By mid-August the Southeast Command had repeatedly asked the OKW for the deployment of regular troops in Serbia. On August 28, General Bader reported to the Southeast Command that the situation in Serbia was worsening daily, with German troops suffering casualties and Partisan attacks on railroads making supply transportation extremely difficult.[24]

On September 4 the exasperated List ordered ruthless reprisals against the rebels, their families, and the population at large; entire localities were to be burned if they failed to inform on the presence of the insurgents. List's instructions may have emanated less from his ideological disposition than from the frustrations of a professional officer desperate over the situation in the area under his command. While not a fanatical Nazi by conviction, List nevertheless displayed racial biases toward the Serbs, whom he considered intrinsically bloodthirsty and rebellious.[25]

A day later, List reported that the "situation in Serbia does not exclude the expansion of the uprising," while the MBS chief of staff echoed that the insurgency was "expanding rapidly due to the rebels' temporary military successes." Although German exploitation of the Bor mine began in September, Partisan attacks on the railroads cut off the supply of ore for the production of copper, so crucial for Germany's war efforts. In the first eight days of September, 414 German troops were killed, wounded, and missing. The number of victims among the collaborationist administration and police was much higher.[26]

This situation elicited a drastic response from Hitler. On September 16, 1941, the OKW issued his order to vest all executive powers in Serbia to the commander of the Eighteenth Army Corps general Franz Böhme. Recommended by List as an "outstanding expert" of the Balkans, Böhme was appointed the "plenipotentiary for the suppression of the uprising in the Southeast" and the commander of all German forces in Serbia, authorized to reestablish order by the "application of sharpest means." These included the execution of a hundred hostages for each German killed and fifty for each wounded. Simultaneously, the OKW ordered the transfer of two combat divisions to Serbia—the 342nd Infantry Division from France and the 113th Infantry Division (in November) from Russia. Two regiments and several battalions were also dispatched from Greece.[27]

As the plenipotentiary for suppressing the resistance, Böhme's jurisdiction surpassed that of the MBS, and in late October he officially replaced Dankelmann, whom Hitler considered "too soft." His appointment indicated that the OKW attempted to compensate for the German manpower shortage by dispatching to the Balkans those officers who had experience in the region.[28]

An Austrian, Böhme was one of many imperial officers who during World War I fought on the eastern front or in the Balkans. They acquired strong anti-Slavic attitudes and participated in reprisals against civilians, carried out by the Austro-Hungarian army. Still, the Austro-Hungarian command believed that reprisals were extreme but temporary measures and that the army should act—as long as circumstances allowed—within the confines of international law.[29]

In contrast, in 1941 the Wehrmacht officer corps was not bound by any political or moral considerations and viewed all Serbs as hostiles capable of understanding only brutal force. An additional factor that fueled such attitudes was the brutalization of warfare on the eastern front, where the German troops waged the most vicious battles of World War II. The German troops, the SS, and the police in Russia murdered thousands of civilians as insurgents or guerrilla helpers and destroyed entire localities marked as "partisan infected." In September a Sipo report mentioned that south of Leningrad the German army "adopted the new methods of the Security Police" in wiping out villages suspected of supporting the guerrillas. In other words, the Wehrmacht endorsed the anticommunist and racist aspects of the Nazi ideological doctrine and became a willing partner of Himmler's repressive apparatus.[30]

If some German officers had reservations about the methods of the *Einsatzgruppen*, they eventually accepted them as long as the participation of the troops in mass executions was kept to a minimum. However, since the SS and police forces in Serbia were too small, the army set out to do the job.[31]

Operation Užice

Böhme's staff officers worked out a plan code-named Operation Užice, which stipulated the deployment of battalion-size combat groups to match the mobility of Partisans. Against 15,000 Partisans (in the first stage of the operation, Mihailović's Chetniks were temporarily left alone), Böhme concentrated between 70,000 and 80,000 German and collaborationist troops and police units, thus achieving the approximate ten to one ratio, conventionally considered necessary for successful antiguerrilla warfare. The NDH forces were deployed along the Sava and Drina Rivers to prevent Partisans from breaking through to Bosnia and Srijem.[32]

What became known in the Yugoslav communist historiography as the "first enemy offensive" began on September 21. Earlier, Böhme, as the commander of the Eighteenth Corps, urged moderation and warned his subordinates of counterproductive, "unguided and spontaneous" reprisals.[33] On his new appointment, however, he was determined to suppress the uprising as quickly as possible by using the most draconian means. On September 25 he gave his troops carte blanche for future actions: "You are marching through the land in which in 1914 German blood was shed by treacherous Serbs. You're the avengers of this blood. Anyone who acts mildly [in regards to the population] endangers the life of his colleagues and will be held responsible regardless of personality before a court martial."[34]

The order asserted that the population at large had joined the rebels and that "women and children [were] running messages and maintaining the bandits' lines of supply."[35] The order effectively targeted the entire population in antiguerrilla warfare and gave troops the green light to shoot anybody who merely looked suspicious. Success would be measured in body counts, which constituted a high ratio of civilian deaths. Simultaneously, in the areas of operations, List ordered German forces to seize all males between fourteen and seventy years of age, to burn houses and barns, and to resettle the remaining population south into the valley of Cer (a mountain in western Serbia, 62 miles west of Belgrade).[36]

Both orders were deliberately too broad, leaving German commanders with wide latitude to act as they deemed fit. The conduct of troops, therefore, depended on the personal disposition of officers, who would either strive merely to fulfill execution orders or initiate a large-scale massacre.[37]

Lieutenant General William Hinghofer, the commander of the 342nd Division, represented the latter category. Serving as an Austrian officer on the eastern front during World War I imbued him with the most radical anti-Slavic and anti-Semitic sentiments. Malleable to the Nazi ideology, Hinghofer declared that suspicion of guerrilla activities alone sufficed for executions, and his subordinates exceeded the 100:1 and 50:1 ratios set by Weichs per Hitler's order, killing even more hostages as the fighting progressed during Operation Użice.[38]

Between September 23 and October 3, the units of the 342nd Division killed and executed up to two thousand guerrillas and suspected communists. On October 2 alone, the troops shot a thousand guerrillas and hostages. On October 25, the division broke the Partisan siege of Valjevo and seized up to 25,000 civilians, who were sent to the Šabac concentration camps, where six thousand were subsequently shot. Villages suspected of helping Partisans were burned, and five thousand people were forcibly removed from the Šabac district. At the same time, the German and collaborationist units sustained losses of 61 killed, 67 wounded, and 93 missing in action.[39] By November 11, troops of 342nd Division operating between Mačva and Valjevo were reported to have killed 905 Partisans in combat, shot 2,685 hostages in reprisals, and shot or sent to concentration camps 21,875 persons, at their own loss of 32 killed and 127 wounded.[40]

The units of the 714th and 704th Infantry Divisions, which since the outbreak of the uprising bore the brunt of Partisan attacks, matched Hinghofer's men in ruthlessness. In retaliation for the Partisan attack on the town of Kraljevo, where the Germans lost fifteen men, the town commandant compiled a list of five hundred hostages. To meet the necessary quota, about 1,200 people were seized, including Jews, Chetniks who refused to cooperate with the Germans, and employees of the airplane factory in Kraljevo, who had been interned on suspicion of sabotage. Among the hostages were forty-eight Slovenian refugees living in the vicinity. On October 15, troops escorted the first group of hostages to the yard of the local railway car factory and shot them. The executions continued for two more days; by October 18, 1,775 people had been killed.[41]

Another large-scale massacre took place almost simultaneously in Kragujevac. On October 14–17, a German battalion of the 714th Division sustained losses of nine soldiers killed and twenty-seven wounded in a collision with Partisans and Chetniks. The guerrillas also shot several German captives. Outraged, Böhme ordered the execution of hostages in accordance with Hitler's September order.[42] On October 19, troops burned down four villages around Kragujevac and shot 422 men, women, and children on the spot. Other units seized all Jews and Serbian suspects in Kragujevac and its vicinity. Since the numbers still fell short of the necessary quota, assisted by SDK members and the SDS, the troops seized the entire male population of Kragujevac between the ages of sixteen and sixty. In vain, the Kragujevac military commandant argued that the residents had obediently cooperated with German authorities. Major König, the commander of the punitive expedition, agreed to release only Zbor members and individuals employed in service of the Wehrmacht, among them medical personnel, pharmacists, and technicians. The headmaster of the local school offered himself as a substitute for his pupils and when his offer was rejected, he cast his lot with his students and was executed. On October 21–22, 2,324 hostages were shot in several groups, making Kragujevac a symbol of Serbia's martyrdom, similar to the Czech village of Lidice and the French town of Oradour-sur-Glane.[43]

The massacres raised protests from Benzler and Turner, who saw them not only as counterproductive, but as potentially damaging, since among the victims were valuable specialists and even collaborationists. When in September 1941 the chief of the Banat administration, Franz Rajt, requested that all potential resisters in the region be shot, Turner turned down the request.[44] Some German commanders also showed more restraint. For example, General Hoffmann, the commander of the 717th Infantry Division, suggested to Böhme that more comprehensive propaganda efforts could convince the population that the resistance was futile.[45]

Still, the massacres increased in scope and intensity. To meet Hitler's necessary quotas of hostages, the Germans used numerous concentration and detention camps, which swelled with prisoners. For example, in Banat alone about 5,700 people were interned in several concentration camps and prisons.[46] In October the administration of the concentration camp Crveni Krst in Niš, which was a major detention site of the district, delivered a thousand Jews, the Roma, political prisoners, and family members of suspected guerrillas as hostages. Similarly, by late November, 3,500 inmates from the camps around Šabac were shot in reprisals.[47] The *Einsatzgruppe* Serbia also organized roundups of civilians, particularly the Serbian intelligentsia as a potential "security threat," and delivered them to the troops for executions.[48]

As a part of Operation Užice, the Bulgarian army and police launched an offensive in southeastern Serbia, rounding up and detaining hundreds of civilians in numerous prisons and concentration camps. Although on a smaller scale than in the German-controlled areas, the Bulgarian troops executed hostages and burned villages suspected of helping or harboring the guerrillas.[49] On September 4, thirty hostages were shot in the Vranje district and the bodies were left in the open for several days. In other instances, the corpses of suspected guerrillas were decapitated and the heads were impaled to intimidate the population.[50] In November 1941, after the villagers in Tulovo of Leskovac district refused to (or were unable to) recognize the corpses of three guerrillas, the Bulgarian commander ordered his unit to open fire on the crowd; after killing a number of civilians, the soldiers murdered the wounded and departed, leaving behind seventeen corpses.[51]

* * *

The Partisan strategy to create the Užice republic succeeded as a political initiative, but the German offensive revealed its serious shortcomings as a military undertaking. Emboldened by their summer successes, the Partisans came to believe that they could face German troops on equal terms. If in the summer German troops had to disperse their forces to pursue constantly moving Partisan and Chetnik bands, the expansion of "liberated zones" entailed the concentration of Partisan forces in specific locations. As a result, the Partisans lost their most crucial tactical advantage—mobility. Conversely, instead of tracking Partisans through forests and mountains, Böhme could concentrate his forces on specific villages and towns.

With Operation Užice in motion, German troops were aggregated into battalion-size combat groups. Supported by armor and artillery, they struck simultaneously at Partisan positions in the Čačak, Šabac, and Užice districts. While some combat groups launched frontal attacks, others occupied villages and deported their populations, depriving Partisans of supplies and manpower. Living in constant fear of German reprisals, peasants became increasingly reluctant to support the guerrillas. With alarming speed, Partisans found themselves under pressure, especially as they lacked firepower to match the regular troops. In this situation, the scarcity of qualified officers began taking its toll. Although some Partisans were veterans of the Spanish Civil War, most were party functionaries lacking elementary military training, much less the experience of leading companies and battalions. During his service in the Austro-Hungarian army, Tito himself was the youngest NCO in his regiment, but he had never led a large formation. The Partisan signal and outpost services were also of low quality.[52]

On November 25, Böhme launched the final stage of the offensive. A combat group of eight thousand German troops and five thousand collaborationist forces launched a two-pronged assault from Valjevo and Kraljevo-Čačak toward the Partisan capital of Užice. Two days later the German troops shattered Partisan positions in the Čačak district. At the same time, two Bulgarian regiments in Niš, Toplica, and Leskovac crossed the demarcation lines into central Serbia. Although the Partisan leadership received reports about the concentration of German and Bulgarian troops, it did not have an emergency plan and still counted on the previous "elastic" tactic of avoiding direct confrontation with the enemy.[53]

The rapidity of the German offensive took the Partisans off guard, and they gave up one position after another. Later, Tito admitted that the Germans "slice[ed] through the liberated territories like a knife through butter."[54] Having realized that the situation was critical, the Partisan command ordered a retreat to Sandžak. The retreat soon turned into a flight and a rout. Four hundred Partisans, who were ordered to hold off the enemy at Užice, were outflanked and wiped out to a man. Other units fled without firing a shot; small groups and single Partisans were separated and wandered through the hills and forests. Tito himself remained with a small detail that lost contact with the main forces and barely escaped the pursuers.[55]

A crucial problem for Partisans was the lack of arms, and, although they produced explosives and used captured guns, their self-sufficiency had its limits. Another major difficulty was the increasing numbers of sick and wounded, particularly given the constant shortage of trained medical personnel. Since the Germans routinely murdered wounded guerrillas—in three days they shot about 160 wounded Partisans—it was imperative for the Partisan leadership to evacuate the hospitals. On November 29, the Partisans abandoned Užice, carrying with them a thousand wounded comrades. Still, many sick and wounded guerrillas were left in the hands of sympathetic villagers;

some hid them in the countryside. Their fate, however, was tragic—most were found and shot by German patrols and collaborationist units. Hence, many Partisans preferred to commit suicide rather than fall into enemy hands. In turn, if previously the Partisans tried to spare German prisoners, now they killed their captives.[56]

It has been observed that civil wars often tend to be more violent than international conflicts. Indeed, Operation Užice exacerbated the Chetnik-Partisan war, which was fought with extreme brutality. Partisans and Chetniks killed each other's messengers, kidnapped and murdered suspected enemy sympathizers, and took hostages among the families of political opponents. In one instance, the Chetniks intercepted and massacred a group of thirty Partisans, including young girls, who had slipped out of Belgrade. Given all of this, any compromise became impossible.[57]

Operating under German command, the Serbian gendarmerie, the SDK units, and the "legal" Chetniks contributed to escalating violence. In late September, "legal" Chetniks captured a group of Partisans near Bor and handed them over to the Germans; most captives were sentenced to death and executed. In October the collaborationist forces reported to have killed four hundred Partisans but collected only 106 rifles—an indication that most victims were civilians. In late November in the village of Jošanice of the Niš district, the Serbian gendarmes killed forty-five captured guerrillas.[58]

As Operation Užice was going on, Axis forces launched antiguerrilla offensives in other parts of Yugoslavia. In Montenegro, the Italian command amassed seventy thousand men and within six weeks defeated the Partisans and reestablished control over the country. Five thousand Montenegrins were shot in reprisals, and the special courts-martial meted out hundreds of death sentences. Suppression of the resistance was accompanied by a merciless bombardment and burning of villages suspected of helping the guerrillas. The troops deported entire communities to detention centers and concentration camps, where tortures of suspected rebels became a norm.[59]

Meanwhile, having delivered a crushing blow to the Partisans, the Germans turned against the Chetniks. On December 6, German troops launched Operation Mihailović, and in four days they captured the Chetnik headquarters, where they took 390 prisoners, including almost the entire command of the movement. The troops also seized arms, horses, a radio transmitter, and 203,000 dinars. Having barely escaped, Mihailović remained on the run for several months, a bounty of 200,000 dinars on his head. By this time, the Gestapo and the Special Police had infiltrated and destroyed many Chetnik cells in Serbia and Banat.[60] Under constant pressure, some Chetnik commanders crossed into Bosnia, hid in the mountains, or subordinated their units to Nedić or Pečanac. In the latter case, they participated in the last phase of the anti-Partisan offensive in December 1941.[61]

In late December, the bulk of Partisan forces left for Sandžak and Bosnia, leaving small units in the northwestern and southern counties of Serbia. The remaining Chetniks of Mihailović's hid in the forests and mountains, but the German command discounted them as ineffective. Accordingly, the OKW ordered the 113d Infantry Division back to Russia; the 342d and 718th Divisions were transferred to Bosnia and were replaced by the units of the First Bulgarian Corps.[62]

Holocaust

A key element of German terror policies in Serbia was the genocide of Jews. Before the war, Serbia had fifteen thousand Jews, two-thirds of whom lived in Belgrade. The assault on Jews began immediately after the outbreak of the April war, when German soldiers joined the local rabble in looting Jewish stores, houses, and apartments. Three weeks after the collapse of Yugoslavia, the field commandant in Belgrade still reported numerous incidents of looting, perpetrated by German military personnel.[63] Anti-Jewish violence was particularly vicious in Banat, where its form (but not its magnitude) resembled the pogroms in the Soviet western provinces in the summer of 1941. Soldiers and some ethnic Germans beat Jews or amused themselves by forcing them to clean latrines and to collect horse manure with their bare hands. Hundreds of Jews were detained in the first concentration camps. Violence was accompanied by widespread plunder, and on April 25, 1941, the military commandant in Banat ordered the population to return all Jewish property, goods, and valuables to the administration.[64]

In the course of a few days, Serbian Jews found themselves under siege. On April 16, a day after Yugoslavia's capitulation, Hans Helm, the Gestapo chief of the *Einsatzkommando* Belgrade, ordered the registration of Jews in Belgrade. On April 21 the military commandant of Belgrade ordered the formation of the Jewish labor force, made mandatory for all adults. Jewish labor details worked up to eighteen hours a day clearing up rubble, burying corpses, and defusing undetonated bombs.[65] Upon the punishment of high fines or incarceration, Jews were banned from using public transportation, had but a few hours to buy groceries, and were prohibited from standing in lines for commodities alongside the "Aryans." In late April, Jews were ordered to wear special labels or yellow stars.[66]

On May 30 General Förster introduced Nazi racial regulations to Serbia, which deprived Jews and the Roma of basic civil rights in accordance with the Nuremberg Laws. Jewish communities were dissolved, Jewish religious services were prohibited, and Jews were fired from the civil service and the education system (alongside Serbs who were deemed "nationally unreliable"). Jewish medical personnel were allowed to treat only Jewish patients, while veterinarians and pharmacists lost their livings altogether. Noncompliance with these regulations was punishable by death.[67] The racial regulations also affected the Roma, who were prohibited from owning property, were fired from civil service, and were ordered to wear a special identification label.[68]

Discriminatory measures were accompanied by systematic robbery that stripped Jews of all material and economic assets. In accordance with MBS orders, the Jewish communities were to pay for "war damages." In June, the Jewish community in Belgrade had to collect a contribution of 10 million dinars for the MBS and pay 16,000 dinar monthly to the Serbian city administration as a penalty for "Jewish-communist" activities.[69] In accordance with MBS orders, all Jewish property and commodities (estimated at 3 billion dinars) were placed under the supervision of Turner's *Verwaltungsstab*.[70] Several German offices and organizations claimed their share of the confiscated Jewish property and businesses. For example, Benzler's Foreign Office took over Jewish property in the regions occupied by Hungarian and Bulgarian forces.[71] In early May, all Jewish property in Banat was transferred to the "supervision" of the ethnic German commissars, who set up front firms that sold Jewish property and goods on discount to German military personnel. In the words of a German officer, officers and soldiers in confiscated Jewish houses and apartments "lived like kings."[72]

All these measures brought about a rapid pauperization of Jews in Serbia and Banat. Already in May, half of the Jewish population—6,800 people—were receiving their meals from charity kitchens organized by the Jewish communities.[73]

In April the German military commandants ordered Jews into makeshift ghettos, which they were forbidden to leave. Some of these ghettos were town quarters, where Jews lived before the war, while in other localities Jews were ordered to move into former military barracks or factories. For example, the Šabac commandant Walther Benne ordered the creation of the so-called Judenlager on the eastern bank of the Sava River in the barracks of the Yugoslav army. The camp's population grew to a thousand and included Jewish refugees from Austria, Czechoslovakia, Poland, and Germany who failed to obtain emigration visas before the war. Soon, Jews were joined by Serbs suspected of political activities, and in September the camp contained 4,900 Serbian and 1,100 Jewish inmates.[74] In Niš 500 Jews, 1,000 Roma, and suspected communists were incarcerated in the Crveny Krst camp near the former Red Cross facility.[75] The ad hoc ghettoization in Serbia was similar to the pre-murder stage in Ukraine and Russia, indicating that it was a short-term measure, and the uprising merely expedited the process of annihilation.

All ghetto and concentration camp inmates carried out hard menial work, cleaning rubble and repairing roads, while the guards brutalized and often murdered them without pretext. Sanitary conditions rapidly deteriorated due to the increasing numbers of prisoners and to the lack of food and drinking water. By the fall, epidemics broke out in several ghettos and camps.[76]

In August, Fuchs and Turner ordered the creation of a special "transition" camp for the Jews and the Roma in the former military garage, Topovske šupe, in Belgrade, previously used for accommodating Serbian refugees from other parts of Yugoslavia. Named in the German parlance as the *Judenlager Autokomanda*, the camp contained five thousand Jews (mostly males from Belgrade) and several hundred Roma. The Jewish community of Belgrade was made responsible for supplying the camp with food and cloth.[77]

In tune with the Nazi racial ideology, the Wehrmacht defined the war against the Soviet Union as a crusade against "Judeo-Bolshevism"—the lethal foe of the Third Reich. Accordingly, the German *Bandenbekämpfung* concepts developed an ideological-racial category that largely conflated the terms *bandits*, *communists*, and *Jews*. In Russia, the Nazi killing units, often in collaboration with the German army, had killed hundreds of thousands of Soviet Jews, including women and children.[78]

Against this background, the Wehrmacht command in Serbia assumed that Jews *must* have spearheaded the Partisan movement, and while all German offices constantly squabbled over their priorities, the identification of Jews with the resistance became the single issue on which they were in full agreement.[79]

The first mass executions of Jews began in July, when General Schröder ordered the seizure of Jews and communists, who would provide the main reservoir for hostages in mass reprisals. In one week alone, between July 22 and 29, the troops and the police shot more than 230 Jews and communists. When German troops lost four men in a clash with the Partisans near Šabac, in retaliation they shot a number of Jewish prisoners from the Šabac concentration camp.[80]

The "Jewish-communist" resistance became the key issue in correspondence between Benzler and Edmund Veesenmayer, Ribbentrop's political adviser for the NDH. Both concurred that the elimination of Jews would incapacitate the resistance and simultaneously expedite the "completion of the Jewish question" in Serbia. Hence, they repeatedly requested that at least eight thousand male Jews be deported to Romania, Poland, or Russia.[81] However, the Romanian government tried to get rid of its own Jews and certainly would not be receptive to such measures. Similarly, Hans Frank (Hitler's viceroy in the so-called

General Government in Poland) was averse to the deportations of thousands of Jews into his domain. Meanwhile, Berlin prioritized the deportations of large Jewish communities to the east and denied Turner's and Benzler's requests. Having consulted the Gestapo "Jewish" expert Adolf Eichmann, the department chief of the Foreign Ministry Martin Luther informed Benzler that the MBS should kill Jews on the spot, since elsewhere in Europe "the local army commanders eliminated a lot more Jews without making a fuss."[82]

Veesenmayer wrote to Benzler that the "draconic implementation [*drakonische Erledigung*] of the Serbian Jewish question" would effectively end all troubles in Serbia. Turner, who repeatedly advocated selective reprisals, envisioned that the murder of Jews served two simultaneous purposes: it achieved the Nazi ideological aim of making Serbia *Judenrein* and mitigated reprisals against the Serbs, thus boosting the waning prestige of the Nedić administration in the eyes of the population.[83]

For Böhme, Fuchs, and Turner, the murder of Serbian Jews offered an opportunity to "empty" concentration and labor camps to allow for the confinement of Serbian civilians. At the same time, the numbers of murdered Jews entered the tally of successful antiguerrilla operations. Although the OKW order of September 16 did not specifically mention Jews, in a rare spirit of close cooperation, the Wehrmacht, the German civil administration, and the SS agreed that wherever possible Jews would be shot first; the Roma community was also targeted due to its alleged "danger to public order."[84]

As a result of such policies, the numbers of Jews shot in reprisals grew rapidly. On October 2 the Partisans killed twenty-two German captives near Topola (between Belgrade and Obrenovac) and two days later Böhme ordered the exact application of the OKW September order. Turner and Fuchs were to deliver 2,100 hostages from Šabac and Belgrade, in the first place Jews and communists. Eight hundred and five Jews and the Roma were taken from the Šabac concentration camp and the Topovske šupe. More than a thousand Jewish hostages were delivered by other camps and on October 9–11 the units of the 342nd Division shot 2,200 people. The commander of a shooting detail, First Lieutenant Walter Liepe, reported that the hostages did not know about their fate until they arrived at the execution site. The execution was photographed and filmed; Security Police details collected the victims' cloth and valuables to hand over to the Nazi aid agency.[85]

The Wehrmacht thus implemented the Holocaust, effectively taking over the "regular" practices of the Sipo and the police, whereas killing Jews fulfilled the necessary quota of hostages and solved logistical problems of ghettoization. On October 10, Böhme and Turner ordered that Hitler's September 16 order be applied to all communists, Jews, "suspicious" Serbian males, and individuals of nationalist and leftist orientation.[86] On October 17 Turner wrote to Richard Hildebrandt, his friend and the supreme commander of the SS and police in West Prussia, that in the "last eight days" two thousand Jews and two hundred Roma had been shot in accordance with 100:1 ratios for thirty-four killed and wounded German soldiers in Valjevo; 2,200 Jews were to be shot in the next eight days.[87]

By the late fall 1941, half of Serbia's Jews—up to eight thousand—and eight hundred Roma had been murdered in reprisals.[88] The first stage of the Final Solution Holocaust in Serbia was complete.

* * *

As Jewish males were being executed, German officials were determining the fate of Jewish women and children. On October 1941, Franz Rademacher, the referent on the "Jewish question" in the Foreign Office, and two of Eichmann's representatives arrived in Belgrade, where they conferred with Turner, Fuchs, and Benzler. The six men decided that since "evacuation" to the east was impossible, all remaining Jews should be collected in one place, where the "Jewish question" would be resolved once and for all.[89]

The place found suitable for this was the site of the former Sajmište fairgrounds on the left bank of the Sava River, which belonged to the territory of the NDH. At the request of the Foreign Ministry, the NDH granted permission for the camp to be erected on the Zemun peninsula. Surrounded on three sides by the river, the site was conveniently isolated from the mainland and inhibited escape attempts. It was also near the Belgrade railway station, making it possible to deport Jews from different localities to the camp.[90]

In December 1941, the Topovske camp was shut down and all remaining Jews were transferred to Sajmište. By late January 1942, seven thousand Jews, including 3,933 women and 1,238 children from all over Serbia, were deported to the camp. Eight hundred Roma, mostly women and children, were also detained in the camp. Still, German policies toward the Roma were not as unbendable as toward the Jews, and Nedić's administration supported the appeal of the Belgrade Roma community to release the sedentary Roma, who were classified as loyal. As a result, 237 such individuals were freed.[91]

The camp was totally inadequate and unprepared for so many inmates, especially with the onset of winter. Having been damaged in the April bombardment, most buildings had neither windows nor doors, while the heating system was inoperative.[92] Wooden benches were erected in three tiers and some collapsed, injuring those sleeping below. A survivor recalled that the "straw on which we slept was not changed and became a stinking, filthy, wet mess." Those who did not bring along warm cloth or blankets, particularly the old and sick, succumbed to cold, which increased due to poor roofing.[93]

The overall supervision of the camp was in the hands of the Gestapo, which made the Jewish council in the camp responsible for food supplies, labor duties, and internal policing. Stripped of financial assets, the council was unable to supply the camp with sufficient foodstuffs. Consequently, inmates received thin soup made from a cup of warm water with a leaf of cabbage and a piece of potato; an irregular ration of 250 grams of coarse bread had to sustain an inmate for several days. But even that amount was dwindling every day.[94] When frozen potatoes became the main nourishment in the winter of 1942, the death toll increased dramatically. Emaciated inmates were particularly prone to epidemics, which spread after Jews sick with typhoid fever were transported to the camp from Bosnia.[95] Jewish medical personnel tried to alleviate suffering, but the lack of medical supplies made their task nearly impossible. Cold and hunger killed five hundred inmates between January and March. Not infrequently, corpses lay among the inmates for days.[96]

Surviving on a few hundred calories a day, all the inmates, including the sick and the old, were awakened at five in the morning to stand for *Appell* (roll call) by the commandant, SS-*Untersturmführer* Herbert Andorfer, or his deputy. German functionaries amused themselves by forcing the inmates to perform "gymnastics" or various menial works. Inmates received their food rations only after standing in long queues, which also formed for the few latrines. Several labor details were dispatched to the city, where they worked ten to twelve hours a day repairing roads and at various construction sites. But the majority of inmates remained inside—as in Ukraine, such order and the makeshift structure of Sajmište indicated that in a short time the camp inmates would be marked for slaughter.[97]

Indeed, in accordance with Nazi genocidal practices, unbearable conditions in the Jewish ghettos and concentration camps expedited mass murder. In early March 1942, Heinrich Müller informed Schäfer that in connection with the "Jewish action" in Serbia, an operative unit—a gas van and two SS drivers—had been dispatched to Belgrade.[98] Andorfer then informed the Jewish camp leaders that the truck would transport the inmates to a "different location." The van began its ride between Sajmište and the firing range at Avala, nine miles south of Belgrade, taking each time a load of fifty-eighty inmates and killing everyone inside within twenty minutes. The truck operated daily except Sundays and holidays, reducing the number of inmates from 5,780 in February to 1,184 in April. Serbian prisoners were brought to Avala to unload the truck and bury the corpses in prepared pits. On May 22, the last gas van to Avala departed with the medical personnel from the Jewish hospital in Belgrade. The MBS received regular reports about the "progress" of the murder. The group of Jews of German origin who carried out clerical tasks in the camp was shot at the end of the month. All in all, between January and May 1942 Sajmište claimed about 6,400 victims.[99]

Executions of remaining Jews were simultaneously carried out in other localities in Serbia, and German officials hastened to announce that the Final Solution was complete. On May 29, 1942, Rademacher reported that the "Jewish question in Serbia is no longer actual. [There] remains only the question of [Jewish] property." On June 8, Schäfer informed Bader and the Southeast Command of the same. Finally, in August 1942, Turner reported to the new German commander in the Balkans that Serbia was the only country in Europe where the "Jewish problem" was solved.[100]

Nevertheless, the Gestapo and the Special Police continued hunting Jews hiding in the countryside or living under false identities. In May and August 1943, thirty-six Jews were brought to the Banjica prison. In November 1943, the Germans murdered the last Jewish prisoners in Crveny Krst. In late September 1944, Partisan troops liberated the last Jewish laborers in the Bor copper mines, mostly citizens of other countries.[101]

After the Jews were murdered, the Sajmište camp became a detention camp (Anhaltelager Semlin) for Serbian and Croatian political activists, the "illegal" Chetniks, and captured Partisans, who labored in harsh conditions at construction sites and road repairs. Between spring 1942 and October 1944, when the camp was shut down, fifteen thousand detainees passed through its gates.[102] Since the Croatian administration refused to supply the camp, according to different sources, the death rate among prisoners reached up to two hundred dead a day. Between May and November 1942, between 3,000 and 4,181 inmates died of starvation, disease, or were killed by the guards. The death rate remained high after the camp was transferred under the jurisdiction of NDH in early 1943.[103]

The last inmates of the camp were Hungarian Jews, who in September 1944 were transferred to Sajmište, from whence they were deported to Hungary and subsequently to the death camps in Poland.[104]

* * *

During anti-insurgency operations in Serbia, the German forces lost up to 203 dead and 520 wounded. The casualties of the civil war were much higher—between April and December 1941, the resistance killed 1,700 and wounded 1,500 Serbian officials, soldiers, and policemen.[105] The German response was overwhelming—between July and December of that year, ten thousand alleged guerrillas and between twenty thousand and thirty thousand civilians, including Jews and the Roma, were killed.[106]

The German repression policies in Serbia passed through two stages. Initially, terror was directed against specific ideological and racial enemies—

the communists, Jews (who allegedly combined both qualities), Chetniks, and the Roma. The outbreak of resistance, however, entailed the end of the terror's predictability and fused Nazi ideology and *Bandenbekämpfung* concepts, effectively eroding the difference between the treatment of civilians and that of guerrillas. Consequently, in addition to overall directives of the German command, which institutionalized mass violence against the entire population, individual commanders established norms of conduct for their subordinates, encouraging them to commit murder.

The defeat of the Partisans in the late fall of 1941 seemingly validated the convictions of those German officials, who advocated unrestricted terror as the sole effective method of antiguerrilla warfare. Indeed, Serbia seemed pacified and the population cowed into submission, and the top German functionaries no longer deemed unrestricted terror necessary. Turner and Benzler in particular insisted that the smooth functioning of the administration depended on a more restrained application of violence. Their opinion prevailed, and in December the new MBS, Paul Bader, who replaced Böhme, halved the reprisal ratio to fifty civilians for one German fatality.[107]

Temporarily, terror against the Serbs lost its intensity and functioned only as a tool of occupation policies rather than as a policy in itself. In contrast, the murder of Jews continued unabated. In contrast to Poland and the Soviet Union, where the *Einsatzgruppen* and the police carried out most of the killing, in the fall of 1941 the Wehrmacht became the key culprit in implementing Nazi genocidal policies. In the spring of the next year, the SS murdered most of the surviving Jews. All in all, approximately 14,800 Jews and 1,200 Jewish refugees lost their lives.[108]

Although by December 1941 the Partisan movement in Serbia had been crushed, it was not wiped out entirely. The gravity of the resistance shifted to NDH, where it benefited from the strong communist presence, the weakness of the Croatian administration, and policy disagreements between the German and Italian commands. In the remote areas of Bosnia-Herzegovina, Partisans were able to find new recruits—especially from the areas affected by the Ustasha's atrocities—to rebuild their strength and to use the Užice republic model as the blueprint for the new liberated territories.

The defeat became a hard but valuable lesson for the KPJ leadership. Although many demoralized guerrillas abandoned the struggle altogether, about two thousand survived the onslaught. Headed by the ideologically committed and determined leadership, they prepared for hardship and sacrifice and had the potential to evolve into an effective nucleus of the future Partisan army.

Figure 1. Crowd gathered around the hanging on Terazijama square, 17 August 1941. Courtesy of Belgrade Historical Archive

Figure 2. Banjica prison. Courtesy of Belgrade Historical Archive

Figure 3. Execution of Banjica inmates at Jajinci. Courtesy of Belgrade Historical Archive

Figure 4. SD functionaries and guards at the Anhaltelager Semlin (Sajmište) camp, 1943 (?). Second from left is a privileged prisoner. Courtesy of Belgrade Historical Archive

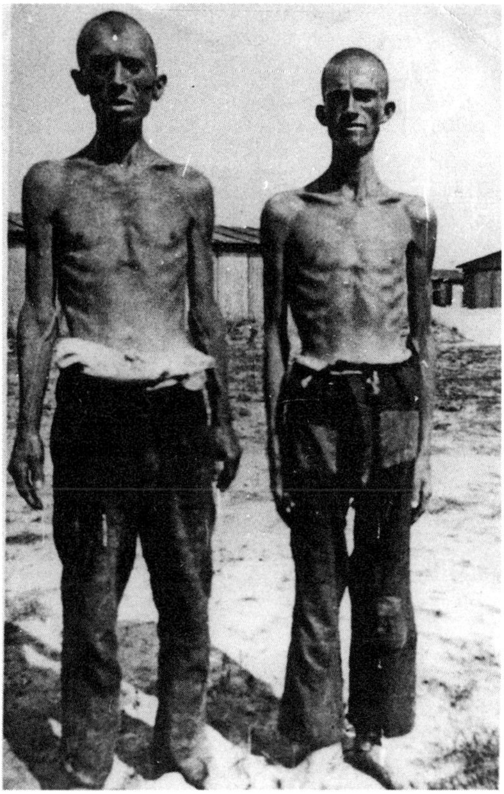

Figure 5. Serbian inmates at Sajmište. Courtesy of Belgrade Historical Archive

242 *картонски регистар* А

Пауновић Благоје, чин. рођен 20-II-1915 год. у Д. Трепчи, срез Љубићски син Вујице и Стасинке рођена Лацковић, одговара због комунизма.

год. 28

Опис: стар 28 година, других података нема. Треба га пронаћи и привести Одељењу специјалне полиције Управе града Београда с позивом на бр. 5386/43.

ПГ 872-43. Т-п. бр. 818-43.

Figure 6. Serbian State Security arrest warrant on a suspected communist. Courtesy of Belgrade Historical Archive

Број 881 „ПОЛИЦИЈСКИ ГЛАСНИК“ Страна 75

38

725 *картонски регистар* A

Петровић Душан, земљ. рођен 1923 године у Селевцу, син Радомира. Отишао је од куће у непознатом правцу.

год. 20
висок
— — —

Опис: стар 20 год., раста високог, очи зелене, косе смеђе, нос и уста правилна, бркове и браду брије, особених знакова има на десној руци, других података нема. Треба га пронаћи и привести Одељењу специјалне полиције Управе града Београда с позивом на Пов. II бр. 2117/IV-43.

ПГ 881-43. Т-п. Пов. бр. 159-43.

726 *картонски регистар* A

Стојановић Драгољуб, зв. **„Фајта“** берберски помоћник из Лесковца, рођен 1915 године, јула месеца 1943 године отишао је у непознатом правцу.

год.28
средњи
— — —

Опис: стар 28 год. раста средњег, лица округлог, коса и очи црне, других података нема. У случају проналаска треба га привести Предстојништву градске полиције у Лесковцу с позивом на бр. 8996/43. У. г. Б. II бр. 10235-43. Т-п. бр. 1948-43.

ПГ 881-43.

727 *картонски регистар* A

Пецић С. Илија, земљ. рођен 1908 године из Ждрела, удаљио се у непознатом правцу.

год. 35
средњи
— — —

Опис: стар 35 год., раста средњег, очи и коса црна, мало проседа, бркове штуцује, других података нема. У случају проналаска треба га привести начелнику среза Млавског с позивом на бр. 7804-43 У. г. Б. II бр. 10178-43. Т-п. бр. 1948-43.

ПГ 881-43.

728 *картонски регистар* A

Новаковић Живадин, земљ. рођен 1921 године из Селевца, син Војислава, на дан 27-VI-1943 године нестао је из с. Селевца.

год. 22
средњи
— — —

Опис: стар 22 год., раста средњег, очи црне, косе смеђе, нос и уста правилни, бркове и браду брије, других података нема. Треба га пронаћи и привести одељењу специјалне полиције Управе града Београда с позивом на Пов. II бр. 2117-IV-43. Т-п, Пов. бр. 159-43.

ПГ 881-43.

729 *картонски регистар* A

Костић Д. Љуба, рударски радник, рођен 1923 године у с. Жидиљу срез Деспотовачки. На дан 7 септембра 1943 године око 10 часова отпутовао је из Равне Реке и до данас се није вратио.

год. 20
средњи
— — —

Опис: стар 20 год., раста средњег, очи зелене, косе плаве, нос и уста правилни, бркови мили плави, браду брије, са обе стране вилице зуби мањкају, коштуњав, других података нема. Треба га пронаћи и привести Команди С.Д.С. округа Моравског с позивом на Ј.Б.бр. 2883/43.

ПГ 881-43. Т-п. бр. 2190-43.

730 *картонски регистар* A

Копривица Миливој, полицијски агент-приправник, рођен 21-III-1915 године у с. Вукојевцу срез Косанички, син Митра и Јане, од 11 септембра 1943 године није се јавио на дужност.

год. 28
мали
— — —

Опис: стар 28 год., раста малог, смеђ, лице мршаво и старачког изгледа, нос мален, уста мала, на једној страни сребрн зуб очњак, других података нема. Треба га пронаћи и привести Управи полиције Ниш с позивом на бр. 33672/43.

ПГ 881-43. Т-п. бр. 2192-43.

731 *картонски регистар* A

Костић Д. Коста, рударски радник, рођен 1911 године из с. Жидиље, на дан 7 септембра 1943 године око 10 часова отпутовао је из Равне Реке и до данас се није вратио.

год. 32
средњи
— — —

Опис: стар 32 год., раста средњег, лице црномањасто, коса и обрве црне, бркове и браду брије, очи црне, нос и уста правилна, танак, коштуњав, других података нема. Треба га пронаћи и привести Команди С.Д.С. округа Моравског с позивом на Ј.Б.бр. 2884/43.

ПГ 881-43. Т-п. бр. 2190-43.

732 *картонски регистар* A

Ранковић Милорад, зв. **„Ценвар“** рођен 1904 године у Новом Кнежевцу, син Богдана и Магде рођ. Јегришка. Одговара за дело из § 278 и 275 к. з.

год. 39
— — —
— — —

Опис: стар 39 год., других података нема. Треба га пронаћи и привести Окружном суду у Кикинди с позивом на Кзп. бр. 101/42

ПГ 881-43. Т-п. бр. 2166-43.

733 *картонски регистар* A

Аћимовић Милина, рођена 1915 године у Бежанији среза Земунског. Побегла у партизане.

год. 28
средњи
— — —

Опис: стара 28 година, раста средњег, коса и очи црне, лице округло, нос и уста правилна, других података нема. Треба је пронаћи и привести станици с.д.п.с. среза Посавског с позивом на бр. 2999/43.

Т-п. бр. 2232-43.
ПГ 881-43.

Figure 7. Serbian State Security arrest warrants for suspected guerrillas. Courtesy of Belgrade Historical Archive

Figure 8. Serbian gendarme escorting a group of Roma. Courtesy of Belgrade Historical Archive

Figure 9. Anti-Semitic poster from the 1941–42 anti-Mason exhibition. Courtesy of Belgrade City Museum

7 "Serbia Is Quiet," 1942–1944

"Compared to the entire Balkans, [Serbia] is quiet," noticed two German officers passing through the country in 1943.[1] Indeed, to an outside observer, Serbia must have appeared as an island of tranquility, especially in contrast to Bosnia-Herzegovina, where in 1942–43 the Axis powers unleashed a series of massive antiguerrilla operations. In the process, they applied the methods used during Operation Užice, murdering tens of thousands of civilians. Meanwhile, the depleted Partisan forces in Serbia confined their actions to small-scale attacks and sabotage acts, while the Chetniks remained largely passive. It appeared, therefore, that small German contingents assisted by the Bulgarian and collaborationist forces would be able to keep the country in check.

This general impression of peace, however, concealed deep-seated antagonisms that split Serbian society along ideological lines. Unable to launch large-scale attacks, Partisans still managed to disrupt the functioning of the collaborationist administration and blocked access to industrial sites. Meanwhile, Mihailović tried to maintain the image of the national resistance leader, simultaneously to avoid collisions with the Germans and to fight the Partisans and occasionally, Nedić's forces. The latter, in turn, were deployed against both Partisans and Chetniks. A vicious civil war among the three forces frequently overshadowed what was supposed to be the war of liberation against the Germans. German responses to the situation were affected by the guerrilla war in the NDH and by continuous tensions between the advocates of relentless terror and proponents of more nuanced policies.

Partisans: Defeat and Recovery

In the winter of 1942, the situation of the Partisans in Serbia seemed hopeless. Up to four thousand poorly armed guerrillas faced fifty thousand enemy forces (7,000 German, 20,000 collaborationist, and 22,000 Bulgarian troops).[2] Suffering hunger, cold, and exhaustion, the Partisans trudged through mountains and forests, where frequent snowfalls inhibited their movements. Sickness and desertion severely depleted Partisan ranks; some units disintegrated, while others, although designated as "battalions," were reduced to platoon- and squad-size detachments. In the Zaječar and Šabac districts, only twenty KPJ members remained at large, while too much emphasis on the communist ideology and attempts of "socialist reconstruction" in the villages reduced potential popular support.[3] The communist resistance so much diminished in intensity that in January 1942, Nedić announced that "communism in Serbia is almost eliminated."[4]

Yet, some astute observers were not deluded. The German defeat at Moscow reinvigorated the Partisan spirits and in December 1941 the *Einsatzgruppe* Serbia reported to Berlin that the resistance might resurge in the spring. In early February the Southeast Command recorded that "Serbia remains an operational zone, where the war continues and unfortunately, will continue for the foreseeable future."[5] The Gestapo-chief Heinrich Müller also admitted that all the anti-insurgency measures had failed to completely eradicate the resistance.[6] Even more alarming were reports of the regional Serbian offices about the guerrillas' disruptions of communication lines, attacks on gendarmerie outposts, and burning of communal archives. In the Niš and Leskovac districts, Partisans even created small pockets of liberated areas.[7]

Forced to keep most German troops for garrison and guard duties in urban and industrial areas, the MBS was perforce to rely on the collaborationist forces, despite misgivings about their reliability. In March, the troops subordinated to Nedić reached their numerical peak—twenty-one thousand policemen and soldiers, and thirteen thousand "legal" Chetniks. In addition, five thousand members of the Russian Defense Corps—recruited among White Russian émigrés—were deployed to protect railroads and industrial sites.[8] Acting under the German or Bulgarian command, these forces were to bear the brunt of antiguerrilla warfare, while the German artillery, armor, and engineer details provided fire power and technical support.

On January 15, 1942, the Wehrmacht and NDH troops launched a large-scale operation against Partisan forces in eastern Bosnia (dubbed by the Yugoslav communist historiography as the Second Enemy Offensive). Simultaneously, under the overall command of General Bader (in March he was appointed the supreme commander of the Axis forces in Serbia and the NDH), a series of antiguerrilla operations began in Serbia and Banat.[9]

In December 1941, Bader advocated a more "measured" approach to anti-insurgency methods, but his forbearance was short-lived, as the January offensive failed to destroy the Partisans completely. On February 8, 1942, Bader ordered that harsher measures be deployed against the guerrillas and their helpers. Consequently, mass executions of civilians soon reached the reprisal scale of Operation Užice.[10] For example, after the Partisans ambushed a regimental commander of the 704th Infantry Division, five hundred hostages were shot in Belgrade. On February 17–19, eight hundred inmates of the Crveny Krst concentration camp, including all Jews and some Roma, were shot.[11]

In March, ten thousand Bulgarian and five thousand collaborationist forces launched another major offensive in southeastern Serbia. Under pressure, the Partisans split into small groups, frequently of between five and ten men, who tried to slip through enemy lines. By late April, the troops reported five hundred Partisans killed and twelve hundred captured; Nedić again declared that the "total elimination [of the resistance] was achieved—there were no more communists in Serbia." The collaborationist press repeatedly trumpeted that the civil war in Serbia was finally over.[12]

This time such declarations seemed warranted. The Partisan command in Serbia admitted to NKOJ that the resistance was all but destroyed. Many guerrillas abandoned the struggle and went home or surrendered to local authorities.[13] Surviving on meager food rations, the remaining guerrillas frequently slept on the bare ground under snow and rain, unable to dry their tattered clothing. The sick and wounded were carried on stretchers, overloaded carts, or horse-drawn litters; many succumbed to gangrene and cold.[14]

Still, the resistance was not destroyed. In July and August, another offensive known as the Aćimović Pursuit (Milan Aćimović supervised the operation) was carried out in southeastern Serbia. It involved fourteen thousand collaborationist and five thousand Bulgarian forces, which blockaded roads and villages, conducted house-to-house searches, and shot civilians. Five hundred houses were burned and three thousand villagers were seized for allegedly helping Partisans.[15]

The antiguerrilla war again generated a draconian response from the German command in the Balkans, whereby the advocates of more drastic measures prevailed over those who desired more comprehensive policies. In the first half of 1942, German and collaborationist troops killed and executed twenty thousand civilians.[16] In October 1942, General Alexander Löhr, who had assumed the Southeast Command, ordered "all visible enemy troops . . . to be exterminated to the last man" and expected his subordinates to carry out his order "without exception and in a brutally harsh spirit." Outraged at the high numbers of prisoners taken in anti-partisan operations in the NDH, Hitler issued an exceptionally severe anti-partisan directive on December 16, 1942, ordering "the most brutal means . . . against women and children."[17]

In contrast to the Chetniks, the Partisans were not overtly concerned about civilian victims. Rather, they expected that German terror would drive more recruits into their ranks. Indeed, a discernible shift occurred in the Partisans' social makeup. If earlier most Partisans were urbanites who remained a socially alien element in the countryside, the resistance gradually swelled with hundreds of peasants antagonized by reprisals and increasing supply quotas. Tito placed a special effort on propaganda work, and as more illiterate peasants joined the ranks, the KPJ held literacy courses in the Partisan camps, facilitating the ideological indoctrination of new recruits. As a result, KPJ membership swelled—in 1943 the communists came to constitute between 7 and 10 percent of the ranks.[18]

While the KPJ stressed the necessity of the national-liberation struggle, it had to live off the land, utilizing all available manpower and economic resources of Partisan-controlled territories. The propaganda campaign for material support of the resistance, therefore, became a cornerstone of political activities of the Partisans. Often the population gave up food, cloth, or horses, out of conviction or fear. In fact, communist sources frequently mentioned "donations" and forcible requisitions from "speculators" and those who were unsympathetic to the resistance.[19]

To convince the population to lend its support, Partisans set up meetings and cultural exhibitions in the villages, which highlighted the KPJ main objectives—the liberation of Yugoslavia and national and social equality for everyone. In November 1942, the Partisan leadership convened a conference in the town of Bihać, Croatia, where it announced the formation of the Yugoslav National Antifascist Liberation Council (Antifašističko vijeće narodnog oslobođenja Jugoslavije, AVNOJ). Made up of communist and noncommunist representatives and headed by Tito, the AVNOJ proclaimed its support for democracy, the rights of ethnic minorities, and the right of private property.[20]

The KPJ organized secret conferences, where the party goals and guidelines for activities were explained to Partisan delegates and to workers' and peasants' representatives. The regional KPJ committees maintained contacts with each other; the committee in southeastern Serbia established links with the Bulgarian communist resistance.[21]

Unlike the Chetniks, the Partisans drew distinct lines between the enemies and allies. Tito made it clear that, regardless of the instructions from Moscow, there would be no more compromise with the Chetniks. In early April 1942, he issued an explicit order to the Croatian Partisan command to "liquidate the Chetniks whenever possible." In correspondence with Moscow, Tito largely succeeded in discrediting Mihailović in the eyes of Stalin, describing him as a traitor and collaborationist. Impressed by these reports, in August 1942, in a message to the Yugoslav government in exile, the Soviet government accused the Chetniks of collaboration with the Axis powers.[22]

Despite severe losses, the Partisans displayed genius for escaping annihilation, relying on stamina, determination, knowledge of the terrain, and discipline. Slackers, cowards, and deserters were court-martialed and executed, while veterans served as models for the demoralized and dispirited. The Partisan leadership shared all deprivations and miseries with their men and led by example. KPJ members—on average there was one communist per ten Partisans—served as propagandists, officers, and political commissars.[23]

Partisans' dedication to the cause translated into numerous instances of heroism and self-sacrifice, and as noted previously they often chose to take their own lives rather than fall into enemy hands. For example, in Banat a member of the KPJ Central Committee, Žarko Zrenjanin, and his comrade Strahinja Stefanović were surrounded in a house by a hundred policemen and soldiers supported by mortars. Both refused to surrender and died in the ensuing battle.[24] The execution of Partisan commander Stevan Filipović entered the resistance mythology. When captured, Filipović withstood all tortures and was sentenced to hang by a collaborationist court. On May 22, 1942, in Valjevo, on the scaffold with a noose around his neck, Filipović defied his tormentors and appealed to the crowd to resist the occupiers.[25]

The Partisan resistance had a profound psychological impact, giving moral strength to those who had resigned themselves to foreign occupation. The communist cross-national appeals gradually succeeded in attracting people of various ethnic, religious, and political persuasions. An OSS report in November 1943 admitted that the Partisan resistance included anyone from a cleric to an "agrarian democrat."[26]

Partisans skillfully used the Axis division of Yugoslavia and, when hard pressed, they crossed into the less dangerous areas in Montenegro or Sandžak. They replenished their ranks, particularly in Croatia and Bosnia, where the Ustasha terror drove thousands of Serbs to join the resistance, and then returned to Serbia.[27] Decimated by arrests, the urban underground strove to rebuild its cells. In January 1942, Dragi Jovanović reported 243 communists and 1,538 resistance members active in Belgrade, and a year later the Special Police accounted for 252 communists and 1,758 resisters in the capital. Partisans also accepted into their ranks those Chetniks and gendarmes willing to switch sides, although the recruitment of such elements undermined the quality of the resistance.[28]

Allied victories in Egypt and Libya directly threatened the German position in Sicily, and the critical situation of the German army at Stalingrad forced Hitler to reconsider the situation in the Balkans. In October 1942, the OKW increased the German forces in Serbia, which grew to thirty-five thousand men (in comparison to 20,000 in NDH). In late December, Hitler named the Balkans the "operational theater of war"—the implication being that the entire region had acquired a new significance. Accordingly, the Southeast Command and the Italian army in Croatia prepared a large-scale operation, aiming at destroying the main Partisan forces in Bosnia. Code-named Weiss, it was a constituent part of the overall plan to secure the Balkans in case of the Allied landing. In January 1943, Operation Weiss was set in motion and inflicted severe casualties on the Partisan army, which lost almost a third of its personnel but managed to break out of the encirclement. In May and June, the Partisans survived the second phase of the offensive, Operation Schwarz, in the Sutjeska valley. The Allies could no longer ignore the situation, and the British mission in Mihailović's staff eventually sent reports to London, confirming that the Partisans bore the brunt of fighting against the Axis.[29]

The MBS dispatched several contingents to Operation Weiss in Bosnia, thereby thinning the German garrisons in Serbia. Conversely, to relieve the pressure on their comrades in Bosnia, the Partisan command initiated a series of attacks on communication lines and industrial sites. In early February, Partisans attacked a mine in the Bor area and torched a hangar with fuel. Such actions had the immediate effect of diminishing industrial production and were more damaging than attacks on gendarmerie outposts.[30]

The MBS responded with another wave of reprisals. By late April 1943, 2,332 hostages, including 1,628 communists and 704 Chetnik supporters, were shot.[31] In June the Germans retaliated by executing nine hundred hostages, including women, children, and the elderly in the Šabac camp. When in the autumn this and other camps were shut down, hundreds of inmates were forced on "death marches," whereby hundreds died on the roads of exhaustion or were murdered by the guards.[32]

Naturally, small-scale Partisan attacks could not seriously endanger German rule in Serbia, but the Partisans remained a real thorn in the side of the German garrisons and the collaborationist administration. Particularly in southeastern Serbia, about 4,000 guerrillas fought the German, Bulgarian, and Chetnik forces. In mid-November near Užice, a large Partisan unit battled for eight hours against eighteen hundred Bulgarian and two hundred

German forces, supported by tanks. The Partisans beat off the attackers and captured several Bulgarian artillery pieces.[33] As a result of Partisan activities, the delivery of agricultural quotas for the troops of occupation became extremely difficult. The MBS General Hans Felber (who replaced Bader) ordered that the collection of agricultural deliveries be conducted under a strong protection of the troops and the police, even at the cost of temporarily decreasing antiguerrilla operations.[34]

On November 21–29, 1943, in the Bosnian town of Jajce, the communist leadership convened the second AVNOJ conference, which declared itself the supreme executive authority in Yugoslavia. Tito was promoted to the highest military rank of marshal of Yugoslavia and became prime minister. The AVNOJ announced that postwar Yugoslavia would be a federal state of six constituent republics and that the NKOJ would act as the temporary government. Crucially, the AVNOJ denied King Peter II the right to return to the country until a popular referendum. The communist revolution entered its decisive phase.[35]

Chetniks: Tactics of Survival

In early 1942, the Chetniks' situation looked more favorable than that of the Partisans. In contrast to his dispersed and hard-pressed rivals, Mihailović had five thousand men under his command in addition to about as many "legal" Chetniks who constituted a potential reserve pool. Many SDS officers were sympathetic to Mihailović, even if they did not support him directly. For example, General Kosta Mušicki, who headed the Nedić forces during the attack on Užice, supplied Mihailović with ammunition and intelligence.[36]

Mihailović still enjoyed the reputation of the leader of the national resistance, and the Yugoslav émigré and the Allied press extolled the Chetnik movement as the "third front" in the Balkans, consistently downplaying or ignoring completely Partisan war efforts.[37] Although the British knew that the Chetniks were largely inactive against the Germans, they continued to support Mihailović, not necessarily because "they believed him to be the most effective leader, but for long-term political reasons." Accordingly, in January 1942 the government in exile promoted Mihailović to brigadier general and appointed him minister of war.[38]

Outwardly, the Chetniks did their part in the resistance. They helped to safety downed Allied pilots and maintained a widespread intelligence network that provided the British with information about German troop movement in the Balkans. Sabotage acts, skirmishes with the SDS and with SDK units, and assassinations of several officials of the Nedić administration also contributed to the impression that the Chetniks were furthering the resistance.[39]

Under closer scrutiny, however, Mihailović's position was vulnerable. He acted as the supreme leader of the Yugoslav resistance but at the same time declared himself an inveterate enemy of the communists, who were fighting the occupiers. On December 3, 1941, Benzler reported to Berlin that although Mihailović remained the "rallying point" for nationalist insurgents, for the time being he was not dangerous because the Chetniks were busy fighting the communists.[40]

In contrast, Mihailović's position vis-à-vis the Germans and Nedić remained blurred. For example, sometimes the Chetniks fought side by side with the collaborationist forces, but when in February 1942 the Chetnik and Partisan units collided in the Požarevac district, both were attacked by the German and Nedić troops.[41] During the Chetnik commanders' conference in July, Mihailović's instruction delineated the tactical objectives of the movement: sabotage and cunning toward the occupiers, a propaganda war against the collaborationist forces except when the latter's "activities were useful for the people," and a merciless struggle against the communists as the "most dangerous internal enemy."[42]

The top German officials remained divided as to the most effective course of action toward the Chetniks. Meyszner and Schäfer viewed them as just as inimical to German interests as the Partisans, while Turner, Benzler, and some military and intelligence experts judged that the Chetniks' anticommunism was stronger than their anti-German sentiments.[43] In March 1942, Benzler wrote to Ribbentrop that weakness of the Germans forces necessitated more flexible policies to facilitate the internal struggle between the communists and the Chetniks.[44]

Regardless of such differences of opinion, Mihailović's vacillation was bound to exasperate the Germans. A perspicacious Chetnik commander Predrag Raković, who cooperated with the SDK in anti-Partisan operations in the Čačak area, predicted that the Chetnik-German collaboration was temporary and after the Germans destroyed the Partisans, they would turn against the Chetniks. He proved right—in late February 1942 the German and the SDK units began disarming their Chetnik allies.[45] Similarly, during a conversation with Nedić in March, Turner suggested that the best solution for the "Chetnik problem" would be getting rid of Mihailović, whose constant maneuvering made him a liability.[46]

Mihailović's other weakness was the loose structure of the Chetnik movement. Unlike Tito, who shared the same privations as his Partisans, Mihailović tended to stay at his headquarters. Most Chetniks were local or "seasonal" fighters, reluctant to operate outside of their home bases and acting only when it suited their own needs. Some Chetnik commanders conducted temporary truces with the Germans and the Nedić forces, receiving from them arms and ammunition and joining their anti-Partisan operations.[47]

Ideologically, the Chetnik leadership clung to its postulate of building the Greater Serbia. Believing that the Allies unequivocally supported the Yugoslav government in exile, the Chetnik ideologists envisioned a postwar unitary state that embraced "historical and ethnic" lands inhabited by the Serbs, Croatians, and Slovenes. On December 20, 1941, Mihailović created by decree an "ethnically pure" Great Serbia that included Montenegro, Bosnia-Herzegovina, Srjiem, Banat, and Bačka. Upon victory, these territories would be subjected to the "cleansing" (*čišćenje*) of national minorities and of "anational elements." The Croats and Slovens would be allowed to practice Catholicism on the condition they would reject the supremacy of the Pope.[48]

These concepts resembled Nedić's *zadruga* vision, indicating the ideological affinity between the VNS and Mihailović, making the contacts between the two so much easier, especially as the war against the Partisans remained Nedić's and Mihailović's priority and was marked by atrocities on all sides. For example, in May 1942 during the anti-Partisan operation in Šumadija, the Chetniks fought alongside the SDS and SDK units. Having discovered a hidden Partisan hospital, the collaborationist forces murdered every patient, wounded and sick guerrillas.[49] In some areas, the Chetnik *vojvodas* coerced Serbian officials to cooperate, or they removed them. They established courts-martial to try alleged communist sympathizers, and special squads known as black trios (*crne trojki*) killed suspected Partisan helpers; the families of the suspected Partisans were not spared, either.[50] Even incarcerated in Banjica, the Chetniks and the Partisans remained hostile to each other; sometimes the prison administration used Chetniks as informants against their enemies.[51]

Meanwhile, the Germans tolerated the semi-open existence of Mihailović's Chetniks as long as the latter fought Partisans. Due to the intercession of Neubacher, there was no major anti-Chetnik offensive until summer 1942, when the British urged Mihailović to increase attacks on railroads to impede the movement of troops and supplies, crucial for German operations in Africa.[52] Concerned about the strategic situation in the Mediterranean, the MBS ordered that 13,400 Chetniks (including "legal" ones) be disarmed and inducted into labor units. Only small numbers, considered battle worthy, were transferred to the SDK. On June 17, Himmler related to Heinrich Müller, the chief of the Gestapo, that the situation in "entire southeastern Europe depended on the destruction of Mihailović" and urged him to use any possible means to this effect.[53]

As the battle in northern Africa reached its apogee, the government in exile insisted that Mihailović increase his activities. On November 7 he issued an appeal for civil disobedience and in November and December the Chetniks carried out twenty-five acts of sabotage on the Belgrade–Salonika railway. This spark of activity temporarily fortified the image of the Chetniks as a determined anti-Axis force. The Allied command in the Middle East praised Mihailović for his contribution to the Allied cause.[54]

In reality, not only did Mihailović's November 7 order and the resulting actions fall short of British expectations, but they provoked drastic German response, which for many justified the "wait-and-see" policies he and the Chetniks had clung to since the beginning of the war. In October, a Bulgarian regiment and units of the SS Prince Eugen Division burned the village of Kriva Reka in the Kopaonik district and murdered 320 men, women, and children (according to other sources, 263 or 600 people); more than a hundred were burned alive in a church.[55] Hundreds of the Chetniks were captured and deported to Germany for forced labor; others were sent to the Banjica prison camp, where they were executed. Simultaneously, the Sipo destroyed several Chetnik cells in Belgrade.[56]

Assuming that the Allied invasion in the Balkans would benefit Mihailović more than Tito, the Southeast Command ordered that Hitler's no-prisoner policy toward Partisans also be applied to the Chetniks.[57] As a result, between September and early December, more than nine hundred Chetniks and their helpers were shot along with five hundred communist sympathizers. On December 12 the chief of the OKW Operations Staff, General Alfred Jodl, reported to Hitler that between fifteen and thirty Chetnik "supporters" were shot in Belgrade every day.[58]

Still, in the winter of 1943, as many as fifteen thousand Chetniks participated in Operation Weiss. To Mihailović's dismay, in the battle on the Neretva River, the Partisans decimated some of his best troops. Furthermore, the German command blamed him for the failure of the operation and disarmed some Chetnik units.[59] Since both the Partisans and the Chetniks derived their moral strength from the large-scale war in Croatia and Bosnia, the debacle on Neretva severely undermined the latter's morale, and their combat effectiveness inexorably deteriorated. In Serbia, the Chetniks suffered a further setback when in the winter and spring of 1943 the Gestapo and *Abwehr* arrested many of Mihailović's supporters within the Nedić administration.[60]

In July 1943, the MBS launched an offensive against Mihailović's headquarters near Čačak. Mihailović and his staff escaped, but more than a hundred Chetniks were shot and 453 captured.[61] In effect, Mihailović was fighting a three-front war. Squeezed between the German and the Nedić forces on one side and Partisans on the other, some Chetnik units scurried between the lines. Some tried to survive by conducting temporary truces with some or all of the enemies.[62] In some instances, Partisan and Chetnik units occupied and divided a single village in two, maintaining a temporary ceasefire; German reports indicate that sometimes it was impossible to differentiate between the Chetniks and Partisans.[63] In late September, Mihailović's Chetniks near Užice fought German and Bulgarian forces, which were assisted by a "legal" Chetnik unit.[64]

If the Chetniks tried to maintain neutrality toward Nedić's forces and often released captured SDS officers and soldiers, they showed no leniency toward SDK members, whom they hated as much as the Partisans. In turn, from the beginning of war, Ljotić blamed the Chetniks for their cooperation with Tito. The clashes between the two forces were extremely brutal, with neither side giving quarter to prisoners or the wounded. For example, in July 1943 in the Kruševac district, the Chetniks ambushed an SDK unit, killing twenty of its members, including a battalion commander and the district chief.[65]

Meanwhile, the Allies increasingly perceived the Chetniks as a liability and criticized Mihailović for a lack of martial energy, whereas the Partisan movement was gaining strength and more popular support. Moreover, in preparation for a potential Allied invasion of the Balkans, Hitler ordered the defense of the coastal areas to be strengthened and ordered Bulgaria to dispatch five more divisions to free up the German troops in Serbia. In July, Hitler stressed Serbia's importance in the Balkan struggle and urgently required the destruction of all "bands"—that is, both the Partisans and the Chetniks—that were active on German communication lines in Serbia and Croatia.[66]

Facing the Allied invasion of Italy, however, Hitler grudgingly consented to Neubacher's reorganizing the anticommunist forces in the Balkans. In November, Weichs, who in August was appointed commander of the German forces in the Balkans, issued a directive stating that local agreements with the Chetnik forces and common actions against the communists were underway, provided that the Chetniks placed themselves under German command. Consequently, some Chetnik commanders negotiated a series of agreements placing them under German command. For example, the representatives of the Southeast Command and Major Vojislav Lukačević arranged for a cease-fire in the area from southeastern Bosnia and Montenegro all the way to the Ibar valley. To ensure better coordination against the Partisans, German liaison officers were dispatched to Chetnik units. Weichs's directive, however, specified that such cooperation applied only to individual Chetnik commanders, but not to Mihailović and those Chetniks who still pursued the anti-German actions. It seemed, therefore, that the directive was the last offer to Mihailović to openly declare on the German side.[67]

At the same time, in preparation for the conference of the Allied foreign ministers in Moscow, the British foreign secretary Antony Eden urged the Yugoslav government in exile to induce Mihailović to carry out a large-scale action in Serbia in order to convince Stalin of the Chetniks' anti-German struggle. Consequently, in October 1943 Mihailović ordered the intensification of actions against the occupying forces.[68] But it was too late. By the opening of the Teheran conference in November 1943, the British had concluded that Tito's Partisans were doing most of the fighting and that the Chetniks had compromised themselves by dealing with the Axis powers. The Allies' patience with Mihailović ran out, and they withdrew support for the Chetnik forces.[69]

With a sense of defeat creeping in, Mihailović called a Chetnik congress, which took place on January 25–28, 1944, in the village of Ba, near Ravna Gora. Presided by Stevan Moljević as the president of the Central National Committee, the congress confirmed the Chetnik adherence to reestablish monarchy in Yugoslavia and expressed expectations that the Western powers would support it. Although intended as "Yugoslav," the congress looked anything but, since among 294 delegates there were only six Croats, Slovenes, and Muslims. The delegates tried to establish the centralized political organ—the Yugoslav Democratic National Union—in the hope that it would counterweigh the AVNOJ. To answer the communists' challenge, the conference settled on a more liberal program that called for the federalist state structure under the monarchy, with Serbia, Croatia, and Slovenia as autonomous national units. Although democracy and parliamentarian rule were accentuated, the territorial borders as well as the status of national minorities within the three national units remained vague. The congress announced itself as the sole representative of Yugoslavia's sovereignty inside the country and confirmed its determination to fight both the Germans and Partisans.[70]

In February 1944 Weichs, Neubacher, and the MBS discussed the situation in Serbia and decided that most Chetnik commanders were not meeting expectations. Meyszner also issued a directive, stressing that, despite agreements with Mihailović, the latter continued to act against the German forces. As a result, in mid-February, the German, Bulgarian, and Nedić forces launched a series of operations against the Chetniks, who suffered heavy casualties.[71]

The Race for Belgrade

In 1942 the bulk of the guerrilla warfare shifted to Bosnia and Herzegovina, but the Partisan leadership never lost sight of Serbia as the critical region for the future political transformation of Yugoslavia. Returning to Serbia became an obsession for Tito, who correctly judged that only in Belgrade could the communists ensconce themselves as the successors to the monarchy. Accordingly, in the summer of 1943, the KPJ leadership established guidelines for the Partisan offensive into Serbia.[72]

In January 1944, Partisan forces in Montenegro advanced into Serbia. Striking in the Ibar Valley, Partisans attempted to establish a base between the Ibar and Morava Rivers, threatening the German communication lines between Serbia and Greece. The attack created a potential link between the Partisans and the Soviet forces that were about to enter Serbia from Bulgaria and Romania. After a series of vicious clashes with the German and collaborationist forces, in March the Partisan offensive ran out of steam.[73]

In April the Partisans launched another attack, simultaneously in the Ibar Valley and in western and southeastern Serbia. According to Gestapo intelligence, between eight and ten thousand Partisans advanced from Montenegro, while the units in southern Serbia were joined by five hundred Bulgarian partisans from Macedonia, whose activities increased dramatically with the offensive of the Red Army in Romania. A vicious battle raged for two months, and all sides suffered severe casualties. The battle-hardened Partisan Proletarian Division lost more than half of its four thousand men; another elite unit—the Krajiška Division—suffered casualties of 50 percent.[74]

Concerned over its communication lines from Greece to Serbia and supplies of raw materials, the Southeast Command beefed up its forces in Serbia. By early 1944 these amounted to 15,000 men, in addition to 31,000 Bulgarians and 17,000 collaborationist forces.[75] Still, deeming its forces as inadequate to deal with the Partisan onslaught, in May 1944 the Southeast Command issued a directive, stressing that the situation necessitated collaboration with the Chetniks.[76]

Mihailović was duly alarmed by the magnitude of the Partisan attack, but his situation became increasingly desperate. Although the Chetnik movement still represented a significant force—twenty thousand fighters—this strength was illusory. Some units bore an impressive designation as "corps" but had no more than two hundred active members.[77] Mihailović tried to avoid fighting the Germans but also wanted to maintain some semblance of contributing actively to the resistance. Nevertheless, in April the British mission with the Chetniks reported that Mihailović's "orders of inactivity . . .

are followed almost without exception . . ." and that a "sort of nonaggression pact existed . . . to the comfort of all concerned."[78] Some Chetnik commanders were fighting alongside German, Bulgarian, and Nedić troops. Supervised by German liaison officers, these forces engaged Partisans in a series of bloody encounters. In the same period, the Chetnik commandos carried out several assassinations of Nedić's officials, including the chief of the Nedić's cabinet, Colonel Miloš Masalović, and its state secretary, Cvetan Ceka Čorčević.[79] The objectives of these attacks are not clear, and some Chetnik commanders may have acted without Mihailović's knowledge in retaliation for anti-Chetnik actions carried out by the Nedić forces. In turn, the Germans and SDK units killed about three hundred Chetniks and their supporters in the Kosmaj and Rudnik areas.[80]

Eager to patch up differences within the anti-Partisan forces, on May 20 Ljotić met with Mihailović's chief of staff, General Miroslav Trifunović, to discuss closer cooperation between the VNS and the Chetniks. Trifunović pledged to cease attacking German personnel and the Serbian administration and to concentrate on fighting the communists. Ljotić, in turn, promised to supply the Chetniks with arms and food.[81] Accordingly, in April, General Felber reported to OKW that the Germans forces, the SDK, and Mihailovic's Chetniks were fighting the communists in southeastern Serbia. In July, Felber further asserted that "for the time being," the Chetnik combat units were not to be treated as hostile."[82]

Simultaneously with the military offensives, the KPJ prepared political measures to prepare the ground for taking over. Contrary to its previous decision to fight "Serbian chauvinism," in June 1944 the KPJ Central Committee decided that Serbia was ideologically ripe for the creation of its own KPJ branch.[83] On June 16, 1944, on the Dalmatian island of Vis, the AVNOJ and the government in exile reached an agreement to create the united Yugoslav government. The last British liaison officers left Mihailović's staff, and on August 28 King Peter dismissed him as supreme commander of the Yugoslav forces. On September 12, the king called on all Yugoslavs to come together under Tito's leadership. In desperation, Mihailović even attempted to establish contacts with the Soviet forces that were about to advance into Yugoslavia from Romania and Bulgaria. Some Chetnik units even joined the Soviet forces in September. The mission, however, failed after the Soviets arrested the Chetnik emissaries, who attempted to contact the Allied missions in Bucharest.[84]

Trying to find a viable solution from this predicament, Mihailović and Nedić came up with a plan of the Chetnik takeover at the time of the German withdrawal, hoping to present the Allies with a fait accompli (as happened with nationalist uprisings in Warsaw and Slovakia).[85] On August 12–13, 1944, three Chetnik commanders reached a formal agreement with Dragi Jovanović and the chief of Nedić's cabinet, Miodrag Damjanović. According to the agreement, Nedić would pay the Chetniks 100 million dinars and supply them with thirty thousand rifles; the VNS representatives handed over the money and ten thousand rifles. On August 20, Nedić and Mihailović met in Topola near Valjevo. They agreed to stop mutual hostilities and turn exclusively against the Partisans. Realizing that his name has been tarnished by collaboration with the Germans, Nedić consented to place his forces under Mihailovic's command. To provide the Chetniks with the remaining twenty thousand rifles, Nedić contacted the Hungarians through his minister of propaganda, Đjorđje Perić, who was authorized to offer territorial compensation to Hungary in exchange for arms.[86]

On August 30, Mihailović declared general mobilization of the "Yugoslav army in the Fatherland," and on September 6 all Chetnik and the Nedić forces were unified under his command. In preparation for the Chetnik coup, Nedić ordered his subordinates to take control of all railroad junctions and all telephone and telegraph stations. Similarly, Mihailović issued instructions for the creation of the administrative organs, which were to secure industrial sites, warehouses, and courts as the new organs of justice—all in the hope that the Allies would support him to prevent a communist takeover.[87]

All of these plans were doomed. The Soviet Army command recognized the NKOJ as an equal partner, while on August 19 Tito issued a directive to the Partisan command in Serbia outlining its main strategic objective: defeat of the enemy forces and the establishment of the "people's power." On September 28, 1944, the Soviet press agency TASS announced that Tito had signed an agreement with the Soviet Union about the joint Partisan-Soviet actions in the northeastern areas of Yugoslavia.[88]

On August 23, Romania declared war on Germany, with Bulgaria following suit on September 8, creating the potential for the entire German force to be trapped in the Balkans. Consequently, the Southeast Command ordered general retreat. With their strategic right flank secured by the Soviet advance, the Partisan command concentrated sixteen divisions of twenty thousand battle-hardened soldiers for the final push on Belgrade. These forces advanced from Sandžak, Montenegro, and the Ibar valley.[89]

Partisan troops swelled with large numbers of volunteers, particularly after the king appealed to his subjects to join Tito. Among these "last-minute partisans" were a thousand Chetniks who switched sides.[90] Between September 8 and 11, Partisans defeated Mihailović's forces near Užice and captured the Chetnik archives; Mihailović, his staff, and a U.S. military mission were saved in the last moment by the timely arrival of an SDK battalion.[91] On October 3 the Partisans captured Bor, liberating the remaining Jewish and Hungarian laborers. By October 12, all of eastern Serbia was liberated, and the area between Kragujevac and Sava was under Partisan control. On October 13 the Germans left Niš, and the next day the battle for Belgrade began. After a week of ferocious fighting, Partisan and Soviet forces entered the battered capital, which had never fully recovered from the April 1941 German bombardment (and was further damaged by Allied bombers in April 1944). Now, German units set off explosives in many buildings, which collapsed or burned, killing people hiding in basements. The Partisans sustained 2,953 casualties, indicating Tito's determination to capture the capital with his own forces (the Soviets lost a thousand men).[92]

On November 9, 1944, in Belgrade, the first session of the Great Antifascist Assembly (acting in the name of the AVNOJ) declared Serbia as an equal member of the Yugoslav Federation. The Partisans immediately began the "socialist reconstruction" by abolishing old political institutions and replacing them with the new "people's organs of power." With thousands of peasants rushing to join the KPJ, a communist functionary mused that the KPJ had already become a "peasant" rather than a "workers'" party.[93]

The eviction of the Germans did not end violence in Serbia, for Partisans set out to settle old scores. In May 1944, Tito had ordered the formation of the special police, which proceeded to hunt down ideological enemies, and in October and November the "revolutionary" tribunals sentenced to death or to long prison terms between six thousand and ten thousand people, including the Chetniks, the members of the collaborationist administration, and individuals considered hostile or unsympathetic to the communists.[94]

Nedić retreated with the German forces to Austria, but in January 1946 the British extradited him to Belgrade, where, according to the Yugoslav official version, he committed suicide in prison. Mihailović managed to avoid capture until March 1946, when he was trapped by the Yugoslav secret police. Three months later, along with seventeen other defendants, he was sentenced to death.[95]

* * *

The defeat of the Partisans in 1941 was the beginning of a long and arduous struggle. They frequently appeared on the brink of total annihilation only to almost miraculously survive, although for a long time they were incapable of seriously threatening the occupation forces. While the Partisan popularity soared in Serbia, the Ustasha terror in Croatia and Bosnia against the Serbian population facilitated the growth of the communist resistance, so that by late

1943 the Partisans had developed into an effective force that posed a serious threat to German troops in the Balkans.

In contrast, the ideological inflexibility of the Chetnik movement and collaboration with the occupying forces eventually undermined its potential. By all accounts, in 1942–43, large Chetnik contingents effectively became an integral part of the occupation forces. Mihailović's shifting alliances with the Partisans, Nedić, and the Germans chipped away the movement's strength, which cracked under the pressure of fighting too many enemies at the same time.

In 1942–44, the civil war in Serbia reached its culmination, often overshadowing the resistance warfare against the occupiers. For Partisans, it was an inevitable and inseparable component of the socialist and national revolution, and those who placed themselves at the service of a foreign oppressor effectively extinguished their membership in the new Yugoslav nation.

Despite Tito's promises to Churchill that he did not intend to impose communism in Yugoslavia, on November 21, 1944, the AVNOJ announced the nationalization of the "enemy's" property and its transfer to the state. Ethnic Germans, Hungarians, Italians, and all individuals declared as "enemies and traitors" lost their citizen rights. The socialist revolution, which the communists had preached throughout the war, had prevailed.

8 Serbs and Jews

All over German-dominated Europe, participation in the persecution of Jews became a key element of native collaboration, demonstrating loyalty or ideological affinity of Germany's allies, satellites, and the right-wing groups.

Collaboration in the Holocaust emanated from a variety of motives—ideological convictions, a desire to please the Germans, or indifference toward a powerless minority. In Serbia, the Council of Commissars and the Government of National Salvation enforced the registration of Jews, published discriminatory decrees, and participated in the systematic robbery of Jewish property. Many officials and policemen also profited from the confiscation of Jewish property and businesses, and some displayed considerable zeal and energy, superseding the orders and expectations of their German masters. Although most Serbian collaborationists participated in the Holocaust indirectly, they became a useful instrument in the hands of the occupiers, responsible for criminal complicity.

On the Eve of Destruction

The Jewish demographics and professional occupations in Serbia (as well as in all of Yugoslavia) displayed patterns traditional to Eastern Europe. Most Jews resided in towns and cities, with at least half being proficient in the Serbian language. Almost 70 percent made their living through trade, commerce, and banking; 20 percent labored in industries, artisanship, and agriculture; and 11 percent served in the civil service, the army, and were occupied in free professions. Jews constituted 30 percent of college and university students and were particularly visible in the medical fields and technology.[1]

Jews in interwar Yugoslavia enjoyed a more tranquil situation overall than their counterparts in Poland, Romania, or Hungary. Concerned about nationalist aspirations in Slovenia, Croatia, Kosovo, and Macedonia, the SCS government was determined from its inception to stem ethnic tensions. Hoping to win the support of the Jewish political and financial circles, Belgrade tried to mitigate anti-Semitic agitation.[2] On June 28, 1919, the SCS constitution guaranteed full equality to all religious minorities; the government showed its will to implement the Minority Treaty, which accorded the religious communities wide autonomy in internal matters.[3]

In general, Jewish-Serbian relations were traditionally marked by a relative tolerance, conditioned by several factors. The small size of the Jewish community mirrored its political insignificance, while the Serbian middle class was also small and its competition with the Jewish merchant and commercial groups lacked the same vehemence as elsewhere in Eastern Europe. That relatively few Jews lived in the countryside eliminated potential frictions with the Serbian peasantry. Similarly, an underdeveloped industrial sector in Serbia attracted fewer employment contenders, mitigating potential Jewish-Serbian tensions.[4]

Anti-Semitism in Serbia (and later in the SCS) was a marginal although not unknown phenomenon. Since the late nineteenth century, it found supporters among the Orthodox clergy and the right-wing activists, who formed small but vocal groups such as the "God-admirers" (*Bohomoljci*). Led by their spiritual leader, Archbishop Nikolaj Velimirović, the *Bohomoljci* blamed Jews for spearheading Marxism, socialism, and liberalism, and in 1926 they disseminated the infamous *Protocols of the Elders of Zion*.[5]

The anti-Semitic agitation gained momentum after the Nazi takeover in Germany. Its main promoters were White Russian émigrés who associated Jews with Bolshevik rule in Russia, the Nazi activists within the ethnic-German community, the Zbor movement, and some right-wing intellectuals. For example, in 1934 the publisher of the newspaper *Vreme*, Stanislav Krakov (who would later became a prominent collaborationist) blamed Jews for the murder of King Alexander in Marseilles, while the Zbor organized anticommunist exhibitions with strong Judeophobic overtones.[6]

The growing influence of Nazi Germany in the Balkans was reflected in changes of the official policies toward Jews. In the early 1930s, the Yugoslav government tolerated the influx of Jewish refugees from Germany and Austria, but in October 1938 it drastically curtailed their numbers. In March 1940, Prime Minster Dragiša Cvetković authorized the Ministry of Education to compile a list of Jewish students in schools and institutions of higher learning.[7] This measure proved a prequel for the decree of October 5, 1940, which banned Jews from the wholesale food business and from trade in raw materials. The decree imposed quotas on Jewish students in schools and colleges (exemption was made for students whose parents had distinguished themselves in service of the state), and foreign Jews were barred from the state education system altogether. Those who failed to obey the decree were liable for imprisonment and a fine of 500,000 dinars ($10,000); a secret circular also banned the promotion of Jewish military personnel.[8]

The October decree emulated the Nazi Nuremberg Laws of 1935, and Yugoslavia thus followed several countries—Hungary and Slovakia (April 1938), Italy (September 1938), Romania (August 1940), and Vichy France (two days before Belgrade)—that adopted racial laws that defined Jews and limited their abilities to practice certain professions. Unlike the decrees in those countries, however, the October decree targeted exclusively the socioeconomic status of Jews—a reflection that Yugoslavia wished to maintain good relations with Great Britain and the United States. Later, Yugoslav politicians justified the decree solely as a gesture to placate Hitler (similar arguments would later be put forth by Nedić's apologists) and denied that it reflected the government's anti-Semitic attitudes. Whatever the case, the decree clearly indicated that Yugoslavia had descended into Germany's political sphere.[9]

Collaboration in the Holocaust

By 1941 all of Hitler's satellites and allies had introduced anti-Jewish measures. Vichy France and Slovakia did it largely of their own volition, while others like Hungary needed "prodding" from Berlin. In Belgium, Holland, and Serbia, the collaborationist administrations seemed to have merely obeyed German orders.

Indeed, bereft of executive powers, the Council of Commissars and the VNS outwardly did as they were told by the Germans. In April 1941, the MBS delegated the Council of Commissars to register the Jews and the Roma, as well as their property. The council relayed the order to its local branches, which registered 11,150 Jews (including 9,200 in Belgrade) and 3,050 Roma. Serbian police and the gendarmerie enforced registration, escorting Jewish labor details and guarding Jews and the Roma at the detention sites.[10]

Serbian local offices registered Jewish property and established specific hours when Jews and the Roma could enter shops. They also banned Jews from various professions, prohibited them from attending movie theaters, swimming pools, and exhibitions, and fired Serbian civil servants married to Jews.[11] While most local Serbian officials were carrying out German orders, some functionaries displayed personal initiative, especially during the

"Aryanization" campaign, since the MBS was not able to identify all Jewish businesses without assistance. They also squabbled over who had priority to use Jewish labor details and especially Jewish specialists. For example, the Belgrade administration complained that at times Serbian officials used Jewish laborers for "individual projects"—repairing or redecorating their houses and apartments.[12]

Facing so many pressing issues such as the resistance and the worsening economic situation, the collaborationist administration did not consider the "Jewish question" a priority. Rather, participation in anti-Jewish measures demonstrated loyalty and adherence to the ideals of the New Order, particularly since the collaborationists aspired to integrate Serbia into Hitler's geopolitical space. Assisting in isolating and robbing Serbian Jews seemed a small price for such a promising future.

Superficially, such attitudes appear reactive rather than proactive. In contrast to Ljotić or Krakov, there are no direct indications that Nedić was an avid anti-Semite. A product of the Serbian officer corps, he was a nationalist and a conservative who viewed internal politics narrowly through a Serbian prism. He was therefore apprehensive of Croats and Muslims, while his anticommunism ensured his determination to combat the resistance.[13]

Since the Serbian conservative and right-wing circles traditionally linked Jews and communism, Nedić might also have harbored suspicious toward the former. In his capacity as war minister, in November 1939 Nedić issued a memo that advised against reactivating officers with German, Hungarian, or Jewish backgrounds. Early in 1940 he ordered that Jewish officers who had converted to Christianity and referred to themselves as "Yugoslavs" in official correspondence had to indicate their religious background (i.e., Judaism) in personnel files. Still, such acts fit squarely into the official policies of the time and did not necessarily indicate that Nedić introduced them on his own initiative.[14]

It seemed, therefore, that German anti-Jewish policies offered Nedić bargaining power with which to obtain minor concessions from the MBS. When Turner advocated "selective" reprisals, in which Serbian hostages would be spared at the expense of Jews, Nedić found that measure fully justifiable and acceptable, especially since it mitigated the image of his administration as a German puppet.[15] Similarly, when the MBS ordered the execution of two hundred Serbs for the killing of the two German NCOs, Dragi Jovanović offered to substitute them with 170 Roma from the Banjica prison.[16]

In several public announcements and speeches, Nedić stressed the leading role of Jews in the resistance, referring to them as the "Jewish-communist bandits" and the most dreadful enemy of the Slavic people.[17] On September 17,

1941, he offered a bounty for the capture of the resistance members, claiming that Jews, the Roma, and other "non-Serb renegades" were the main culprits behind the chaos and civil war.[18] On March 28, 1942, Nedić complained to Turner about the clandestine activities of the Masons, Jews, and British agents in Serbia. Turner assured him the Jewish question was "as good as solved" and the remaining Jews and the Masons would soon be eliminated.[19]

After the Nazis murdered most Jews in spring 1942, Nedić wrote that, due to the German efforts, "the [Serbs] got rid themselves of the Jews, and now it was up to us to rid ourselves of other immoral enemies standing in the way of Serbia's spiritual and national unity." In June 1942 he wrote to Bader that in the Osnabrück POW camp, 340 Jews and a number of "leftist" officers carried out communist propaganda and requested that the camp administration "undertake necessary measures to this effect."[20]

Although such declarations could be construed as an attempt to curry favor with the Germans, they appear in a different light if placed in the context of Nedić's vision of the *zadruga* state. As mentioned before, the creation of this state entailed the national regeneration of Serbia, in which there was no place for ethnic minorities such as Croats or Albanians, much less for the Jews.[21] To this end, on August 26, 1942, with the consent of the MBS, Nedić decreed the appropriation of the remaining Jewish property (after most of it was confiscated or used by the Germans) as "belonging to the Serbian state." Two days later, all Jewish property was transferred to the Serbian Mortgage Bank. The monies accrued from the sale of Jewish property were transferred to the Serbian National Bank, and the Serbian administration used it to pay for the occupation costs.[22]

Unlike Nedić, Ljotić was ever consistent in his ideological views, and long before the war he was promoting virulent anti-Semitism. Abhorring democracy and secularism, Ljotić praised Hitler's anti-Jewish policies and blamed Jews for all political and social ills. He consistently stressed that the Zbor fought alongside Germany against communism, the Jews, and Masonry. Since religion and national identity in Serbia were tightly entwined, Ljotić pronounced that Jews were to be excluded from membership in the Serbian nation.[23]

Accordingly, since the outbreak of the war, Zbor members were active parties in the persecution of Jews. In April 1941 they participated in violent assaults and roundups of Jews in Belgrade; some received Jewish property as a reward for their activities.[24] Members of the SDK served as informants for the Special Police, denouncing Jews who were in hiding or who did not wear the yellow star. The SDK command was appalled that some Jews were living in Belgrade under Christian identities and constantly reported to the

VNS that Jews spearheaded the resistance and "demoralized" the Serbian population. SDK detachments also searched for Jews in the countryside and took part in the execution of Jewish and communist hostages.[25]

* * *

Despite mutual suspicions and rivalries, the Council of Commissars, the VNS, and the Zbor acted in perfect unity when promoting virulent anti-Semitic ideology and emulating Nazi racial propaganda. From the outset, the collaborationist press aimed at igniting anti-Semitic prejudices in Serbian society as well as playing up to the Germans. One of its most prevalent staples was the association of Jews with communism and the Soviet Union. For example, in a foreword to Milosav Vasiljević's book *Istina o SSSR-u* (The truth about the USSR), Ljotić called the USSR the embodiment of "Jewish-Marxist ideology."[26] Poised to portray the communist resistance as an "alien" force, some authors emphasized that all communist leaders were mostly Jews (or petty criminals), financed by "Jewish-Masonic" secretive cells. The members of the so-called Anticommunist League and similar associations stigmatized the communists and Jews as the new enemies who replaced Serbia's traditional foes, the Ottomans.[27]

Most such articles undoubtedly fell into the gutter press, which derived their vocabulary from the Nazi anti-Semitic newspaper, *Der Stürmer*. Catering to the most base instincts and playing on ugly human emotions, derogatory headlines took up most of the space on the pages, making the articles themselves superfluous. The communists and Jews were portrayed crudely as villainous creatures with crooked noses and deformed faces. Headlines such as "England in the Hands of Jews," "Jews, Banking, and Bolshevism," and "Jews and the War" ascribed all human miseries to Jews. For example, Nedić's minister of justice, Čeda Marković, described Jews as "the creators of the ultimate evils—revolutions, democracy, and political freedoms."[28]

Nedić's chief of propaganda, Lazar Prokić, called Jews a "decaying venomous race," while Stanislav Krakov and the editor in chief of *Naša borba*, Ratko Parežanin, claimed that Tito was a Jew, Lenin and Stalin were "Jewish creations," and if the communists prevailed, they would turn Serbia into a "Jewish" state.[29] Obvious incongruities did not trouble the authors, who portrayed Jews as the most determined and ferocious enemies of Serbia and at the same time as cowards and liars who "duped" the Serbs into the war.[30]

Vehement racism became a leitmotif in the publications of Ljotić and his close associates, who stressed that the future of Serbia depended on removal of Jews. Ljotić promoted "social and hygienic purity" as a prerequisite for Serbia's national regeneration, whereby Jews would be removed from the country. In contrast, Milorad Mojić, a Zbor's founding member and its general secretary, openly called for the extermination of Jews in the name of "Christian civilization."[31]

Mojić penned the *Laws and Deeds of Jews* pamphlet, which claimed that Judaism encouraged Jews to dishonor gentile women and to kill non-Jews.[32] After the discovery of the mass graves in Katyn (where in April 1940 the Soviet security police executed thousands of captured Polish officers), the press immediately blamed Jews for allegedly dominating Soviet security services.[33]

Such demented language and images were not simply a result of religious, ethnic, or racial prejudice but served a clear functional purpose—to portray the resistance as an "alien" force that caused Serbia's suffering and to deflect popular resentment toward German occupation onto Jews. In other words, Jews were portrayed as the embodiment of evil, which could be overcome only by a full mobilization of Serbian society and an alliance with Germany.

A "classic" element of the anti-Semitic imagery was the purported Jewish-Masonic conspiracy—allegedly a secretive force whose tentacles spread everywhere. Yugoslavia traditionally hosted a number of important Masonic lodges, which claimed several hundred members, including banking managers, doctors, lawyers, university professors, judges, and civil servants. A number of Serbian politicians, including members of the nationalist Serbian Cultural Club, also became prominent Masons. In the late 1930s, Masonic lodges in Belgrade counted five hundred members, who supported the monarchy and traditionally displayed pro-French and pro-British proclivities.[34]

The Masons' liberal inclinations, their international connections, and secret ceremonies enraged the Serbian right and the Orthodox Church, and the pro-Axis shift in Yugoslav politics resonated in the increased vilification of the "Judeo-Masons." In summer 1940, the Zbor organized a vicious anti-Masonic propaganda campaign, led by the radical anti-Semites Lazar Prokić, Danilo Gregorić, and Milosav Vasiljević. Playing up to Hitler, the Yugoslav government banned some Masonic publications and closed some Masonic lodges. Under pressure, in August 1940 the grand lodge Yugoslavia announced its dissolution.[35]

After the German invasion of Yugoslavia, the Gestapo arrested a number of prominent Masons; some wound up on the list of hostages and were shot in reprisals. The collaborationist administration hastened to follow, and in August the Council of Commissars blacklisted the Masons as "nationally unreliable" elements and fired them from civil service.[36] The anti-Masonic propaganda campaign escalated concomitantly with the persecution of Jews and utilized a similar rhetoric. On October 22, 1941, *Novo Vreme* blamed the Masons and Jews for provoking "all wars, revolutions, and political assassinations." The paper labeled the Masons as the most dangerous international organization, prophesizing that humanity will live in peace only after Masonry, communism, and Jewry were eradicated.[37] A multitude of newspaper articles and booklets blamed Jews and the Masons for both the March coup and the civil war. On March 27, 1942, the one-year anniversary of the officers' coup in Belgrade, Nedić echoed this trend, accusing the "Jewish-Mason-communist mafia" for breaking the Tripartite Pact that allegedly guaranteed Serbia's integrity and independence.[38]

The myth of the Masonic-Jewish conspiracy appealed to collaborationists for a particular reason. While Ljotić and his Zbor associates may have truly believed in the existence of such a conspiracy, most Serbs had virtually no knowledge of the Masons and their customs. Hence, the collaborationists calculated that linking the Masons with a more familiar group—Jews—would render the imagined threat more believable.[39]

The anti-Masonic drive culminated in a special exhibition whose ideological essence was the fusion of anti-internationalist, anti-communist, and anti-Semitic vitriol. Preparation for the exhibition began under the supervision of the MBS, the *Einsatzkommando* Belgrade, and the Council of Commissars soon after the uprising broke out in summer 1941. For this purpose, the council collected 1,465,000 dinars (including 673,000 dinars provided by the propaganda department of the Southeast Command). The supervisory committee was headed by a longtime German agent, Stevo Klujić, and the chiefs of the VNS propaganda department, Lazar Prokić and Đjorđje Perić. Eighty individuals selected for their "pronounced anti-Jewish, anti-communist, and anti-Mason orientation" were to run the show.[40]

"The Handiwork of the Masons, the Jews, and the Communists" exhibition opened in Belgrade on October 22, 1941, in the Yugoslavia, the former grand Masonic lodge. It was divided into five pavilions, each devoted to a specific theme—the Masonry, Jews, the Comintern, the USSR, and Victory. Among the guests of honor were top German and Serbian dignitaries, and Perić inaugurated the exhibition by delivering a speech about the mortal dangers of the "Jewish-Masonic-communist" conspiracy.[41]

According to a visitor (apparently an individual of pro-communist leaning), the exhibition was carefully prepared. The Special Police provided photographs, documents, and brochures from its archive as well as other related texts and pamphlets. The largest collection was devoted to the alleged Jewish-Mason plot, and a place of honor was accorded to the notorious *Protocols of the Elders of Zion*. Fifteen well-trained young guides explained to visitors the meaning of the numerous posters, pamphlets, cartoons, and statistical charts. The so-called Soviet hall displayed caricatures of Soviet statesmen, with emphasis on their real or purported Jewish background. Determined to make the exhibition a massive public event, the Serbian administration decreed it compulsory for school students and government employees.[42]

The press predictably called the exhibition a great success, claiming that eighty thousand visitors attended. During the three months of the exhibition (it ran until January 19, 1942), 116,290 copies of various items were sold, and a hundred thousand leaflets and pamphlets were distributed in Belgrade. Money raised at the exhibition also funded the so-called winter help—financial and material donations to the German army in Russia.[43]

The "Jewish-Masonic" conspiracy theme reappeared at the second exhibition, which opened in late August 1942 to commemorate the one-year anniversary of the Government of National Salvation. This time the anti-resistance theme predominated, although numerous documents emphasized the "Jewish connections" of the guerrillas; photographs of people allegedly murdered by the communists and Jews were prominently displayed. In Belgrade the exhibition was attended by 35,000 people, and to boost its standing, Nedić again made it compulsory for civil servants and school students. Later, the exhibition was moved to other cities and towns.[44]

* * *

Although blocked from expanding by the Germans, the Serbian police and gendarmerie continued to play important roles in the occupation. They alleviated the constant shortage of German manpower in the fight against the resistance, guarded Jewish ghettos and camps, hunted Jews in the cities and the countryside, and cordoned off execution sites. On October 27–31, 1941, the Serbian gendarmerie rounded up two thousand Roma in Belgrade and its environs.[45]

Numbering just six functionaries, the "Jewish" department of the Belgrade Gestapo was incapable of hunting down Jews without local assistance. Hence, they heavily relied on several native police structures, created specifically to deal with the "Jewish question." Section 7 of the Special Police specialized in apprehending Jews and the Roma. Like many Special Police functionaries, its chief, Jovan Nikolić, held a law degree from Belgrade University. He entered police service in 1931 and by 1938 had been praised by his superiors as efficient and energetic. During the war, Nikolić and his subordinates excelled in hunting Jews who had escaped from the ghettos and camps.[46]

Similarly, the "Jewish" section of the Ministry of the Interior maintained special registries of Jews, the Roma, Jewish property, and Serbian civil servants married to the Jews. The ministry regularly reported to the Council of Commissars and to the VNS on all issues pertaining to Jews and the Masons.[47]

The Special Police, the Ministry of the Interior, and local police and administration offices issued arrest warrants on Jews who escaped from detention places and handed over the captives to the Gestapo.[48] While some Serbian functionaries merely fulfilled German orders, others acted with the zeal of efficient man-hunters, especially since there were financial rewards for apprehending Jews. To demonstrate their loyalty and efficiency, police agents and informants often reported that their Jewish targets were linked to the resistance, especially as such denunciations required no proof. For example, one agent informed his superiors that a group of Jewish laborers clearing rubble in the town of Donje Grade had established contacts with the communists and were conspiring to blow up an ammunition depot.[49]

In autumn 1941, the Special Police initiated a mass hunt for Jews in hiding, searching several hospitals and clinics in Belgrade and identifying Jewish patients with false identities.[50] Escaping from the ghettos and concentration camps alone was a grievous offense (in accordance with the Nazi regulations), but the police reports emphasized that recaptured Jews were communist guerrillas or individuals dangerous to public order. In November 1941, prisoners Ladislav Grinski and two Reves brothers escaped from Topovske šupe, but they were caught by Croatian border guards at the Sava River. The guards handed them over to Special Police functionaries, who viciously beat the captives and sent them back to the camp as "elements dangerous to public security and state order." The three men were then hanged in front of the assembled camp population.[51]

In December, Special Police agents apprehended Berta Filatović, who had assumed an identity as a Roman Catholic. The chief of the Special Police, Ilija Paranos, reported to the Gestapo that Filatović was "dangerous for public order and security" and sent her to the Banjica prison camp. Similarly, when the Special Police functionaries arrested Elvina Kolb, who had converted to Christianity, and Elsa Kovać, who was living under an assumed identity, the log entries on their arrests indicated that both individuals held a "leftist orientation" and spread "alarmist rumors."[52] Section 3 of the Special Police, which was responsible for border safety, also tracked down Jews trying to escape to Macedonia or to the Italian zone of occupation in Croatia. In 1942 this department alone apprehended twenty-two Jews.[53]

Popular Attitudes

Due to Yugoslavia's rapid collapse, it is impossible to talk about Jewish reaction to the Holocaust, since the Nazi assault on Jews was rapid and crushing. After the country was occupied, most Jews were imprisoned in ghettos and camps and their options for survival were extremely limited. Individual Jews and some families tried to escape death by crossing into the Italian and Hungarian zones of occupation or to Turkey via Bulgaria. Others hid among Serbian refugees fleeing the Ustasha terror in NDH and elsewhere in Yugoslavia.[54]

In order to survive, most escapees had to seek contacts with the resistance or among sympathetic Serbs. Helping Jews, however, endangered not just the sympathizers but also their families, since the MBS decreed on May 30, 1941, that such acts were punishable by death.[55] Mass reprisals and daily roundups in Serbia were constant reminders of the ever-present danger to those opposing the German regime, which considered helping Jews a dangerous form of opposition.[56]

Hence, although the persecution of Jews provoked revulsion among many Serbs, few dared to express such sentiments in the open and even fewer risked their lives (and the lives of their families) to carry help to the persecuted minority. In July 1941, the chief rabbi of Yugoslavia, Isaak Alkalaj, wrote to the government in exile that the survival of Jews depended predominantly on the good will of their compatriots. These came from different social backgrounds and represented three groups: those who helped specific individuals such as acquaintances or friends, those who helped anyone, and those who helped for profit.

The first group, the so-called selective helpers, included relatives, friends, colleagues, and former fellow workers of the threatened Jews. The retired general Vojin Čolak-Antić convinced the Germans to spare his peer from the military academy, Colonel Avram Berahi, and his wife. Between December 1941 and January 1942, petitions by Christian relatives resulted in the release of fifty-four Jews and six non-Jews from imprisonment.[57]

Personal connections entailed creating small networks of those involved. With the help of several railroad employees, Olga Igić hid her Jewish friend, Sidonia Jaar, and moved her from place to place. Igić's brother-in-law, Vojislav Pantić, then obtained "Aryan" papers for Jaar, who consequently enlisted as a laborer and was sent to Germany, where she survived the war.[58] Fifteen-year-old Geza Kapon owed his survival to his school director very appropriately named Spasenjie ("salvation" in Serbian) Prica and his deputy, who supplied Kapon with a new identity card.[59]

Jewish children who had grown up in Serbian neighborhoods and were accustomed to Serbian customs could pass for ethnic Serbs. In July 1941, fifteen-year-old Julian Kempnjej knocked on the door of his schoolmate Aleksandar Pejić, whose family presented him to the neighbors as their third child. Kempnjej lived with the Pejić family until the liberation of Belgrade.

Similarly, the mother of nine-year-old Tugomir Brukner entrusted him to the family of Milja Arsenijević in a village near Čačak. The family, which had fourteen members, took Tugomir in until the end of the war.[60]

The other group, the so-called good Samaritans, did not discriminate between friends, acquaintances, and total strangers, instead acting out of compassion, religious convictions, or patriotic opposition to the occupiers. Helping total strangers involved more risks, since the helpers often had to rely only on themselves. For example, apparently acting alone, Dr. Milosav Stojadinović achieved a remarkable feat, hiding about eighty Jews in his apartment near the German security headquarters in Belgrade. Although marrying Jews was prohibited, some Orthodox priests registered Jewish brides under false names.[61]

Sometimes entire Serbian communities participated in rescue efforts. For example, when Anita Milin and his parents were hidden by a friendly family in the village of Ploc near Kopaonik, the whole village, including a priest who supported Ljotić, silently accepted the presence of Jews in their midst. The Serbian Jewish Šomolo family moved from place to place, covering hundreds of miles from eastern Serbia to Banat and then back, finding refugee among peasants in the area.[62]

The third group of Serbs willing to assist were those who used Jews' tragic situation for their own personal enrichment. During the German invasion of Yugoslavia, some locals participated in attacks on and robberies of Jewish apartments and houses in several localities. The scale of robberies was sufficiently high that the German administration repeatedly issued orders that stolen Jewish goods be returned to respective authorities. In May 1941 the MBS imposed the death penalty for purchasing stolen Jewish property.[63]

Similarly, some Serbs and ethnic Germans took advantage of the "Aryanization" campaign. When the administration in Banat put up for sale confiscated Jewish property, local ethnic Germans profited most from the subsequent transactions. According to some sources, a number of Serbs in Belgrade bought 48 percent of the "Aryanized" Jewish houses and apartments (ethnic Germans and "Reich" Germans bought 31 and 21 percent, respectively).[64] By mid-September 1942, Serbs had bought a third of the 133 Jewish enterprises and businesses.[65]

Although other motives such as pity could have been involved, for the helper the trade was profitable enough to risk his life. For example, a Special Police agent reported to Paranos that Tereza Šljivić-Fišer and her mother hid Jews, apparently in exchange for money and valuables.[66] Conversely, only individuals with means could pay for shelter or bribe Serbian officials to obtain false identity cards. Thus, Stjepan Singer paid the huge sum of 400,000 dinars (20,000 German marks) for forged identity cards and reached Lisbon in July 1942.[67]

Many Jews who escaped to the mountains and forests joined the Partisans, who were impartial to ethnic background. All in all, 4,500 Jews joined the communist resistance in Yugoslavia, and some received the highest decorations for valor and sacrifice. In contrast, Chetnik attitudes toward Jews varied according to circumstances and the stance of local commanders. Chetnik aspirations to build a homogeneous Serbia entailed the removal of all non-Serbs, and Pečanac's Chetniks participated in the roundups and executions of the Roma as "Partisan spies."[68]

To emphasize the "non-Serbian" character of the communist resistance, Chetnik propaganda stressed Partisans' ethnic diversity and described their leadership as criminal, "asocial," and headed by Croats, Jews, and Muslims.[69] Some Jewish accounts detail Jews being persecuted and murdered by the Chetniks. For example, in October and November 1941 and March 1942, the "legal" Chetniks captured several Jews, robbed them, and delivered them to the Crveny Krst concentration camp in Niš.[70]

Nevertheless, in the southeastern counties controlled by the Chetniks of Pečanac, a number of Jews were sheltered by the local peasants, most likely with the connivance of the local *vojvodas*.[71] According to some Serbian émigré sources, several Jews served with the Chetniks, even on Mihailović's staff. In June 1942 the Sipo in Belgrade ordered the Special Police to arrest Emil Piskar, a Jew who was a Chetnik currier.[72] Apparently, Chetnik commanders employed or impressed Jewish specialists into service. For instance, the physician Ladislav Deutsch provided the Chetniks with medical services, in exchange for which the local Chetnik commander removed his pregnant wife Julia to a friendly village, where she survived the war.[73]

* * *

The Holocaust in Serbia generated a broad variety of responses, from active persecution of Jews to efforts to help or save them. Participation in the Holocaust was inseparable from the general collaboration of the Serbian administration. The latter had no power or authority at its disposal to resist the Germans' policy of killing Jews, and furthermore, it displayed no willingness to do so. Instead, the collaborationists adopted an opportunistic approach to the "Jewish question," considering anti-Jewish measures as unavoidable, a small price to pay to appease or impress the Germans, and even necessary in order to safeguard public order.

Nevertheless, the Nazi ideological crusade against "Judeo-Bolshevism" converged with the aspirations of the principal collaborationists, who perceived themselves as the champions of Serbia's regeneration and closely emulated Nazi xenophobic and racial tenets. The Ljotić group had displayed outright anti-Semitic manifestations long before the war, but it was able to put them into practice only under German occupation. In contrast, to a certain degree the anti-Jewish actions of the Council of Commissars and the VNS partially evolved into a sort of collateral damage, whereby anti-Semitism was frequently a secondary motive. If Nedić did not hate Jews, he was nonetheless certainly indifferent to their fate, particularly since their small numbers made them easily dispensable and convenient scapegoats who could be sacrificed for the good of Serbia. Yet, as the war progressed he increasingly acted as an anti-Semite who viewed the removal of Jews as a building block of the country's national regeneration.

Accordingly, the Zbor, the Council of Commissars, and the VNS were quick to associate Jews with communism, and the resistance and collaborationist propaganda consistently portrayed them as the most sinister force, both domestic and international. Key collaborationists used the Jewish question as a launching pad for their own ambitions. Like his French counterpart Philip Pétain, Nedić embraced collaboration as a long-term project, which in the end entailed some autonomy for Serbia. Ljotić saw it as the path to Serbia's total absorption into the German geopolitical space. Both envisioned the new Serbia as a reactionary and antimodernist state opposed to cosmopolitanism, liberalism, communism, democracy, and urban decadence. In this state, there was no place for Jews (or for any other minority).

Given the small size of the Jewish community in Serbia, the Germans would unquestionably have destroyed it without the aid of the collaborationist regime. Still, the Council of Commissars and the VNS contributed in tracking down Jewish refugees and escapees. Serbian officials and policemen were driven by various motives—from the sense of professional duty to xenophobia, anticommunism, or greed. Although they performed auxiliary tasks, without their help the Final Solution in Serbia would have been less effective and would have taken longer, possibly according some Jews more time to hide and survive.

While a number of individuals benefited at the expense of Jews or remained onlookers, others risked their lives to help their Jewish compatriots. Rescue efforts in Serbia were significantly affected by a relative tolerance, which had characterized Jewish-Serbian relations before the war. Indeed, although the collaborationist propaganda inaugurated a vicious anti-Jewish defamation campaign, the MBS and the Southeast Command were skeptical of its quality and effects.[74] Therefore, in contrast to Poland, Romania, or Ukraine, where

Jewish refugees often faced hostile neighbors, Jews could often rely on their Serbian compatriots, both in urban areas and in the countryside.

Constantly exposed to the Nazi terror and the vicissitudes of the civil war, many Serbs appreciated and sympathized with the plight of Jews. Some offered help, which was often conditioned by a prewar relationship, while others risked their lives by harboring refugees and helping strangers.

The exact number of Serbian Jews who survived due to the efforts of their compatriots is difficult to establish with certainty. It is safe to say that most survivors who returned to their homes after the liberation of Serbia in the fall of 1944 owed their lives to their Serbian friends, neighbors, and simply decent people. Indeed, in the former constituent republics of Yugoslavia, Serbia holds the highest number of saviors—by January 2009, the State of Israel had awarded 125 people the honorable title of "Righteous among the Nations" (followed by 102 in Croatia, 40 in Bosnia, 9 in Macedonia, and 6 in Slovenia).[75]

9 Living with the Enemy

After the disaster of the April war wiped out the rapturous enthusiasm of the March coup, for more than three years the Serbian population endured constant hardship and violence. How did the average individual react to the brutal realities of war? As a rule, peasants and workers did not leave memoirs for posterity, while the communist historiography conventionally portrayed Yugoslavia's population divided into three groups: the collaborationist minority led by the "native bourgeoisie," the communist resistance, and the "silent" majority, which eventually came to constitute the main human reservoir for the Partisans.[1]

Such a clear-cut division, however, was more wishful thinking than reality. As the war went on, thousands of volunteers indeed joined the Partisan forces, but this process was slow and assumed large proportions only in 1944. Before then, in the face of overwhelming German power, most Serbs resigned themselves to the realities of occupation, albeit remaining "passive patriots," pledging silent loyalty to the king and to the government in exile.

Similar attitudes prevailed all over German-occupied Europe, where economic deprivations and fear of German terror left little time for political activism. To provide for their families, men had to work, returning to the daily routines that accorded minimal economic security and a modicum of social stability. In other words, living with the enemy effectively meant laboring for the enemy and entailed threading a dangerous balance between accommodation and collaboration.

Peasants and Workers

For a short time after the collapse of Yugoslavia, life in the countryside appeared to be returning to normal. In the summer of 1941, peasant cooperatives were able to deliver their required allotments to collection points, and most families had access to the food supplies accumulated before the war. As food scarcity in urban areas increased, peasants could profit by raising prices on their products or selling them to black marketers (although at the risk of German reprisals). After most German troops were transferred to the eastern front, villagers rarely saw German soldiers, who were garrisoned primarily in cities and towns. Fulfilling German orders provided a tentative guarantee of security, particularly since the German and collaborationist propaganda characterized enemies in ideological rather than in racial terms (with the exception of Jews and the Roma). The Serbian administration appointed reliable notables, teachers, or professionals as mayors and village elders, who functioned as intermediaries between their communities and the Germans. Similarly, the reappearance of gendarmes in their familiar blue uniforms was undoubtedly comforting to many Serbs.[2]

Eventually, however, the situation changed for the worse as numerous restrictions and regulations seriously affected villagers' lives. In April and May, the MBS introduced a variety of labor duties for peasants, including providing troops with transportation and billeting. Numerous pass controls and permits drastically reduced the opportunities for hunting and fishing; all boats, vessels, and river installations were placed under the jurisdiction of the military commandants. In some areas, peasants were ordered to sow rye, barley, and hemp exclusively, required by the Wehrmacht. Those who violated such orders were subject to imprisonment or forced labor. To prevent guerrilla attacks, the MBS prohibited grain cultivation within 500 meters of all communication lines, and existing fields within that perimeter were destroyed.[3]

Meanwhile, the outbreak of resistance resulted in the reduction of general agricultural output, and from January 1942 Serbia was also compelled to supply the Bulgarian occupation forces. Before the war the grain yield per hectare was 1,170 kilograms wheat and 1,240 kilograms corn, but in 1942 it fell 22 and 15 percent, respectively.[4] Simultaneously, the ever-rising allotment quotas and taxes effectively nullified any surplus. For example, since the wheat harvest in 1941 was 8,000,000 metric quintals, for 1942 Benzler's office established a quota of 10,000,000 metric quintals and authorized military commandants to collect the required crop quota regardless of the agricultural output.[5] It will be recalled that Serbia had to pay for the occupation costs, which in 1942 amounted to about 100 million dinars. In addition, Serbia's food supplies to Germany were worth 96,641,000 prewar dinars, besides those collected for the MBS.[6]

On average, peasants had to surrender about half of their harvest. So, of 500 kilograms grain, they were allowed to retain 260 kilograms and were compelled to sell the rest to the administration at fixed prices. This arrangement allowed the countryside to sustain itself for some time. However, with the tax rate rising 200 percent every six months, many families were barely at a subsistence level.[7]

Since the occupation troops relied mainly on horse-drawn transport, they requisitioned horses and forage, causing a litany of complaints from the district chiefs to Belgrade. For example, the Kraljevo chief reported that his district was completely stripped of hay and straw.[8] In addition, military commandants often imposed higher quotas than did the MBS, and they fined villages for late deliveries. Consequently, if before the war, there were 140,000 horses and 1,100,000 cattle in Serbia, in early 1943 there were 119,947 and 827,734, respectively. Before the war, there was one horse per 19 hectares of land and one cattle head per 2.4 hectares, but in 1943 the ratios went down to 1:22 and 1:3.2, respectively.[9]

Low agricultural productivity in combination with requisitions and confiscations affected the populace's diet. In winter 1942 the military commandants and the Serbian administration reported rising numbers of deaths from starvation.[10] This did not result in any countermeasures, since the MBS's position from the beginning of the occupation was that the "needs of the population should play no role [in economic planning]."[11]

As a result of deteriorating rural conditions, however, the countryside's grudging and sulky obedience mutated into passive resistance and eventually sabotage. Peasants turned to barter, slaughtered domestic animals, farmed less land to produce just enough to sustain their families, hoarded harvests, or sold their products on the black market.[12] The last tactic assumed mass proportions and became a universal fact of life under occupation, as prices on all goods and commodities skyrocketed. Indeed, the illegal smuggling of food supplies into towns and cities in exchange for clothing and manufactured goods became so commonplace that some individuals devoted their energies to this trade. The MBS and the Serbian administration considered black marketing a form of resistance, punishable by imprisonment or the death penalty. To the same end, the Germans requisitioned larger amounts of food than assigned and demanded that the Serbian authorities impose higher taxes to meet the costs of the occupation.[13]

Most Serbian industries and communication lines were either damaged or shut down during the April war, and the MBS's first orders were to make them operational again. Given their limited employment opportunities, many Serbian industrial workers left for the countryside or volunteered at various labor projects, such as the construction at the Belgrade–Salonika and Belgrade–Sofia roads, which employed six thousand laborers in May 1941.[14] Thousands went to Germany as volunteers, and thousands were rounded up by the Serbian police. By December 1941, Serbian laborers in Germany numbered thirty thousand, but Berlin requested more, especially individuals with experience in metal works, industries, and agriculture.[15] Serbian workers (as well as other laborers from Eastern Europe) received minimal payment and were subjected to Nazi racial regulations. By the end of the war, Serbia had provided the second largest labor force from the Balkans (after Croatia)—63,000 laborers to Germany and 65,000 to Italy. In addition, half of the two hundred thousand Serbian POWs in Germany were used as labor.[16]

The Serbian administration also carried out the mobilization of labor for various duties. Sometimes working details were paid, but often they had to pay for food supplies. In October 1941, the Bor mine and in November the lead and zinc mine in Trepča became partially operational, and both became crucial sources of raw materials for Germany's war effort. By 1944 the Bor copper ore mines and the Trepča lead mines provided 50 percent of the lead and 98 percent of the aluminum of Germany's total consumption.[17] Concomitantly, the numbers of laborers at the Bor mines peaked from 3,042 in May 1941 to 9,025 in January 1943 (although some sources mention as many as 30,000). In addition, 11,000 Belgrade residents were directed to the mine for a two-month labor duty. Contract laborers also arrived from other parts of Yugoslavia but also from Hungary, Poland, and a few from Western Europe.[18]

The Serbian administration tried to attract more laborers into the mines by promising good working and living conditions. At the same time, it used the mines (and other industries) as indoctrination sites for Serbian males. However, the Bor mine soon acquired a notorious reputation due to poor sanitary conditions. Some mine officials used the plight of miners to extract bribes for labor exemptions. Many laborers became sick, and in December 1943 the Nedić administration complained to the German direction of the mine about the plight of Serbian laborers. The Germans agreed to release some sick and emaciated laborers but demanded that these be replaced.[19]

To replenish the thinning labor force, the MBS and the Serbian administration used the Bor mines as a forced labor site for various transgressions such as black-market activities, corruption, shirking labor duties, or participation in the resistance. Captured guerrillas, Jews, and the Roma were placed at the mine indefinitely and subjected to particularly harsh treatment. They worked in the deepest shafts without ventilation, were flogged by the guards, and if they became too emaciated to work, were shot and thrown into the Lazar River.[20]

Urban Conditions

Unlike the countryside, Serbia's urban areas felt the impact of war immediately, especially those cities and towns subjected to German bombardment. Metropolitan Josif Cvijović, who was expelled by the Bulgarians from Skopje, arrived in Belgrade in early May 1941 and observed empty streets, ruined and burned houses, damaged roads, and water pipes ripped apart.[21] Twenty thousand buildings and houses were ruined or damaged, and Belgrade's clinics and hospitals were overcrowded by thousands of wounded and injured people. The city heating system was never fully repaired after damage early on, and the destruction of the city's water pumps forced residents to take water directly from the Drina River, increasing the danger of epidemics. The disruption of electricity and transport was compounded by limited food supplies and the advent of cold. Coal and timber could be obtained only on the black market at increasing prices. The curfew imposed by the military commandant office limited residents' movements, especially straining those queueing for basic commodities.[22]

The communist historiography proudly claims that "every sixth resident of Belgrade was a member of the resistance movement."[23] In reality, facing material shortages, labor duties, blackouts, and curfews, most city residents had little time for political activities. In addition, after the cessation of initial hostilities, the Belgrade military commandant dispatched Jewish and POW labor details to clear the rubble and to repair roads. Soon public transport, the post, and the telegraph resumed. On April 24, electricity was restored to Belgrade, and the next day trams began circulating in the city. Some stores and public facilities were reopened, railways began operating on schedule, and several water pumps were repaired and returned to use. On May 5, the MBS health department began vaccinating residents against typhus and paratyphoid. Most residents accepted these measures as signposts of returning to normal life conditions and grudgingly adapted to German occupation as a permanent reality.[24]

Return to normalcy, however, was but partial. During the April war, the population of Belgrade fell from 320,000 to 238,000, but by early May thousands returned home. In addition, thousands of people from other urban areas as well as from the countryside arrived in the capital, looking for better economic conditions and social opportunities. Accordingly, by mid-June the city population rose to 296,000, and adequate food supplies rapidly became a pressing issue.[25]

On July 11, 1941, the Council of Commissars ordered that prices on labor, property, and services revert to prewar levels. The order, however, was impossible to implement, but most importantly, it did not affect the prices of basic commodities, which had skyrocketed. For example, the price of 1 kilogram of beef rose from the prewar 11.50 dinars to 20–24 dinars, 1 kilogram of potatoes from 1.40 to 4–4.5 dinars, 1 kilogram of butter from 30 to 88 dinars, and 1 kilogram of wheat flour from 400 dinars to 2,500 dinars. Accordingly, the fixed salaries of civil servants and workers made feeding their families extremely difficult. Problems with food supplies increased as the war progressed, and in February 1942 the bread ration in Belgrade was reduced from 400 to 265 grams and in April to 200 grams per person.[26] Despite severe penalties, the black market became an essential source of supplies.[27]

The city administration tried to supply the city from its reserves and from the countryside. While the distribution of bread was temporarily solved, milk, fat, and meat quickly became scarce, and soon Thursday and Friday were declared to be meatless days. In autumn 1941, the administration introduced street kitchens, which provided dinners for the price of 10 dinars.[28]

In search of food, some Belgrade residents crossed the border to the suburb of Zemun, which belonged to the NDH, and others ventured to the countryside, exchanging shoes and clothing for meat and fat. To prevent speculation, German checkpoints regularly frisked people, confiscating foodstuffs and manufactured goods.[29]

Such measures, however, only drove up food prices, so the administration repeatedly reduced rations, causing a decline in public health. In 1941 a daily ration of flour was 227 grams per individual, but in 1943 it fell to 107 grams. In the same period, the monthly sugar ration dropped from 1.35 kilograms to 5 grams.[30]

Table 9.1 Prices on Basic Foodstuffs (in dinars)

Foodstuff	Official Price, April 1941	Black-Market Price, June 1942	Official Price, June 1943	Black-Market Price, June 1943
Wheat (100 kg)	350	5,000	500	40,000
Corn (100 kg)	250	2,500	285	35,000
Fat (1 kg)	55	450	84	2,100
Sugar (1 kg)	33	260	62	1,200
Pork (1 kg)	23.5	150	33.5	600
Salt (1 kg)	8	8	20	30
Wheat bread (1 kg)	4.5	90	350	350

Source: USHMM, RG-49.010M, reel 17, box 19, folder 5, report of the Kragujevac district administration, October 1941; Schlarp, *Wirtschaft*, 446.

The guerrilla war further caused traditional markets to shrink, and it rapidly limited food deliveries to towns and cities, while the Wehrmacht claimed the lion's share of foodstuffs collected in the countryside. Due to the separation of Banat from Serbia's economic zone, prices rose rapidly and Partisan attacks on the railroads disrupted supply deliveries to the city. In November 1941, in his report to the government in exile, Dr. Sekulić described the situation in the capital as critical.[31] By the end of 1941, Neuhausen warned that if starvation affected industries, productivity would fall and unrest could erupt throughout the country. In January 1942, Belgrade's bakeries were mixing corn and grain to bake bread; meat and milk rations repeatedly fell. The death rate increased substantially as a cumulative effect of malnutrition and disease. Despite a good harvest in 1941, the threat of potential famine forced the MBS to require increased foodstuffs from Banat. In summer 1942, the food supplies for Belgrade fell so low that Nedić complained to Bader that despite "much talk (in regards to the economic situation), nothing was done" and the city population, including him, did not receive bread for a month.[32]

In April 1943, the supply situation in most urban areas reached its nadir, as only a quarter of the urban population received bread. Huge lines stood in front of grocery stores. Coal was barely accessible, 1 kilogram of fat was sold at 1,500 dinars, a loaf of bread at 400 dinars, and many people could no longer remember the last time they had seen meat.[33]

Besides the critical situation with food supplies, the population had to deal with other pressing issues. Cities and towns lacked coal and timber, and the MBS and the OKH monopolized the purchases of textiles, manufactured goods, and leather. The paucity of these materials resulted in black market prices skyrocketing. Simultaneously, the devaluation of the dinar (by 1944 the mark to dinar ratio stood at 1:250) provided German military personnel with unprecedented purchasing opportunities, and soon after the conquest, most food supplies simply disappeared from stores.[34]

Despite the war, however, life went one, and thousands of students attended regular schools. Although as noted earlier Belgrade University was closed, the MBS allowed students to take exams in a few disciplines. In October 1942, 728 students graduated with degrees in law, technology, and medicine. Numbers of graduates rose to 1,344 in February 1943 and to 2,864 in December.[35] Some medical specialists found employment in various hospitals and clinics, and some engineering graduates were employed in the few remaining industries, receiving salaries and rations prescribed by official standards. However, most graduates had to fend for themselves, as the rest of the population was doing.[36]

In late 1943, some urban areas were subjected to Allied bombing. In October, Niš was heavily bombed and suffered three hundred casualties, and from April 1944 the U.S. military began regular air assaults on Serbia from bases in southern Italy.[37] Belgrade was subjected to particularly vicious bombing since it was a crucial railroad junction for oil supplies from Romania to Germany and a fuel depository for the German army. On April 16–17, almost exactly three years after Strafgericht, six hundred Allied bombers attacked Belgrade and Zemun, aiming at German communications lines. In order to avoid the German antiaircraft defense, the bombers dropped their ordnance—including 100- and 150-kilogram bombs—from a high altitude. This strategy resulted in limited damage to German facilities, with living quarters in downtown Belgrade, the electricity system, and water pumps taking the brunt of the bombing: 687 buildings were damaged, and about 1,160 residents and 200 German personnel were killed. The bombing continued through the summer, generating a flow of refugees into the countryside.[38]

In August 1943 the chief of staff of the Southeast Command described the situation in Serbia as extremely unstable. The VNS officials were dissatisfied and unreliable, workers were "infected" with communism, and many people supported Mihailović. The same month Nedić complained to Bader that economic hardship caused by German requisitions generated profound popular resentment, strengthening the resistance.[39]

Culture under Occupation

Since the beginning of occupation, the Germans and the collaborationist administration used the media and culture to convey official ideology. To demonstrate that life had returned to normal and to dampen communist and nationalist propaganda, in late April 1941 the MBS authorized the reopening of places of entertainment and recreation.

Cinemas, athletic events, and theater performances were to spread the image of Serbia's ostensible cultural and intellectual revival under German hegemony. Concerned about the effects of the communist and Chetnik propaganda, the Council of Commissars and the VNS were eager to involve the cooperation of Serbian intellectuals and artists. Films and dramas were to facilitate the "reeducation" of the population, particularly youngsters, in the spirit of national duties and patriotism.

Especially in entertainment, the pool of willing candidates to restart artistic careers was large enough. The war had disrupted Yugoslavia's cultural life, rendering hundreds of artists and actors without any income. In addition to many entertainers living in the capital, about 120 performers arrived in Belgrade from other parts of Yugoslavia. According to a renowned Serbian playwright, many actors and intellectuals found themselves in a spiritual limbo—they blamed the government for the humiliation of the April war, despised the Germans, and feared the communists. The occupation presented them with a limited choice—to starve or to accept that plying their trade entailed compromise with the conqueror and forsaking their artistic and intellectual independence.[40]

All troupes and individual actors had to come before a special commission to prove their reliability and to receive permission before resuming work. The commission consisted of reliable Serbian officials, who strove to make sure that all performances emphasized the "return" to national traditions. Any play or performance that promoted "alien" values, such as the emancipation of women, were banned. In August 1941 in an interview with the magazine *Srpska scena* (Serbian scene), the director of the National Theater, Jovan Popović, stated that prewar leftist tendencies "almost destroyed the importance of the [Serbian] theater as an educational institution."[41]

The new Serbian culture, therefore, needed a total break with the past, and entertainment was utilized as a tool of "national regeneration." The revenues from theatrical plays and musical festivals were frequently collected for refugee relief, while attending the theater, the cinema, and exhibitions was considered a patriotic duty. Nedić himself escorted peasant delegations to theatrical plays to demonstrate the revival of the Serbian national spirit.[42] Serbian folklore groups traveled around the country, performing traditional songs. Some renowned opera singers such as Krsta Ivić and Anka Arankelović frequently performed in towns and the countryside, while the concerts of German musicians and singers highlighted German–Serbian cultural exchange.[43]

On July 11, 1941, the National Theater (known as the Drama Theater under occupation), which was badly damaged during the April bombardment, reopened with *Figaro's Wedding* (the theater became fully operational in June 1942).[44] In 1941–42 there were 100 theater performances; in 1942–43 the number of plays rose to 254. Accordingly, official propaganda hailed intellectual and artistic collaboration as vivid proof that Serbs lived free under German tutelage.[45]

Besides entertainment, theaters offered warmth in the winter and for a brief moment helped patrons forget the war's harsh realities. In fact, most directors focused on neutral topics such as the world classics and costume dramas that were traditionally popular. Thus, Molière's *Tartuffe* and *Le malade imaginaire* (*The Imaginary Invalid*) and Beaumarchais's *Le Mariage de Figaro* constantly attracted large crowds. The National Theater also staged Goethe's *Stella*, while the orchestra of the National Opera under Chief Conductor Stevan Hristić (a signatory to the August appeal) performed Puccini's *Tosca* and Verdi's *Rigoletto* and *Aida*.[46]

Several actors, ballet dancers, and opera singers achieved stardom. Relja Burić gained fame playing Romeo and Don Carlos, while the press particularly favored Olga Spiridonović for her role as Shakespeare's Ophelia. Among the most popular opera singers were Žarko Cvejić, who sang in a major concert on March 12, 1942, in Belgrade; Slobodan Malbaški (who later joined the Partisans); and Natasha Bošković, particularly known for her performance in Bizet's *Carmen*), and her partner Miloš Ristić became the top ballet dancers. After the war, some performers emigrated out of fear of communist reprisals; Spiridonović and Cvejić were blacklisted by the Yugoslav authorities.[47]

Soccer clubs were also reactivated, and matches between the Serbian teams or between Serbian and German teams attracted many fans. The official press highlighted sports, car races, films, and plays, depicting Belgrade as a major entertainment center. Attendance at theaters and athletic events almost doubled regardless of the quality of the entertainment. Thousands flocked to theaters, cinema, cafeterias, cabarets, and museums, which offered the only diversion from the tribulations of daily life.[48]

The most popular source of entertainment and the key tool of mass propaganda was film; by April 1944, 743,403 viewers had attended cinemas. After the April war, the Yugoslav film distribution network Avala-film was abolished as "Jewish," and in late 1941 the German firm Ufa-film bought two movie theaters. The Belgrade film producer Tesla was also taken over by German companies. Mobile cinemas were dispatched to towns and villages. Founded in 1942, Banat-Film operated five mobile and twenty-two brick-and-mortar cinemas.[49]

Permission to open a movie theater depended on the political reliability of its owner, who had to prove that he was of "Aryan" stock and had no communist connections. The MBS Propaganda Department and the Serbian Ministry of Education and Religion evaluated the ideological contents of all films and banned those judged "immoral" or antireligious. German and Serbian officials responsible for propaganda regularly reported to their superiors about attendance and audience reactions to films.[50]

Naturally, German and Serbian officials considered films conveying ideological messages to be of primary value. Thus, the press reported the deeper meaning of *Ohm Krüger* (1941, *Uncle Kruger*) by Hans Steinhoff. Set against the background of the Anglo-Boer War, it portrays in darkest tones British colonial practices and predicts Europe's grim future if the Allies win the current war. In particular, the major newspapers praised Erich Waschneck's *Die Rothschilds* (1940, *The Rothschilds*)—the first anti-Semitic film shown in Serbia—which purports that Jews are intrinsically avaricious and treasonous.[51]

The film *Better War than the Pact* (1942) condemns the "Serbian clique" for the April catastrophe and promotes the image of stability and peace under German occupation, while the Serbian-made documentary *New Serbia*, which appeared in 1943, highlights the achievements of the Nedić administration.[52]

By Veit Harlan, the director of the notorious *Jud Süß*, *The Golden City* (1942) portrays an innocent country girl who runs away to Prague to find her lover but instead is seduced and abandoned by her cousin. In desperation, she drowns herself. The film fit well into the propagation of Nedić's *zadruga* vision, reminding viewers of the "corrupting" influences of city life in contrast to the order and tranquility of the countryside.[53] Newspapers praised Harlan's historical drama, *The Great King* (1941), dedicated to Friedrich the Great (with a clear analogy to Hitler), but its popularity with audiences derived from its flashy visual effects rather than from its ideology.[54]

Indeed, comedies and opulent musicals were much more popular than historical or documentary films. Quality played a secondary role, as most people were happy to forget themselves even in the most ordinary melodrama. For example, theaters were packed when shows like *Women Are No Angels* (1943), directed by Willy Forst; the *Romantic Adventure* (1940) by Mario Camerini; *My Daughter Lives in Vienna* (1940) by Emerich Emo; or *Love Premiere* (1943) by Arthur Rabenalt were played. The Serbian short film *The King of the Air* (1931?) featured the famous acrobat Dragoljub Aleksić. The sequel to *The King of the Air*, titled *Innocence without Protection* (1942), was the first Serbian sound production. Although criticized by the Ministry of Education and Religion as "naive and primitive," the film garnered 62,000 viewers in Belgrade alone.[55]

Kingdom of Nonexistence

Regardless of one's sympathies and political affiliations, the war eventually intervened in everybody's life. One researcher aptly referred to Serbia in wartime as the "Kingdom of Nonexistence" (*carstvo nepostojanja*), implying that the population was perpetually uncertain about what tomorrow would bring.[56] Exhausted economically and psychologically due to requisitions, confiscations, labor duties, and taxation, people sought solace within their own families, in the church, or in their villages, waiting for the outcome "like a bear sleeping in the winter." One district chief mused that the population lived in a "lethargic state."[57]

The majority of Serbs undoubtedly accepted the occupation as inevitable. The popular World War I slogan "for King and Fatherland!" no longer had appeal, and old ideals evaporated when they came up against what appeared to be an inexorable enemy. In a report to the government in exile, Dr. Sekulić wrote that "overall disorganization, chaos of retreat, and the fast [German] conquest deeply affected our nation. The young King Peter and the coup of 27 March faded into bright memory."[58]

Although their traditional loyalties to the monarchy were shattered, many people still expected that one day the king would return, and they saw Mihailović as his representative. They grudgingly accepted the Serbian administration as the lesser of two evils, less pernicious than the Germans. According to police reports, most Serbs were suspicious of the communists and sympathetic to the Allies. Despite the German successes on the eastern front, they believed that Russia would emerge victorious. The worsening economic situation contributed to popular attitudes' becoming more hostile to the collaborationist regime as the war progressed.[59]

German reprisals caused widespread outrage. The August 1941 public hanging at Terazijama summoned solidarity across all walks of life. According to German reports, teachers brought their pupils to the square to show them what constituted "German culture."[60] Anti-German leaflets and graffiti on walls predicted an end of the occupiers, as did numerous anonymous threats to German and Serbian officials.[61]

German military personnel frequently behaved in a crudely and condescendingly manner toward the Serbs. German soldiers tore up the portraits of the King and destroyed other national symbols. Such behavior added to popular discontent; the police reported numerous cases in which local residents comported themselves "insolently" toward the German and collaborationist officials.[62]

But even remaining neutral did not guarantee personal safety. Not only did German reprisals engulf innocent bystanders, but supplying the Germans with food or livestock or refusing to turn over horses to the guerrillas could be interpreted as a sign of hostility by either side. To combat the resistance, the MBS ordered local residents to perform guard duties on neighborhoods, roads, and communication lines. Failure to do so resulted in German reprisals, but appearing at these points was fraught with exposing oneself to attack by the guerrillas.[63]

In fact, the resistance forces frequently were as oppressive and brutal as the Germans, especially in the countryside. Partisans and the Chetniks requisitioned supplies and kidnapped or murdered individuals suspected of helping the other side. Partisans and the Chetniks had similar logistical problems, for their existence depended entirely on supplies obtained in villages. (Indeed, across Axis-occupied Europe, resistance movements could not survive merely on the goodwill of the population.) At times they established cordial relations with peasants, but as often as not they simply seized foodstuffs, horses, or cattle by force. The communist Yugoslav historiography emphasized peasants' voluntary cooperation in sabotaging deliveries of agricultural quotas.[64] In reality, the villagers often acted under duress, for complying with the orders of the administration could elicit the retribution of the Partisans. Conversely, the refusal to surrender food or a horse to the Partisans could prove as fatal, and the villagers faced the unsatisfying alternatives of complying or informing on the intruders to the German or Serbian police. In the latter scenario, Partisans and the Chetniks retaliated swiftly, often against alleged traitors' whole families. Surviving relatives of the kidnapped or murdered individuals were then likely to collaborate with the police, informing on the alleged resisters.[65]

The guerrillas forcibly mobilized young men, particularly when the influx of volunteers was low. When they needed to replenish their losses, they confiscated vehicles, motorcycles, carriages, and horses. Failure to appear at mobilization points or to turn in allotments was punished "in accordance with the laws of wartime," which included reprisals against the culprit's family or the burning of his house.[66] Partisan tribunals executed individuals suspected of collaboration with the enemy; reprisals were also carried out against those who did not publicly display sympathy toward the communists. "Revolutionary" justice could be dispensed by kidnapping and murdering potential political opponents.[67]

In late 1941 and early 1942, KPJ reports indicated the rapid decline of popular support, as peasants had by then acquired a justifiable fear of German reprisals, the collaborationist police, and the Chetniks. These reports, however, fail to mention that the countryside was as weary of the Partisans. The latter could ill afford to use German methods, particularly in liberated zones, where they relied on the willingness of the population to supply them with food and horses. In these areas, the communist leadership largely succeeded in curbing the potential excesses of its forces. However, if the Partisans tried to show restraint toward the population, they were impervious to inflicting violence on "traitors," "deviants," or unsympathetic villages. Hence, the arrival of a Partisan (or Chetnik) unit to such a village more often than not meant trouble for its residents, especially as the civil war often split families—sometimes one brother joined Tito and the other fought under Mihailović.[68]

War severely affected public morality as the line between right and wrong became increasingly blurred. The struggle for survival entailed the decline of moral constraints—according to a German who participated in the shooting in Jajinci, locals near the execution site often dug up graves to sell the victims' clothing, money, and shoes.[69] Attracted by bounties on the guerrillas, some individuals informed the police of the Partisans' and Chetniks' whereabouts, while the peasant "self-defense" units turned against the guerrillas. After a bounty of 100,000 dinars was announced for the capture or killing of Partisan commanders, in February 1943 a small group of Partisan veterans in southern Serbia was betrayed by their host. Surrounded by the gendarmes, the Partisans lost ten in the ensuing firefight, and only two managed to escape.[70]

The constant population flow between the countryside and the cities facilitated the German and Serbian security organs in saturating the countryside with informants and agents provocateurs who infiltrated Partisan and Chetnik forces. Mihailović himself barely escaped several attempts on his life from such agents.[71]

Communist ideology emphasized that in the "class" war the poor supported the revolution, while the rich fought for the old order. In reality, such a clear-cut division did not eventuate since often the relatively well-to-do peasants sided with Partisans, while the poor ones joined the Chetniks. Djilas once admitted that the townspeople of the Partisan "revolutionary" capital Užice were rather reserved if not outright hostile toward the Partisans.[72]

When pushed to the extreme, the peasants resisted. When pressed into service by Partisans, some peasants deserted their units, while others fled their villages, hid in the forests, or collaborated with police. In several instances, the peasants turned against Partisans. In late autumn 1941 in parts of southwestern Serbia, peasants organized themselves into self-defense units that fought off the Partisans. Leaders of these units requested arms and ammunition from the Serbian administration, which reported to the MBS that the situation should be utilized to wipe out the communists.[73] In September 1941, Partisans forcibly mobilized men in the Morava district and burned the houses of those who refused. The peasants retaliated by killing thirteen and handing over twenty-five Partisans to the Germans. In March 1942, peasants in the Kolubar district informed the Serbian administration about the location of a Partisan unit, which was subsequently attacked by the SDS and suffered heavy casualties. In the vicinity of Jagodin (85 miles south of Belgrade), where the Partisans attempted to mobilize the peasants, the so-called *kulak* elements murdered thirty Partisans and handed over the rest to the Germans, who shot them.[74]

Those who suffered assaults or requisitions by Partisans or the Chetniks often sought retribution. Settling personal scores and financial rewards were strong incentives to contact the Gestapo or Special Police. Some informants hoped that fingering resisters would save the lives of innocent people—in July 1942, an anonymous Belgrade resident tipped off the Gestapo that Vukašin Bogdanović allegedly possessed a radio transmitter and wanted to join the Partisans. The informant stressed that he "did not wish one hundred Serbs to die because of one individual." Bogdanović was lucky, however, since the Gestapo found a broken and useless transmitter and released him.[75]

Many of those wanting to avoid the fratricidal war were forced to make choices. When the SKOJ committee in Niš called on youths to boycott the labor draft, many responded by fleeing into the countryside. Unable to remain in hiding indefinitely, eventually they had to face the decision to join the guerrillas or to comply with the orders of the administration. In some counties of the Leskovac district, the Partisans forbade the villagers from fulfilling the requisitions orders of the administration, which exposed them to German reprisals.[76]

Initially, the peasantry was well disposed to the Chetniks, but discipline in the latter's ranks was in general lower than in the Partisan army. The Serbian administration reported numerous abuses by both "legal" and "illegal" Chetniks who robbed, mistreated, or murdered villagers. As a result, some residents invited German officers to billet in their homes as a way to ward off intruders. In some instances, the German military commandants banned "legal" Chetniks from entering the town due to their poor reputation.[77]

Besides Partisans and the Chetniks, Serbian villagers feared the SDK and SDS units, which frequently imposed their own taxes on villages and mishandled the residents. In June 1942, the Užice district chief complained about the abuses of SDK members, who were despised and feared by the population.[78] Italian soldiers and Albanian auxiliaries crossed into southern Serbia from Kosovo and raided neighboring villages under the pretext of searches for the guerrillas. Similarly, Bulgarian border guards and soldiers from Macedonia often crossed into Serbia to rob or kidnap villagers.[79]

Criminal groups engaged in robberies, and violence proliferated during the war. A number of criminals escaped from prisons during the April war, causing grave problems in the countryside. Some guerrilla units evolved into roving bands, terrorizing peasants for food or clothing. As the war progressed, the fine line between political and criminal violence eroded.[80]

In March 1943, the Serbian administration of the Morava district reported to Belgrade that the situation had worsened dramatically, since the district was inundated by the Partisans, the Chetniks, and criminal bands that terrorized the population.[81] In some areas, local offices and police stations virtually ceased to exist as various armed formations moved through the land. The population lived in constant fear and had to surrender food, livestock, and money to armed intruders.[82]

Crime was as omnipresent in cities and towns. Under the pretext of searches, unidentified armed groups carried out robberies, assaults, and kidnappings. In a single night of August 5, 1941, eleven people were kidnapped in Belgrade. In the first half of November, the Serbian police in Belgrade recorded eleven murders, six armed robberies, and three arsons.[83]

* * *

The period between April and July 1941 was the most tranquil time in wartime Serbia. Germany appeared to be invincible, and traditional patriotism was overweighed by the pragmatic realization that in order to survive the war, one had no other choice but to "live with the enemy." Such "involuntary" collaboration entailed compliance with the orders and regulations of the enemy forces. Grudgingly, most Serbs supplied the Germans with food, accommodation, and transport. Some Serbian industries were put to work, providing employment to workers, and for some time German rule showed a certain degree of forbearance. Especially in comparison to Bosnia, Croatia, or Kosovo, where the anti-Serbian terror gained momentum, Serbia appeared relatively tranquil.[84]

Soon, however, the situation changed for the worse. Peasants in particular found themselves in the midst of a guerrilla war. Since the opposing forces—especially Partisans and the Chetniks—had logistical problems, their existence depended entirely on supplies obtained in the villages. Although sometimes the guerrillas made arrangements with villages, more often they took everything by force. Acceding to the guerrillas' threats could provoke German reprisals, whereas refusal would expose villagers to the insurgents' wrath.

The effects of the occupation on daily lives varied from one segment of the population to another, from city to the countryside, and from winter to spring. But as the war in Europe dragged on, the Germans demanded ever higher quotas of food supplies and raw materials. German taxation and allotments, combined with guerrilla warfare, traumatized Serbia's economy. Initially, the food crisis affected the cities and towns, but eventually the countryside suffered, as well. Eventually, the entire county was affected by rationing, curfew regulations, and the lack of water and electricity. Ultimately, due to Serbia's strategic importance in the Balkans, German food policies were never as radical as in neighboring Greece, which was decimated by horrible famine. Although city dwellers in Serbia fared worse than the rural population, the paucity of rationed food resulted in poor subsistence for most people.

Unremitting increases in allotments and the cost of living forced rapid readjustments in civilians' lives. Like many in occupied Europe, most Serbs were not heroic resistance fighters, instead driven to engage in "bread-and-butter collaboration." They focused on providing for their families, which accorded them a sense of seclusion from the war and compelled them to accept miseries as a constant life companion under occupation.

Conclusion

The German occupation of Serbia was hastily prepared, lacked organizational coordination, and was driven by false calculations that the country no longer posed a military threat. As a result, German rule was shaped by competing power structures that significantly impeded more constructive occupation policies. In accordance with Hitler's vision, each German conquest entailed the utilization of economic and human resources of the defeated nation. In this context, Serbia's contribution to the German economy was significant. According to a British study, 24 percent of Germany's wheat and 13 percent of its corn came from Serbia (Banat provided up to 51 and 32 percent, respectively).[1] At least two hundred thousand Serbs labored for Germany in various capacities.

The war and occupation severely undermined Serbia's economy. Besides human losses, the economic devastation seemed beyond repair. Structurally, 92,435 buildings and houses, 6,500 libraries, 19 museums, 1,670 schools, 52 churches and monasteries, 63 synagogues, and over 60 other academic institutions were totally or partially destroyed or damaged. A hundred thousand villagers lost their homes. The total war cost for Serbia amounted to 51 billion dinars.[2] For a small country, which long remained a German hinterland in the Balkans, the damage was staggering.

The country was subjected to a crippling occupation cost at the devalued exchange rate of the national currency. As a result, Serbia paid almost fifty times over the actual cost of a German garrison and lost thousands of able-bodied men to POW camps and forced labor. The food supply system broke down, the national currency value plummeted, and inflation soared. Prices on basic commodities increased almost tenfold, while real wages were a quarter of those in 1941. The collapse of the transportation system especially resonated in urban areas, for food supplies could not be delivered on time or at all. The black market proliferated, taking on a life of its own. However, while in the winter of 1941–42 some areas in Serbia seemed on the brink of starvation, relatively good harvests alleviated the potential of famine.

Since Yugoslavia was not a part of the *Lebensraum* (living space) planning, and as long as it augmented Germany's capacity to fight the "big" war, the Nazi leadership did not apply the same ideological-racial criteria to the South Slavs as to the Russians, Poles, and Ukrainians. The immediate Nazi targets were Serbia's Jews and the Roma, and almost all of the former were killed in the genocide. However, when in the summer of 1941 the armed uprising shattered Serbia's ostensible tranquility, it set a stage for ideologically motivated mass reprisals that ultimately engulfed the entire country. Imbued with Nazi extermination ideology, the Wehrmacht suppressed the uprising with extreme brutality, rooted in convictions that terror alone could achieve desired results.

The war exacted a horrible death toll on Yugoslavia—1 million people or 6.3 percent of the prewar 15.7 million total. The German army lost 14,100 German soldiers and officers, and these numbers clearly indicate 1:100 "overkill" in relation to German fatalities—a testament to the scale of German reprisals and the ferocity of the civil war, which was partially the progeny of the interwar period. As in Ukraine, Poland, Greece, and France, German occupation in Serbia unleashed a civil war, in which neither side was willing to compromise and which claimed as many or even more lives than German terror. In total, Serbia sustained between 141,000 and 167,000 deaths (300,000 people were deported or incarcerated in prisons and concentration camps). These included 34,000 people killed by the occupation forces and 46,000 deaths in prisons and camps. Approximately 33,000 Chetniks and members of the collaborationist structures and 42,000 communist guerrillas (including those killed by the Germans), lost their lives.[3] In contrast, the German troops in Serbia suffered a thousand casualties.[4]

Ever short of manpower, the Germans sought reliable local elements who could help to maintain order and enforce supply deliveries. In Croatia the Germans actively participated in the buildup of NDH military forces, whereas in Serbia they opposed any strengthening of the collaborationist administration. The latter could have substantially reinforced German rule, but suspicions of Serbian nationalism among the German military, combined with rivalries among different German offices, inhibited the Council of Commissars and the VNS from becoming effective executive organs.

Collaboration with the enemy is rarely an unconditional process, and its practitioners expect specific rewards. Certain of German victory, some civil servants and policemen were lukewarm to Nazi ideology but functioned as vital cogs of the occupation system. Others engaged in collaborationism or "voluntary" collaboration, which translated into zealous support and close emulation of the Nazi regime. The activities of the Zbor movement represented a logical continuation of its prewar opposition to liberalism and communism. In comparison, many members of the Council of Commissars and the VNS appeared to be docile bureaucrats without ideological convictions, propelled to power solely by circumstance. Under close scrutiny, however, they accepted collaborationism as the only condition to "reinvent" the traditional parochial Serbia and to spare it from what they saw as more dangerous than German occupation: democracy, communism, and multiculturalism. As a result of this ideological transformation, Milan Nedić effectively became both an ideological soldier with his own agenda and a willing tool in the hands of the occupying power, which established ideological and institutional parameters for collaborationism.

Consequently, although acting within narrow functional confines, collaborationists actively participated in upholding German rule, facilitating the efforts of the thinly spread German troops and security forces. In the same vein, they promoted anti-Semitism as a key element of their own political and ideological program. While Zbor's traditional anti-Jewish sentiments were reinforced by Nazi racial policies, the Council of Commissars and the VNS adopted an extremely opportunistic approach to the "Jewish question," considering participation in the Holocaust unpleasant but unavoidable. Such attitudes entailed practical commitment to the Final Solution in the form of enforcing Nazi regulations and conducting a vicious anti-Semitic defamation campaign. Besides fulfilling German orders, however, the collaborationists considered the removal of Jews as crucial for their own objectives. The Holocaust effectively reinforced Nedić's plans for creating the *zadruga* state, in which Jews or other ethnic minorities had no place. Undoubtedly, given the small size of the Jewish community in Serbia, the Germans would have been able to accomplish genocide on their own, but without native help it would have taken more effort and time, giving some Jews a precious margin to escape.

Apologists for collaborationism in Europe have maintained that it had a mitigating effect on Nazi policies and that otherwise the populations of German-occupied countries would have suffered much more devastation. In other words, by active collaboration with the Germans, the Council of Commissars and the VNS spared Serbia from the fate of Poland. There is no indication, however, that the collaborationist administration exerted any moderating influence on German policies in Serbia. To the contrary, despite Nedić's timid protests, in 1941 German reprisals went unabated. Their temporary mitigation in the winter of 1941–42 had nothing to do with Nedić but was affected by the more pragmatic policies of the MBS, which took into account the weakened resistance and the changing strategic situation in the Balkans. Similarly, German policies of exploiting Serbia's economic resources and manpower force were implemented without taking into consideration the livelihood of the population at large.

In early July 1941 the communist uprising laid bare the frailty of the German order in Serbia, revealing the common European pattern—German occupation brought to the surface political divisions within subjugated societies. In Serbia (as well as in the rest of Yugoslavia), well suited and accustomed to guerrilla warfare, resistance arose from nationalism and political calculations. The two main resistance forces—the Partisans and the Chetniks—initially joined efforts, but eventually the rift between the two became irreparable due to opposite political goals. The former were determined to destroy the old political order, while the latter vowed to uphold it. At first, as the traditional monarchist and nationalist organization, the Chetniks enjoyed more popular support than their rivals, but the situation gradually changed. The loose organizational structure of the Chetnik movement and its exclusionary nationalist ideology proved a crucial handicap for Mihailović. From the outset, the Chetnik movement suffered a sort of political identity disorder—on one hand it represented the Yugoslav government in exile, which was at war with Germany and ideologically remained within the Allied camp. On the other hand, Mihailović was determined to avoid a head-on confrontation with the Germans and spent most of his resources and energy fighting the Partisans. Combined with sporadic but costly clashes with the Germans and the Nedić forces, Mihailović's "selective collaboration" effectively sapped the movement's strength.

In contrast, the communists' aims were well-defined before the war and translated into the gradual evolution of the Partisan movement. Small at the beginning, it developed into a well-organized force of dedicated fighters. Although the Partisans were frequently surrounded and decimated, they would break through and regroup. The centralized command and discipline of the Partisan forces facilitated their ability to survive and persevere even in the most difficult times. The eventual success of the communist resistance could be traced to the Užice Republic, which created the model that would supplant Yugoslavia's old political and social order. After the defeat in 1941, the Partisan attacks had a limited effect on German rule in Serbia, but they chipped away at the occupation system, reminding the population that the struggle went on and staking a claim to Yugoslavia's future. Against the background of the war between Germany and the Allies, the guerrilla war in Yugoslavia was unquestionably a subsidiary conflict and Partisan efforts in Serbia seemed more so. Still, in combination with Allied victories, such activities had increasingly powerful political and psychological effects.

The resistance movement also has its critics, who argued that fighting the Axis powers entailed the deaths of thousands of innocents, and that the achievements of the resistance were unimpressive, while the Partisan and civilian losses were extremely high.[5] This perspective is at least debatable, for the resistance inhibited a "perfect" occupation, which would entail the occupiers' unlimited access to the country's manpower and economic resources, crucial for Germany's war effort. The resistance attacks on industrial sites certainly affected Germany's economic potential and contributed to the Allied victory.

Contrary to postwar national mythologies, most people in Yugoslavia (as elsewhere in Hitler's Europe) were not heroic resistance fighters. Of approximately 3 million Serbian adults, no more than 100,000 (or 4 percent) were associated with the forces of resistance and collaboration, roughly split into two equal parts.[6] The occupation induced a survivalist mentality, and the overwhelming majority of Serbs accommodated themselves to Nazi rule in multiple ways. Economic miseries and the risk of death caused profound pessimism, which manifested itself as seclusion from the outside world and focus on providing for family. The threat of violence—whether by Germans, Partisans, or Chetniks—was a powerful deterrent to engage in resistance, but when it became too unbearable or too indiscriminate, it eventually forced many individuals to choose sides.

Having survived the vicissitudes of foreign occupation, the population expected socioeconomic and political reforms. The communists, who were untainted by collaboration, appeared to be the only "Yugoslav" force that could guarantee peace and stability in a country ripped apart by confessional and social conflicts. After the liberation of Yugoslavia, Tito instituted a political system based on the Soviet model. On November 29, 1945, the monarchy was abolished and the Federal Peoples' Republic of Yugoslavia was proclaimed, whereby 90 percent of the votes were cast in favor of the People's Front—the coalition of pro-Partisan parties. The January 1946 constitution, also based on the Soviet model, established six constituent republics: Serbia, Croatia, Slovenia, Bosnia-Herzegovina, Macedonia, and Montenegro, and two autonomous regions within Serbia—Kosovo and Vojvodina. Noncommunist parties were shunted to the country's political margins and political opposition was crushed. Yugoslavia entered a new, long, and relatively stable phase.

Notes

Introduction

All translations of non-English sources are mine unless noted otherwise. Explanations of abbreviations for archival materials appear at the beginning of the bibliography.

1. Piekalkiewicz, *Krieg*, 65.
2. For example, Shepherd, *Terror*; Schmider, *Partisanenkrieg*.
3. Schmider, foreword, 183.
4. Studies by Jozo Tomasevich, Christopher Browning, and Sabrina Ramet lead in the field.
5. Cohen, *Secret War*.
6. Karapandžić, *Građjanski rat*; Parežanin, *Drugi svetski rat*. Derived from the Russian language, *Partisans* was the term used by the Yugoslav communist resistance to refer to its forces.
7. Dimitrijević, *Vojska*, 11.
8. Jelavich, *History*, 2:263; Brborić, "Ministarski savet," 169–80.
9. Roschwald, "Europe's Civil Wars," 538–40.
10. For example, Dejanović et al., *Niš*; Glišić, *Užička republika*.
11. Lašić-Vasojević, *Enemies*; Topalović, *Srbija*.
12. Jareb, "Allies or Foes?," 155; Dimitrijević and Nikolić, *Đeneral Mihailović*.
13. Tomasevich, *Peasants*, 238.

Chapter 1. Background, 1918–1941

1. On June 15, 1389, on the Kosovo field, the Serbian army was crushed by Ottoman troops. The memorialization of the battle became a crucial element in Serbian national identity and cultural traditions.
2. Banac, *National Question*, 147–48, 150–52.
3. Kazimirović, *Srbija*, 2: 417, 441; Drapac, *Constructing Yugoslavia*, 100.

4. Djokić, *Elusive Compromise*, 37–38; Eberhardt, *Groups*, 364.
5. Dejanović et al., *Niš*, 29–30; D. Aleksić, *Privreda*, 36–39.
6. Kazimirović, *Srbija*, 1:188–89, 191; D. Aleksić, *Privreda*, 21, 23, 51.
7. Biondich, *Balkans*, 126–30.
8. Tomasevich, *Peasants*, 238.
9. Rothschild, *East Central Europe*, 245–46; Djokić, *Elusive Compromise*, 72–74.
10. Pavlowitch, *Serbia*, 129–31; Lampe, *Yugoslavia*, 174.
11. Ž. Jovanović, *Seljaštvo*, 18–23; Banac, *National Question*, 189, 191–92.
12. Jelić-Butić, *Četnici*, 12; Pisarev, "Serbia," 135–36.
13. Lampe, *Yugoslavia*, 202; Sundhaussen, *Geschichte*, 287.
14. Lampe, *Yugoslavia*, 122; Popović, *Jevreji*, 97–98.
15. Kazimirović, *Srbija*, 2:369; *Istorijski arhiv*, 2:35–36; Dedijer, *Tito*, 126.
16. Banac, *National Question*, 330, 332.
17. IAB, BdS collection, file H-351, "Andrija Hebrang"; Pavlowitch, *Serbia*, 134.
18. Kazimirović, *Srbija*, 2:372–76; Borković, "Osnivački kongres," 11–12.
19. Dedijer, *Tito*, 128; Vujošević, *Tito*, 38.
20. Petranović, *Srbija*, 48–49; Swain, "Comintern," 39.
21. Glišić, *Beograd*, 1:55–61, 98; Borković et al., *Komunistička partija*, 1:37.
22. B. Gligorijević, "Politički pokreti," 37, 43, 53–54.
23. Ibid., 67–68; Božović and Stefanović, *Milan Aćimović*, 209–10.
24. Ljotić, *Light*, 35–36, 47, 57–59.
25. Falina, "Between 'Clerical Fascism,'" 249.
26. Kerenji, "Antisemitism," 40–45; Byford, "Willing Bystanders," 298.
27. B. Gligorijević, "Politički pokreti," 79–80; Sundhaussen, *Geschichte*, 288.
28. Lumans, *Himmler's Auxiliaries*, 118–19; Kreso, *Njemačka okupaciona uprava*, 27, 30.
29. Drapac, *Constructing Yugoslavia*, 107.
30. Formed in the 1920s, the Little Entente was a defense alliance of Czechoslovakia, Romania, and the SCS against Hungary. In turn, each alliance member signed a defense treaty with France.
31. Lampe, *Yugoslavia*, 133–37; Hoptner, *Yugoslavia*, 41–43, 46–47, 60.
32. Hoptner, *Yugoslavia*, 88; Simeunović, "Relations," 74.
33. Kreso, *Njemačka okupaciona uprava*, 27; Simeunović, "Relations," 74.
34. D. Aleksić, *Privreda*, 26–27, 107–8; Lampe, *Yugoslavia*, 179.
35. Hoptner, *Yugoslavia*, 121–22; Djokić, "'Leader,'" 155.
36. Kazimirović, *Srbija*, 2:408–9, 534.
37. Dragnich, *Serbia*, 117–18; Lampe, *Yugoslavia*, 194.
38. Wuescht, *Jugoslawien*, 91.
39. Tomasevich, *War: Chetniks*, 30; Kazimirović, *Srbija*, 2:632–33.
40. Ristović, *Niemački novi poredak*, 22–23; Petranović, *Srbija*, 63.
41. Kazimirović, *Srbija*, 2:469; Petranović, *Srbija*, 72.
42. Slijepčević, *Istorija*, 3:43–44; D. Đorđević, *Ožiljci*, 1:41.
43. Nikolić, *Strah*, 16–19; Petranović, *Srbija*, 76.

44. Shimizu, *Die deutsche Okkupation*, 91.
45. Piekalkiewicz, *Krieg*, 67; Dedijer, *Tito*, 137.
46. Petranović, *Srbija*, 89–91; Kazimirović, *Srbija*, 3:693–94.

Chapter 2. Invasion and Occupation

1. Wuescht, *Jugoslawien*, 159–62; Čulinović, *Okupatorska podjela*, 40–41f.
2. USHMM, RG-49.010M, reel 18, box 36, folder 8, Belgrade administration report, 25 June 1941; Kreso, *Njemačka okupaciona uprava*, 37–39.
3. Rings, *Life*, 35.
4. Božović, *Beograd*, 11; Glišić, *Beograd*, 1:94.
5. Kreso, *Njemačka okupaciona uprava*, 40–41; Dejanović, *Niš*, 101.
6. Dedijer, *Tito*, 137–39; Piekalkiewicz, *Krieg*, 99–100.
7. Petranović, *Srbija*, 104–5; Kreso, *Njemačka okupaciona uprava*, 31, 47–48; Bogdanov-Senko, *Antifašistički pokret*, 22–23.
8. USHMM, RG-49.005M, reel 1, undated report to government in exile, 2–3.
9. Mešterović, *Lekarev dnevnik*, 10, 13; D. Đorđević, *Ožiljci*, 1:45.
10. Božović, *Beograd*, 120; Kreso, *Njemačka okupaciona uprava*, 56.
11. Nikolić, *Strah*, 22–23; Z. Jovanović, *Seljaštvo*, 41, 43–45; Lampe, *Yugoslavia*, 199.
12. Sundhaussen, "Improvisierte Ausbeutung," 60.
13. Ibid., 55–56; Čulinović, *Okupatorska podjela*, 46–47.
14. Magaš, *Croatia*, 553–55.
15. Marjanović, "German Occupation," 263–64; Kulić, *Bugarska okupacija*, 1:8.
16. Strugar, "Sistem Bugarske okupacjie," 1:254; Stojiljković, "Bugarska kao saveznica," 2:249.
17. Tomasevich, *War: Occupation*, 86–91.
18. USHMM, RG-49.010M, reel 21, box 53, folder 2, Zaječar administration report for 1941, 1; Strugar, "Sistem Bugarske okupacjie," 1:267.
19. Stojiljković, "Bugarska kao saveznica," 2:270–71; Kulić, *Bugarska okupacija*, 1:190–96, 210–11.
20. Momčilović-Brkica, *Banat*, 30–31; Božović, "Juraj Špiler," 228.
21. Kreso, *Njemačka okupaciona uprava*, 138–39; Perica Višnjić, "Nemački okupacioni system," 92.
22. Manoschek, "*Serbien*," 33.
23. Quoted in Čulinović, *Okupatorska podjela*, 420.
24. Ibid., 46–47; Ristović, *Niemački novi poredak*, 44.
25. Browning, "Harald Turner," 351.
26. Rings, *Life*, 32.
27. AVI, file 75/47, "Presuda" [Harald Turner], card 16, MBS jurisdiction chart; Perica Višnjić, "Nemački okupacioni system," 86–87.
28. AVI, file 75/47, "Presuda" [August Meyszner], card 16, MBS jurisdiction chart; Browning, "Harald Turner," 351.
29. NARA, T-501, reel 249, OKH memo, April 23, 1941, frame 0001046–47; Perica Višnjić, "Nemački okupacioni system," 86.

30. Umbreit, "Zur Organisation," 52–53; Browning, "Harald Turner," 351–52.

31. Marjanović, "German Occupation," 266; Herzog, *Gründzuge*, 146.

32. AVI, file 1128/46, "Presuda" [August Meyszner], testimony of Konrad Listemann; Perica Višnjić, "Nemački okupacioni system," 91.

33. AVI, file 75/47, "Presuda" [Harald Turner], card 16, testimonies of Vasil Dragiža and Hermann Schacht; Glišić, *Teror*, 32; Begović, *Logor Banjica*, 2:270–72.

34. AVI, file 75/47, "Presuda" [Harald Turner], card 17, testimonies of Darinka Jovičić, Pers Jovanović, Milka Joksimović, and Zora Mitrović; Glišić, *Teror*, 153–54.

35. Madajczyk, *Faszyzm*, 2: 15; Mazower, *Hitler's Empire*, 236–37.

36. AVI, file 1128/46, "Presuda" [August Meyszner], testimony of Konrad Listemann; Kroener et al., *Organisation*, 1:100.

37. Lemkin, *Axis Rule*, 248–49.

38. USHMM, RG-49.002*1, the MBS decrees, 22 May 1941, microfiche 2, 49; Madajczyk, *Faszyzm*, 2:50, 229, 257; Vegh, "Le système," 499, 511.

39. Shepherd, *Terror*, 84.

40. Božović, *Beograd*, 120; Kreso, *Njemačka okupaciona uprava*, 56.

41. Živković, "Kontribucije," 185–86; D. Aleksić, *Privreda*, 144–46, 200; Schlarp, *Wirtschaft*, 188, 197.

42. Pavlović, *Hitler's Disorder*, 50; Tomasevich, *War: Occupation*, 633–34.

43. USHMM, RG-49.010M, reel 17, box 19, folder 2, K. Stanarević, "Doprinos Srbije i Banata," frame 401; D. Aleksić, *Privreda*, 308; Živković, "Kontribucije," 191, 195–99.

44. Kroener et al., *Organisation*, 1:255; Lampe, *Yugoslavia*, 220.

45. D. Aleksić, *Privreda*, 214–15; Živković, "Kontribucije," 193.

46. USHMM, RG-49.010M, reel 17, box 19, folder 2, K. Stanarević "Doprinos," frame 398.

47. YVA, M29 FR/138, meeting of Turner and Nedić, 28 March 1942, 11; Tomasevich, *War: Occupation*, 648.

48. Seckendorf and Keber, *Okkupationspolitik*, 37–38.

49. Kreso, *Njemačka okupaciona uprava*, 58; Živković, *Ratna šteta . . . Nemačka*, 498–504.

50. AVI, file 75/47, "Presuda" [Harald Turner], card 16, testimony of Adolf Josten; Shepherd, "Bloodier than Boehme," 193.

Chapter 3. Germans and Auxiliaries

1. Shimizu, *Die deutsche Okkupation*, 127.

2. AVI, file 75/47, "Presuda" [Harald Turner], card 16, interrogation of Georg Kiessel; Umbreit, "Die Rolle," 34–37.

3. Božović, *Beograd*, 86–87; Borković, *Kontrarevolucija*, 1:26–29.

4. Božović and Stefanović, *Milan Aćimović*, 17–21.

5. Božović, *Beograd*, 80–81.

6. NARA, T-120, reel 200, Benzler's telegram to the Foreign Ministry, 29 April 1941, frame 153198; Kreso, *Njemačka okupaciona uprava*, 89–90.

7. Perica Višnjić, "Nemački okupacioni system," 87–88; Kreso, *Njemačka okupaciona uprava*, 80–81.

8. USHMM, RG-49.010M, reel 17, box 19, folder 2, Morava administration report to Ministry of Interior, 28 June 1941; AVI, file 75/47, "Presuda" [Harald Turner], card 17, testimony of Walter Uppenkamp; Pavlowitch, *Serbia*, 136.

9. Kreso, *Njemačka okupaciona uprava*, 80–81; D. Aleksić, *Privreda*, 156–58.

10. *Službene novine*, no. 95, 6 August 1941, 2.

11. Madajczyk, *Faszyzm*, 2:170; Borković, *Milan Nedić*, 284–87.

12. USHMM, RG-49.005M, reel 1, undated report to government in exile, 23; Nikolić, *Strah*, 98.

13. USHMM, RG-49.010M, reel 20, box 53, folder 2, commission's findings, 30 May 1941, 4–7; Glišić, *Teror*, 35.

14. Glišić, *Teror*, 36–37.

15. Čulinović, *Okupatorska podjela*, 408.

16. NARA, T-501, reel 249, MBS report, 13 August 1941, frame 000884; Kreso, *Njemačka okupaciona uprava*, 156.

17. Browning, "Harald Turner," 356; Borković, *Kontrarevolucija*, 1:67, 72–73.

18. USHMM, RG-49.010M, reel 17, box 19, folder 2, districts chiefs' reports to Ministry of Interior, 17 and 21–22 July 1941.

19. *Obnova*, no. 12, 18 July 1941, 2.

20. *Novo vreme*, no. 89, 16 August 1941, 3.

21. Ibid., no. 86, 14 August 1941, 3; ibid., no. 87, 15 August 1941, 1; USHMM, RG-49.005M, reel 1, undated report to Ministry of Propaganda, 4; B. Đorđević, *Srpska kultura*, 68.

22. Borković, *Kontrarevolucija*, 1:96–97; Tomasevich, *War: Occupation*, 68, 179; Božović and Stefanović, *Milan Aćimović*, 66–67.

23. AVI, file 75/47, "Presuda" [Harald Turner], card 16, testimony of Harald Turner; Božović, *Beograd*, 362–65.

24. Borković, *Milan Nedić*, 11–14.

25. Tomasevich, *War: Occupation*, 180; Krakov, *General*, 1:143–45.

26. Madajczyk, *Faszyzm*, 2:351.

27. USHMM, RG-49.005M, reel 1, Sekulić's report to Ministry of Propaganda, 4; Borković, *Kontrarevolucija*, 1:88–89.

28. Tomasevich, *War: Occupation*, 181; Borković, *Milan Nedić*, 315–16; Wuescht, *Jugoslawien*, 57.

29. NARA, T-501, reel 256, Turner's letter to the MBS, 11 November 1941, frames 1173–74; Kolanović, "Nezavisna Država," 195.

30. *Novo vreme*, no. 101, 30 August 1941, 3; Borković, *Milan Nedić*, 27; Krakov, *General*, 1:130.

31. Bjelajać, *Generali*, 77, 144–45; Stefanović, *Zbor*, 137.

32. YVA, M29 FR/125, MBS situational report, 6 November 1941, 13; *Službene novine*, no. 105, 9 September 1941, 1–3; Borković, *Kontrarevolucija*, 2:239–41.

33. Ž. Jovanović, "Poljoprivreda," 144.

34. Ž. Jovanović, Seljaštvo, 62–64; Ž. Jovanović, "Poljoprivreda," 145.

35. *Novo vreme*, no. 103, 2 September 1941, 3; VNS declaration, 2 September 1941, in Cvijić and Casović, *Milan Đ. Nedić*, 16–17; Kostić, *Za istoriju*, 46–48.

36. Kolanović, *Zagreb-Sofija*, 167–68, 234.

37. IAB, UGB collection, folder 2192/15-1-5, personal file of Dušan Gavrilović, 2; ibid., folder 2206/29-H-2, personal file of Milan Nadlački, 13.

38. USHMM, RG-49.010M, reel 18, box 25, folder 1, Valjevo administration report, undated; D. Aleksić, *Privreda*, 317.

39. YVA, M29 FR/125, MBS situational report, 6 November 1941, 27; Tomasevich, *War: Occupation*, 209; Živković, "Kontribucije u Srbiji," 195–99.

40. NARA, T-501, reel 256, Turner's letter, 11 November 1941, frames 1173–74; Tomasevich, *War: Occupation*, 182.

41. USHMM, RG-49.002*1, Turner's memo, 21 September 1941, microfiche 4, 445–47; Kroener et al., *Organisation*, 1:199.

42. Topalović, *Srbija*, 242–43; Božović, *Specijalna policija*, 76–78; Borković, *Kontrarevolucija*, 1:59, 376–79.

43. USHMM, RG-49.002*1, report on evacuation of Serbs from Croatia, microfiche 2, 120; Milošević, *Izbeglice*, 21–22.

44. USHMM, RG-49.002*1, report on resettlement of Slovenes, microfiche 2; Milošević, *Izbeglice*, 131, 246.

45. USHMM, RG-49.008M, reel 24, box 168, folder 2, testimonies of Serbian refugees, 1–30; RG-49.010M, reel 18, box 25, folder 1, conference of the Ministry of Interior, 25 April 1942, 1–3; Milošević, *Izbeglice*, 132.

46. *Obnova*, no. 573, 22 May 1943, 3; no. 580, 30 May 1943, 3; USHMM, RG-49.010M, reel 18, box 34, folder 3, letter of the Commissar for Refugees to the Serbian Artisan Association, 16 December 1943; Commissar for Refugees' report to Nedić, December 1943.

47. Dedijer and Miletić, *Proterivanje Srba*, 803–5; Ristović, "Zwangsmigrationen," 320.

48. NARA, T-120, reel 200, Benzler's telegram to the Foreign Ministry, 3 May 1941, frame 153210; NARA, T-501, reel 245, MBS report, 5 September 1941, frames 000518–19, 000523, 000526.

49. *Novo vreme*, no. 61, 17 July 1941, 3; ibid., no. 63, 19 July 1941, 3; *Službene novine*, no. 124, 11 November 1941, 1–2; ibid., no. 4, 13 January 1942, 4–5; Milošević, *Izbeglice*, 273, 286; Roš, *Slovenski izgnanci*, 118–22, 139, 184.

50. Glišić, *Beograd*, 1:366–67.

51. USHMM, RG-49.010M, reel 16, box 9, folder 1, appeal to refugees to enlist in labor force; Milošević, *Izbeglice*, 258–59, 289–90.

52. USHMM, RG-49.010M, reel 16, box 1, folder 2, VNS conference with district chiefs, 6 February 1942, 9–10; Dejanović et al., *Niš*, 233.

53. Milošević, *Izbeglice*, 283–84.

54. NARA, T-120, reel 200, Benzler's telegram to the Foreign Ministry, 15 September 1941, frame 153422; NARA, T-501, reel 245, MBS report, 5 September 1941, frames 518–19, 523–26; NARA, T-501, reel 256, frames 1104–11, 1024–34; *Obnova*, no. 573, 22 May 1943, 3; Milošević, *Izbeglice*, 306.

55. Kulić, *Bugarska okupacija*, 2:26, 54; Bosiljčić, *Istočna Srbija*, 58–59; Stojiljković, "Bugarska kao saveznica," 2:288–90.

56. USHMM, RG-49.005M, reel 1, report of unknown provenance from Bulgarian-occupied Serbia, November 1941.

57. NARA, T-120, reel 200, Benzler's telegram to Foreign Office, 4 January 1942, frames 153482–84; Ristović, "M. Nedić," 685–86.

58. Čirković, *Ko je ko*, 303; Tomasevich, *War: Occupation*, 77–78.

59. Božović, *Stradanje Jevreja*, 49–54; Browning, "Final Solution," 63–66.

60. AVI, file 75/47, "Presuda" [Harald Turner], card 17, trial of the commander of the 64th police battalion Adolf Josten; YVA, M29 FR/138, MBS report, 6 January 1942, 3–4; Browning, "Harald Turner," 362–63.

61. Ristović, *Niemački novi poredak*, 112–13.

62. USHMM, RG-49.008M, reel 21, box 130, folder 6, Belgrade administration report, 22 December 1941.

63. Kreso, *Njemačka okupaciona uprava*, 192–93; Browning, "Harald Turner," 353.

64. NARA, T-175, reel 126, Turner's report to Himmler, 16 February 1942, frame 2651816; Borković, *Kontrarevolucija*, 1:295, 297.

65. *Obnova*, no. 349, 25 August 1942, 3; Borković, *Kontrarevolucija*, 1:293–94; Borković, *Milan Nedić*, 99–100.

66. Kroener et al., *Organisation*, 1:255; Lampe, *Yugoslavia*, 220.

67. YVA, M29 FR/138, meeting between Turner and Nedić, 28 March 1942, 4–8, 13–14; Borković, *Nedić*, 154–55; Tomasevich, *War: Occupation*, 185.

68. NARA, T-120, reel 200, Benzler's telegram to the Foreign Ministry, June 23, 1942, frame 153626.

69. Karchmar, *Draža Mihailović*, 1:296; Schmider, *Partisanenkrieg*, 434–35.

70. Madajczyk, "'Restserbien,'" 466–67, 469.

71. Borković, *Milan Nedić*, 147–48.

72. NARA, T-120, reel 200, Benzler's telegrams to the Foreign Ministry, 4 and 22 November 1942, frames 0153723 and 0153813; Madajczyk, "'Restserbien,'" 467–68.

73. NARA, T-501, reel 256, Nedić's letter to General Bader, 1 January 1943, frame 000912.

74. NARA, T-501, reel 256, Meyszner's letter to Bader, 15 January 1943, frames 000924–26, and Nedić's letter to Bader, 22 January 1943, frames 000927–37; Madajczyk, "'Restserbien,'" 470–71.

75. Wuescht, *Jugoslawien*, 318–19; Tomasevich, *War: Occupation*, 198–99.

76. Kreso, *Njemačka okupaciona uprava*, 194–95.

77. NARA, T-501, reel 249, MBS memo to Nedić, 3 March 1943, frames 000113–14; Tomasevich, *War: Occupation*, 213; Borković, *Kontrarevolucija*, 2:132–33.

78. IAB, BdS collection, file N-720 "Nikola i drugi," 14; Tomasevich, *War: Occupation*, 184–85; Ramet, *Three Yugoslavias*, 134–35.

79. Borković, *Kontrarevolucija*, 2:169–73.

80. Borković, *Milan Nedić*, 226–32; Herzog, *Gründzuge*, 156; Neubacher, *Sonderauftrag Südost*, 134–35.

81. Marjanović, "Neubacher Plan," 490, 498; Neubacher, *Sonderauftrag Südost*, 155–57.

82. *Obnova*, no. 719, 9 November 1943, 5; Božović, *Specijalna policija*, 228–29; Borković, *Milan Nedić*, 102–3, 105.

83. Hoptner, *Yugoslavia*, 121; Ristović, "M. Nedić," 685.

84. B. Jovanović, *Crna Gora*, 22–26; Burgwyn, *Empire*, 88.

Chapter 4. Collaborationism

1. Jelavich, *History*, 2:263; Deroc, *British Operations*, 154–55.

2. Gross, "Themes," 27.

3. Ljotić, *U revoluciji*, 241–49, 253–24, 307–12; Wuescht, *Jugoslawien*, 58.

4. *Novo vreme*, no. 64, 20 July 1941, 1, 3; USHMM, RG-49.010M, reel 18, box 27, folder 9, "Ideoložki stav Zbor," "Stav Zbora u unutrašnjoj politici"; B. Đorđević, *Srpska kultura*, 122–27.

5. Filipović, *Logori*, 82; Borković, *Kontrarevolucija*, 1:171–73.

6. Stefanović, *Zbor*, 152; Kostić, *Za istoriju*, 50.

7. *Službene novine*, no. 49, 19 June 1942, 18; Kreso, "Opšti uslovi," 80.

8. USHMM, RG-49.010M, reel 17, box 20, Kragujevac district administration to Nedić, 13 February 1942; Stefanović, *Zbor*, 148–49; Borković, *Kontrarevolucija*, 1:168–69.

9. Stefanović, *Zbor*, 31; Slijepčević, *Istorija*, 3:151–52, 173–75.

10. USHMM, RG-49.005M, reel 86, trial of Philip Dmitrijević; Glišić, *Teror*, 66; J.Š., "Kragujevačka tragedija," 148.

11. USHMM, RG-49.002*1, Turner's memo, 21 September 1941, microfiche 4, 445–47; Borković, *Kontrarevolucija*, 1:299–300, 2:294.

12. USHMM, RG-49.010M, reel 16, box 1, folder 2, Nedić to Dragi Jovanović, letter 11 April 1943, 1; Nedić's speech, 31 May 1943, quoted in Cvijić and Vasović, *Milan Đ. Nedić*, 127–28.

13. IAB, "Suđenje . . . Bećareviću" file, interrogation of Bečarevič, 52; USHMM, RG-49.010M, reel 17, box 19, folder 2, Ministry of Interior (?) report, July 1941; Božović and Stefanović, *Milan Aćimović*, 12–15.

14. Čirković, *Ko je ko*, 392–93; Božović, *Specijalna policija*, 67–68.

15. IAB, "Suđenje . . . Bećareviću" file, interrogation of Vujković i Gubarev, 2, 5, 12, 29–30; IAB, UGB collection, folder 2192/15-g, personal file of Sergije Golubev, 2–4.

16. IAB, "Suđenje . . . Bećareviću" file, interrogation of Bečarevič, 35, 55; Božović, *Stradanje Jevreja*, 222.

17. Božović, *Specijalna policija*, 39, 70–72; Begović, *Banjica*, 1: 36, 46–48.

18. Božović, *Specijalna policija*, 85, 346–49; Dejanović et al., *Niš*, 254–63, 280–84, 287, 285, 319, 473; Filipović, *Logori*, 66, 70, 73–74, 84–86, 95–97.

19. Glišić, *Beograd*, 2:419.

20. *Istorijski arhiv*, 1:322–23; Božović, *Specijalna policija*, 387–91, 397, 418–22; D. Marković, *Zabranjeni život*, 43–45.

21. IAB, "Suđenje . . . Bećareviću" file, interrogation of Bečarevič, 3–5, 42–46, interrogation of Gubarev, 178–79; Božović, *Specijalna policija*, 327–28, 332–33, 336, 346–49.

22. IAB, BdS collection, file A-125, *Einsatzgruppe* Serbia report, 21 November 1941; Milinčević, *Hronika*, 1:94–97.

23. *Obnova*, no. 349, 25 August 1942, 3; Topalović, *Srbija*, 242–43; Borković, *Kontrarevolucija*, 1:59, 376–79.

24. Božović, *Specijalna policija*, 468–69.

25. Božović, "Juraj Špiler," 217–19, 222, 239; Bogdanov-Senko, *Antifašistički pokret*, 96–100.

26. IAB, "Suđenje . . . Bećareviću" file, interrogation of Bećarević, 71; Momčilović-Brkica, *Banat*, 30–31, 191–94; Božović, "Juraj Špiler," 225, 236, 232–34.

27. Bjelajać, *Generali*, 46–48, 136; Wuescht, *Jugoslawien*, 57, 136; Borković, *Milan Nedić*, 17–18; Lampe, *Yugoslavia*, 195–96.

28. Wuescht, *Jugoslawien*, 57; Kazimirović, *Srbija*, 4:1111, 1113, 1159.

29. Nedić quoted in Ramet, *Three Yugoslavias*, 633, n114.

30. RG-49.010M, VNS conference, February (?) 1942, digital file 747/11; AVI, file 75/47, "Presuda" [Harald Turner], card 16, testimony of Aleksandar Pelivanovič, 11–12.

31. Tomasevich, *Peasants*, 181, 186–87.

32. Ž. Jovanović, *Seljaštvo*, 62–64; Ž. Jovanović, "Poljoprivreda," 145.

33. Ramet and Lazić, "Collaborationist Regime,“ 21.

34. *Novo vreme*, no. 367, 14 July 1942, 5; Ristović," M. Nedić," 646–47, 666–68.

35. *Novo vreme*, no. 227, 28 January 1942, 3; Ramet and Lazić, "Collaborationist Regime," 26.

36. IAB, BdS collection, file N-65, memo of the Sipo/SD, undated, 7–9, 11; IAB, UGB collection, file 2206/29-H-10, trial of Dragoljub Nikolić, 2–6; Slijepčević, *Istorija*, 3:50.

37. Čulinović, *Okupatorska podjela*, 446.

38. *Novo vreme*, no. 96, 24 August 1941, 3; no. 110, 10 September 1941, 1; USHMM, RG-49.010M, reel 16, box 1, folder 2, conference of Nedić and Aćimović with the district chiefs, 27 December 1941, 5–8.

39. USHMM, RG-49.010M, reel 21, box 48, folder 1, notes about the 1941 uprising, 4–6; Nedić's speeches quoted in Cvijić and Vasović, *Milan Đ. Nedić*, 65, 124–25.

40. *Novo vreme*, no. 212, 6–10 January 1942, no page; Ristović, "M. Nedić," 645; Kazimirović, *Srbija*, 4:1122.

41. "Godišnjica Vlade narodnog spasa [1 September 1942]," in Cvijić and Vasović, *Milan Đ. Nedić*, 94–95; "Srpski put [8 November 1942]," in ibid., 100.

42. Ristović, "M. Nedić," 645; Kazimirović, *Srbija*, 4:1122.

43. Borković, *Milan Nedić*, 24; Karapandžić, *Građanski rat*, 28; Krakov, *General*, 1:101, 133–34.

44. "Ponedeljak," n. 47, 6 July 1942, 1; USHMM, RG-49.010M, reel 16, box 1, folder 2, conference of Nedić and Aćimović with the district chiefs, 27 December 27, 1941, 5–8.

45. USHMM, RG-49.010M, reel 16, box 4, folder 2, VNS report, January 1942; YVA, M29 FR/138, meeting between Turner and Nedić, 28 March 1942, 10; *Službene novine*, no. 22, 17 March 1942, 2.

46. Kreso, *Njemačka okupaciona uprava*, 132–33.

47. *Novo vreme*, no. 64, 20 July 1941, 1, 3; B. Đorđević, *Srpska kultura*, 122–27; Stefanović, *Zbor*, 128, 131.

48. Borković, *Kontrarevolucija*, 2:18–20; Ristović, "M. Nedić," 650–52.

49. Ramet and Lazić, "Collaborationist Regime," 28.

50. Ristović, "M. Nedić," 650–52; B. Đorđević, *Srpska kultura*, 113–15.

51. Karapandžić, *Građjanski rat*, 174–75; Rutar, "Employment," 49–50.

52. *Obnova*, no. 186, 11 February 1942, 7; *Službene novine*, no. 22, 17 March 1942, 1–2; Kreso, *Njemačka okupaciona uprava*, 125.

53. *Novo vreme*, no. 194, 16 December 1941, 5; ibid., no. 195, 17 December 1941, 3; ibid., no. 198, 20 December 1941, 3; USHMM, RG-49.010M, reel 18, box 34, folder 10, student tests, 25 June 1943.

54. Borković, *Kontrarevolucija*, 2:82, 98.

55. Kreso, *Njemačka okupaciona uprava*, 135–36; Borković, *Kontrarevolucija*, 2:82–85, 88–89, 92.

56. YVA, file M29 FR/125, MBS report, 6 November 1941, 22; USHMM, RG-49.010M, reel 17, box 19, folder 6, Morava administration to Ministry of Interior, 22 December 1941; Ristović, "M. Nedić," 655.

57. USHMM, RG-49.010M, reel 17, box 20, folder 4, Belgrade district chief's report to Ministry of Interior, 1 February 1942.

58. Borković, *Kontrarevolucija*, 2:92–93; Krstić, *Nepokorena mladost*, 12–15.

59. Glišić, *Beograd*, 2:432–33; Kostić, *Za istoriju*, 96.

60. IAB, "Suđenje . . . Bećareviću" file, interrogation of Bećarević, 38; Krstić, *Nepokorena mladost*, 26–27, 60, 69–73, 82–85, 108–14, 152; Glišić, *Beograd*, 2:431–35.

61. USHMM, RG-49.010M, reel 18, box 36, folder 1, Miodrag Popović's reports to Ministry of Education and Religion, 9–10 May 1943; Krstić, *Nepokorena mladost*, 29–36.

62. USHMM, RG-49.010M, reel 17, box 20, folder 1, Niš police report, 14 January 1942; ibid., folder 1, Ministry of Interior report to Nedić, 15 January 1942; Dedijer and Miletić, *Proterivanje Srba*, 870.

63. YVA, M29 FR/125, Southeast Command report, 6 November 1941, 3–4; Borković, *Milan Nedić*, 44–45.

64. USHMM, RG-49.008M, reel 21, box 164, folder 4, Niš police report, 25 June 1941; ibid., box 132, folder 2, Ministry of Interior report, 26 June 1941.

65. Božović and Stefanović, *Milan Aćimović*, 54, 63; Božović, *Specijalna policija*, 60, 73; Borković, *Kontrarevolucija*, 1:133.

66. AVI, file 75/47, "Presuda" [Harald Turner], testimonies of Rolf Winkler, Stanko Misojčić, and Marinko Dukić; Božović, *Specijalna policija*, 73–74; Glišić, *Teror*, 78.

67. NARA, T-175, reel 126, Turner's report to Himmler, 16 February 1942, frames 2651816–19, 2651821; USHMM, RG-49.002*1, Turner to Aćimović, memo 22 June 1941, microfiche 2, 342.

68. USHMM, RG-49.002*1, Turner to Aćimović, memo 22 June 1941, microfiche 2, 341; IAB, "Suđenje . . . Bećareviću" file, interrogation of Vujković, 98, 113; D. Marković, *Zabranjeni život*, 171–72.

69. USHMM, RG-49.002*1, Special Police report about erection of the Banjica camp, microfiche 2, 1:30, 32; Begović, *Logor Banjica*, 1:27, 30–32.

70. IAB, UGB collection, folder 2192/21-J-30, personal file of the camp guard Jevrem Jovanović, 11; ibid., 2192/21-J-29, personal file of the camp guard Milosav Jovanović, 21; Stanković, "Sećanja," 1:96–97.

71. Begović, *Logor Banjica*, 2:66, 79–81, 99–102; Kuprešanin, *Banjica*, 75–78, 81.

72. Parežanin, *Drugi svetski rat*, 347.

73. IAB, UGB collection, folder 2206/29-H-5, personal file of Dimitrije Nešić, 2–3.

Chapter 5. Resistance Movements

1. *Documents on German Foreign Policy*, 12:445.

2. Božović, *Beograd*, 35, 92–93, 129; Glišić, *Beograd*, 1:119.

3. Tomasevich, *War: Chetniks*, 127–29; Dejanović, *Niš*, 221–24, 316–17.

4. Karchmar, *Draža Mihailović*, 1:80–81.

5. Vučković, *Balkan Tragedy*, 56; Tomasevich, *War: Chetniks*, 118–22.

6. USHMM, RG-49.005M, reel 1, Miloš Sekulić's report, undated, 5–6; Petranović, *Srbija*, 221.

7. Judt, introduction, 6; D. Đorđević, *Ožiljci*, 1: 31–34; Karchmar, *Draža Mihailović*, 1:69–71.

8. USHMM, RG-49.005M, reel 1, Serbian administration report, July 1941, 62; Karchmar, *Draža Mihailović*, 1: 84–85; D. Đorđević, *Ožiljci*, 1:53.

9. Nikolić, *Strah*, 201–2; Ž. Jovanović, *Seljaštvo*, 175–76, 183.

10. Karchmar, *Draža Mihailović*, 2:924–25.

11. Minić, *Oslobodilački ili građanski rat*, 195–97; Pavlowitch, *Hitler's Disorder*, 55.

12. Jelić-Butić, *Četnici*, 19–20; Tomasevich, *War: Chetniks*, 125–26, 130–31.

13. Tomasevich, *War: Chetniks*, 166–70; Karchmar, *Draža Mihailović*, 2:573–74; Petranović, *Revolucija*, 2:91–93.

14. Kazimirović, *Srbija*, 3:920–22; Petranović, *Revolucija*, 2:18.

15. Petrović, "Četnička organizacija," 185–88; Petrović, "Četništvo," 81, 84–85.

16. Petrović, "Četništvo," 83–85; Borković, *Kontrarevolucija*, 1:183–84; Tomasevich, *War: Chetniks*, 127–29.

17. Petrović, "Četnička organizacija," 193–95; Petrović, "Četništvo," 86–87; Dedijer, *War Diaries*, 1:23.

18. Dedijer, *Tito*, 135; Kazimirović, *Srbija*, 2:475, 625.

19. Dedijer, *Tito*, 145–46; Borković et al., *Komunistička partija*, 1:25–28, 32–33; Bjelica, "NOP odredi," 107–9.

20. Glišić, *Beograd*, 1:55–61, 98; Vujošević, *Tito*, 63; Bošnjak, *Diverzantska dejstva*, 24–25.

21. Djilas, *Wartime*, 4–5; Vujošević, *Tito*, 74–75.

22. Borković, et al., *Komunistička partija*, 1:38, 46, 48–49, 52–53; Jončić, "Rušenje organa," 660–61; Dedijer, *Tito*, 153–54.

23. M. Marković, *Rat*, 33–34; Wheeler, "Pariahs," 131–32; Bošnjak, *Diverzantska dejstva*, 29–30.

24. Dedijer, *Tito*, 151–52; M. Marković, *Rat*, 44, 46–47.

25. Terzić et al., *Oslobodilački rat*, 1:74–78; Burgwyn, Empire, 89–90.

26. NARA, T-501, reel 249, MBS reports, summer 1941, frame 884; NARA, T-501, reel 295, frame 000135; USHMM, RG-49.002*1, Southeast Command report, 29 July 1941, microfiche 4, 351; Dedijer, *War Diaries*, 1:20, 36.

27. USHMM, RG-49.010M, reel 16, box 1a, folder 3, Ministry of Interior memo; USHMM, RG-49.010M, reel 17, box 19, folders 3–4, lists of German and collaborationist losses, frames 723–24, 729, 732–33, 771.

28. USHMM, RG-49.010M, reel 16, box 1a, folder 3, Ministry of Interior memo to Nedić.

29. IAB, UGB collection, file IV-Q-44, 280/24, *Einsatzgruppe* Serbia report, 2, 21.

30. NARA, T-312, reel 452, Southeast Command situational reports to OKW, September 3, 5, 7–8, 1941, frames 8037089–90 and 8037092–95; Božović, *Beograd*, 282–83.

31. AVI, file 75/47, "Presuda" [Harald Turner], card 16, testimony of Hermann Schacht; Miša, *Nemački zatvori*, 270; Božović, "Juraj Špiler," 233–34.

32. IAB, UGB collection, file SP-IV-1/1, 163/1, Ministry of Interior report on Velika Kikinda situation, 13 October 1941, 6; Momčilović-Brkica, *Banat*, 77–80, 169–70.

33. USHMM, RG-49.010M, reel 17, box 19, folder 3, Ministry of Interior report, 1–15 July 1941.

34. Bjelica, "NOP odredi," 116, 122; Jončić, "Rušenje organa," 662–63; Dedijer, *War Diaries*, 1:164–65.

35. Ž. Jovanović, "Seljaštvo," 691–93, 696–700; Bokovoy, *Peasants*, 5–7.

36. Dudić, *Dnevnik*, 53, 168, 225; Glišić, *Užička republika*, 82, 84, 157; Bosiljčić, *Istočna Srbija*, 157–58.

37. Burgwyn, *Empire*, 92; Roš, *Slovenski izgnanci*, 232–39; Judt, introduction, 3.

38. Ž. Jovanović, *Nova vlast*, 117–19.

39. Ž. Jovanović, *Nova vlast*, 24–25; Jončić, "Rušenje organa," 662–63; Dudić, *Dnevnik*, 185.

40. M. Marković, *Rat*, 51–52; *Istorijski arhiv*, 1:19.

41. Borković et al., *Komunistička partija*, 1:291–92; Ž. Jovanović, *Seljaštvo*, 139–40; Ž. Jovanović, *Nova vlast*, 130–34, 137.

42. Djilas, *Wartime*, 101; Nikolić, *Strah*, 219–20; Dudić, *Dnevnik*, 48–49, 51–52, 106, 113–15.

43. Vujošević, *Tito*, 70–72.

44. Dedijer, *Tito*, 158–59; D. Marković, *Zabranjeni život*, 177.

45. USHMM, RG-49.008M, reel 6, box K32, folder 6, Svetozar Vujković's report to Belgrade city administration, 10 August 1942; IAB, UGB collection, file IV-Q-44, 280/1, district chiefs' report to Special Police and to Ministry of Interior, 1 August 1941, 5–8; Bošnjak, *Diverzantska dejstva*, 64–65.

46. Glišić, *Beograd*, 1:160–67.

47. IAB, "Suđenje . . . Bećareviću" file, interrogation of Bećareviću, 171–72; Božović, *Beograd*, 241.

48. Kuprešanin, *Revolucionarni likovi*, 110; Borković, Komunistička partija, 1: 330; D. Marković, *Zabranjeni život*, 26–27, 69.

49. IAB, "Suđenje . . . Bećareviću" file, interrogation of Bećarević, 3–5, 42–46; ibid., interrogation of Gubarev, 178–79; Božović, *Specijalna policija*, 327, 332–33, 336.

50. D. Marković, *Zabranjeni život*, 27–29, 31, 73–74; Begović, *Logor Banjica*, 1:60–61.

51. Begović, *Logor Banjica*, 2: 236; Kuprešanin, *Revolucionarni likovi*, 111; Borković et al., *Komunistička partija*, 1:331.

52. Božović, *Podzemna borba*, 11–12, 15.

53. Kazimirović, *Srbija*, 3: 844; Tomasevich, *War: Chetniks*, 122–23; Karchmar, *Draža Mihailović*, 2:565.

54. USHMM, RG-49.010M, reel 18, box 25, folder 1, the *Einsatzkommando* Belgrade to the Ministry of Interior, 4 July 1941.

55. YVA, M29 FR/126, MBS situational report, 6 October 1941, 11; Karapandžić, *Gradjanski rat*, 73–75; Karchmar, *Draža Mihailović*, 1:195.

56. Tomasevich, *War: Chetniks*, 145–46; Glišić, *Užička republika*, 99–100; Karchmar, *Draža Mihailović*, 1:205.

57. USHMM, RG-49.010M, reel 16, box 1, folder 2, letter of unknown provenance to Nedić, October 1941; Petrović, "Četnička organizacija," 196–97; Karapandžić, *Gradjanski rat*, 255–57.

58. IAB, UGB collection, file IV-Q-44, 280/4, Valjevo district chief's report, 18; Glišić, *Užička republika*, 91; D. Mitrović, "Mere nemaca," 629–30.

59. Karapandžić, *Gradjanski rat*, 66–69.

60. Minić, *Oslobodilački ili građanski rat*, 157; Stefanović, *Zbor*, 125; Borković et al., *Kontrarevolucija*, 1:375.

61. USHMM, RG-49.005M, reel 1, "Komunistička akcija"; D. Mitrović, "Mere nemaca," 629–30.

62. Latas, *Saradnja četnika*, 27.

63. Roberts, *Tito*, 41–43.

64. Borković et al., *Komunistička partija*, 1:53–54; Vujošević, *Tito*, 71; Ristanović, "Ustanak," 43.

65. Glišić, *Užička republika*, 121–24; Ž. Jovanović, *Nova vlast*, 35, 39; Djilas, *Wartime*, 92–95.

66. *Istorijski arhiv*, 1: 131, 149–53, 182; Glišić, *Užička republika*, 127, 136–37; Djilas, *Wartime*, 92–93, 99.

67. Macura, "List 'Borba,'" 161–2; M. Aleksić, "Užičke 'Vesti,'" 151.

68. Glišić, *Užička republika*, 191; Glišić, *Beograd*, 1:207; Tomasevich, *War: Chetniks*, 147.

69. Jončić, "Rušenje organa," 669.

70. Lampe, *Yugoslavia*, 211, 213.

71. Kačavenda, "Parizansko-četnički odnosi," 48.

72. Slavin, "Yugoslaviia," 143.

73. Marjanović with Stanišić, *Collaboration*, 13–15; Tomasevich, *War: Chetniks*, 147–48.

74. Marjanović with Stanišić, *Collaboration*, 18.

75. Kazimirović, *Srbija*, 4:1177–79; *Istorijski arhiv*, 1:117.

76. Karchmar, *Draža Mihailović*, 1:244–50; Petranović, Srbija, 267; Marjanović with Stanišić, *Collaboration*, 20–26.

77. Tomasevich, *War: Chetniks*, 149–50; Dedijer, *War Diaries*, 1:44; Pavlowitch, *Hitler's Disorder*, 64.

78. AVI, file 75/47, "Presuda" [Harald Turner], testimony of Kosta Kosić; AVI, file 75/47, "Presuda" [Harald Turner], information sheet of the State Security Department, 8 December 1946; Minić, *Oslobodilački ili građanski rat*, 98–100, 120–21; Karchmar, *Draža Mihailović*, 1:277.

79. Janković, *Grupa*, 46–47.

80. Petranović, *Revolucija*, 1:321–23; Hoare, "Partisans," 210.

81. Minić, *Oslobodilački ili građanski rat*, 51.

Chapter 6. Repression

1. Shepherd, introduction, 3.

2. Milazzo, *Chetnik Movement*, 11.

3. Blood, *Bandit Hunters*, 14–25; Strazhas, *Deutsche Ostpolitik*, 53–54, 215–19.

4. Laub, *After the Fall*, 101; Madajczyk, *Polityka*, 2:235.

5. Pospieszalski, "Nazi Terror," 65–66.

6. Madajczyk, *Faszyzm*, 2:423, 425–27; Radziwończyk, "Rola," 241–42.

7. Förster, "Operation Barbarossa," 4:491; Manoschek, "*Serbien,*" 41–42; Čulinović, *Okupatorska podjela*, 421 n84.

8. Miša, *Nemački zatvori*, 14–22; Nikolić, *Strah*, 37.

9. Ramet, *Three Yugoslavias*, 137; Bogdanov-Senko, *Antifašistički pokret*, 26–28.

10. Živković, *Ratna šteta . . . Nemačka*, 214–15; Erpenbeck, *Serbien 1941*, 19; Božović, *Beograd*, 36–37.

11. Shepherd, *Terror*, 88; Glišić, *Teror*, 33–35.

12. Laub, *After the Fall*, 125.

13. IAB, file "Suđenje . . . Bećareviću," indictment of Bećarević, 3; Kreso, *Njemačka okupaciona uprava*, 153–54; Božović, *Stradanje Jevreja*, 140–41.

14. *Obnova*, no. 11, 17 July 1941, no page; Čulinović, *Okupatorska podjela*, 424–25.

15. Browning, "Wehrmacht Reprisal Policy," 32.

16. USHMM, RG-49.002*1, list of executions, July 1941, microfiche 2; Božović, *Beograd*, 256.

17. USHMM, RG-49.002*1, German police chief's report, 29 July 1941, microfiche 4, 354; AVI, file 75/47, trial of Walter Benne, Fritz Trothe, and Rolf Winkler; Miša, *Nemački zatvori*, 77–78.

18. IAB, UGB collection, file IV-Q-44, 280/24, *Einsatzgruppe* Serbia report, September 1941, 2; USHMM, RG-49.002*1, press report on reprisals in Skela, 15 August 1941, microfiche 4, 326; AVI, file 75/47, testimony of T. Baumgarten.

19. IAB, UGB collection, file 2339, card 157/15, anonymous letter to Dankelmann, undated; Milinčević, *Hronika*, 1:85–93.

20. USHMM, RG-49.010M, list of captured, wounded, and killed guerrillas, reel 17, box 19, folder 3, frame 753; Browning, "Wehrmacht Reprisal Policy," 33.

21. NARA, T-175, reel 126, Turner's report to Himmler, 16 February 1942, frames 2651816–19, 2651821; USHMM, RG-49.002*1, Turner's order to Milan Aćimović, 22 June 1941, microfiche 2, 342; Božović, *Beograd*, 62.

22. USHMM, RG-49.002*1, *Einsatzgruppe* Serbia report, 5 October 1941, microfiche 4, 483; YVA, M29 FR/126, *Verwaltungsstab* report, 6 October 1941, 5, 18.

23. NARA, T-501, reel 246, MBS report, 21–31 August 1941, frame 000203; Bošnak, "Partizanske diverzije," 388–91; Bosiljčić, *Istočna Srbija*, 17–18.

24. YVA, file M29 FR/138, MBS situational report, 31 August 1941, 22; Borković et al., *Kontrarevolucija*, 1:77.

25. Kreso, *Njemačka okupaciona uprava*, 153–54; Pavlowitch, *Hitler's Disorder*, 50; Marjanović, "German Occupation," 276; Browning, "Wehrmacht Reprisal Policy," 34–35.

26. Kroener et al., *Organisation*, 1:195.

27. Hubatsch, *Hitlers Weisungen*, 128; Browning, "Wehrmacht Reprisal Policy," 35; Hehn, *German Struggle*, 47–49.

28. Shepherd, *Terror*, 120–21.

29. Gumz, *Resurrection*, 22, 51–52, 136, 196–205; Manoschek, "Extermination," 169.

30. Reitlinger, *House*, 232.

31. Shepherd, "Bloodier than Boehme," 189–91; Madajczyk, "'Restserbien,'" 463.

32. Strugar, *Iugoslaviia*, 43; Terzić, *Oslobodilački rat*, 109–10; Bambara, *La guerra*, 111.

33. Schmider, *Partisanenkrieg*, 59.

34. Božović, *Stradanje Jevreja*, 147.

35. Kreso, *Njemačka okupaciona uprava*, 71; Čulinović, *Okupatorska podjela*, 392; Shepherd, "Bloodier than Boehme," 195; Manoschek, "Extermination," 169.

36. USHMM, RG-49.002*1, memo by Turner, 21 September 1941, microfiche 4, 445–47; USHMM, RG-49.002*1, MBS order, 25 September 1941, microfiche 6, 461.

37. Shepherd, *Terror*, 10.

38. Browning, "Wehrmacht Reprisal Policy," 36–38; Shepherd, "Bloodier than Boehme," 189–209; Dejanović, *Niš*, 252–53.

39. USHMM, RG-49.002*1, MBS order, 27 September 1941, microfiche 4, 467; ibid., 9 October 1941, microfiche 4, 494; ibid., *Einsatzgruppe* Serbia report, 5 October 1941, microfiche 4, 484; NARA, T-312, reel 452, Southeast Command reports to OKW, 1–2 October 1941, frames 8037146–48.

40. AVI, file 1128/46, "Presuda" [August Meyszner], card 27, interrogation of commander of 64th Police Battalion Adolf Josten; Erpenbeck, *Serbien*, 162.

41. AVI, file 75/47, "Presuda" [Harald Turner], card 16, testimony of Herman Schacht; Roš, *Slovenski izgnanci*, 282; Schlarp, *Wirtschaft*, 198.

42. Begović, *Logor Banjica*, 2:270–72; Glišić, *Beograd*, 1:116, 170–71; Božović, *Specjalna policija*, 43.

43. YVA, file M29 FR/138, MBS reports, 16–30 October 1941, 1–4; AVI, file 75/47, "Presuda" [Harald Turner], card 17, trial of commissar of Secret Field Police Rudolf Berg; Karapandžić, *Gradjanski rat*, 109–11.

44. AVI, file 75/47, "Presuda" [Harald Turner], card 16, Turner to Rajt, letter 20 September 1941.

45. Schmider, *Partisanenkrieg*, 73; Glišić, *Teror*, 61.

46. Miša, *Nemački zatvori*, 127–28.

47. AVI, file 75/47, "Presuda" [Harald Turner], testimonies of Darinka Jovičić, Pers Jovanović, Milka Joksimović, and Zora Mitrović; YVA, file M29 FR/61, Camp Šabac situation report, 18–24 October 1941, 190; Mirčetić, "Niški koncentracioni logor," 107–9; Filipović, *Logori*, 85, 128.

48. AVI, file 75/47, "Presuda" [Harald Turner], testimony of Vasil Dragiža; Glišić, *Beograd*, 1:291–93; Božović, *Stradanje Jevreja*, 97–98.

49. Mitrovski, *Bulgarian Army* et al., 112–13.

50. Živković, *Ratna šteta . . . Bugarska*, 33; Glišić, "Zločini Bugarskog okupatora," 2:315–16.

51. Kulić, *Bugarska okupacija*, 2: 46–7, 454–57; Mitrovski et al., *Bulgarian Army*, 117–18.

52. Dedijer, *Tito*, 31; Bjelica, "NOP odredi," 116; Glišić, *Užička republika*, 77–78.

53. USHMM, RG-49.005M, German report on Partisan movement, digital file 742/44; Dedijer, *Tito*, 169; Stefanović, *Zbor*, 162.

54. Glišić, "Nemačka ofansiva," 96–97; Hoare, "Partisans," 209.

55. YVA, M29 FR/134, MBS (?) reports on Partisan activity, fall 1941, 4–5; Mešterović, *Lekarev dnevnik*, 83; Djilas, *Wartime*, 105–7; Dedijer, *Tito*, 169.

56. Petranović, *Srbija*, 443–44; Djilas, *Wartime*, 113.

57. Petranović, *Srbija*, 265–66; Djilas, *Wartime*, 98.

58. USHMM, RG-49.010M, Zaječar administration report, fall 1941, reel 21, box 53, folder 2, 2; Dejanović et al., *Niš*, 226; Schmider, *Partisanenkrieg*, 75.

59. Madajczyk, *Faszyzm*, 1:463; Bambara, *La guerra*, 80; Terzić, *Oslobodilački rat*, 74–76.

60. AVI, file 75/47-K16, "Presuda" [Harald Turner], testimony of Franz Tritschler, chief of department 4A1 [communist] of Sipo in Belgrade, 19 February 1947; Borković, *Kontrarevolucija*, 1:268–70, 279–80; Nikolić, *Strah*, 71.

61. YVA, M29 FR/134, German police report, December 1941, 4; Pavlowitch, *Hitler's Disorder*, 66; Nikolić, *Strah*, 72; Krakov, *General*, 1:285.

62. Dejanović et al., *Niš*, 235; Kulić, *Bugarska okupacija*, 2: 53.

63. Kreso, *Njemačka okupaciona uprava*, 56; L. Ivanović, "Teror," 291–92.

64. B. Ivanović, "Uništenje," 376–78; Löwenthal, *Crimes*, 11.

65. Janjetović, "Arbeitskräfterekrutierung," 350–51; Božović, *Stradanje Jevreja*, 42, 61.

66. Löwenthal, *Crimes*, 3–5; L. Ivanović, "Teror," 295–96.

67. USHMM, RG-49.007M, reel 1, MBS anti-Jewish regulations, 30 May 1941, frames 000008, 000011, 000013, 000022; AVI, file 75/47, card 16, trial of Harald Turner, 5–6.

68. USHMM, RG-49.002*1, microfiche 2, MBS anti-Jewish regulations, 22 May 1941, p. 89; USHMM, RG-49.002*1, microfiche 22, note on the persecution of Jews and the Roma; Božović, *Stradanje Jevreja*, 18, 141.

69. USHMM, RG-49.010M, reel 17, box 20a, folder 2, *Einsatzkommando* Belgrade report, June 1941, 2; IAB, UGB collection, file 2326, III-8/A, Jewish community to Belgrade city administration, undated letter, 7–9; L. Ivanović, "Teror," 298.

70. USHMM, RG-49.010M, reel 16, box 1, folder 2, amendment to MBS anti-Jewish regulations of 30 May 1941; AVI, file 75/47, "Presuda" [Harald Turner], interrogation of Harald Turner and Georg Kiessel; Schlarp, *Wirtschaft*, 297, 301.

71. Browning, "Final Solution," 57.

72. B. Ivanović, "Uništenje," 376; Bogdanov-Senko, *Antifašistički pokret*, 35; Manoschek, "Extermination," 165–66.

73. USHMM, RG-49.005M, reel 1, report to Council of Commissars propaganda department, 23; Löwenthal, *Crimes*, 46–47.

74. AVI, file 75/47, "Presuda" [Harald Turner], trial of Walther Benne, Fritz Trothe, and Rolf Winkler, members of Kreis commandant office in Šabac; file 75/47, "Presuda" [Harald Turner], card 16, trial of Harald Turner, 17; Begović, *Logor Banjica*, 2:25; Löwenthal, *Crimes*, 40–41.

75. AVI, file 75/47, "Presuda" [Harald Turner], trial of Niš field commandant Karl Freicher von Bottmer; Dejanović et al., *Niš*, 264.

76. Bogdanov-Senko, *Antifašistički pokret*, 36–37; B. Ivanović, "Uništenje," 383–84; R. Mitrović, "Sudbina," 268.

77. B. Ivanović, "Uništenje," 384–85; Koljanin, "Antisemitski stereotipi," 90.

78. Shepherd, *Terror*, 69.

79. YVA, file M29 FR/138, MBS report, fall (?) 1941, 22–23; Browning, "Wehrmacht Reprisal Policy," 36–38; Dejanović et al., *Niš*, 252–53.

80. USHMM, RG-49.002*1, Turner's memo, 21 September 1941, microfiche 4, 447–48; USHMM, RG-49.002*1, German police report, 29 July 1941, microfiche 3, 353; AVI, file 75/47, "Presuda" [Harald Turner], court charges against Walter Benne, Fritz Trothe, Rolf Winkler, and Adolf Josten; Manoschek, "*Serbien,*" 42–43, 62–63.

81. Manoschek, "Vernichtung," 221.

82. Manoschek, "*Serbien,*" 102; Shelach, "Sajmište," 245.

83. NARA, T-120, reel 200, Veesenmayer to Benzler, 10 September 1941, frame 153416; Browning, *Origins*, 323; Božović, *Stradanje Jevreja*, 19–20.

84. YVA, M29 FR/126, MBS report, 6 October 1941, 5–6, 11; Manoschek, "Vernichtung," 221.

85. YVA, M29 FR/61, Lieutenant Liepe's report, 13 October 1941, 3–5; USHMM, RG-49.002*1, MBS order, 2 October 1941, microfiche 4, 480; AVI, 75/47, "Presuda" [Harald Turner], trial of Walter Benne, Fritz Trothe, and Rolf Winkler.

86. USHMM, RG-49.002*1, order of Böhme, 10 October 1941, microfiche 4, 502; Manoschek, "Extermination," 174.

87. Browning, "Wehrmacht Reprisal Policy," 39.

88. Božović, *Stradanje Jevreja*, 19–20.

89. AVI, file 75/47, "Presuda" [Harald Turner], indictment of Harald Turner and Georg Kiessel; Božović, *Stradanje Jevreja*, 62–63; Shelach, "Sajmište," 245–46.

90. Romano, *Jevreji*, 14; Browning, "Final Solution," 55–90; Shelach, "Sajmište," 245–46.

91. USHMM, RG-49.007M, reel 1, MBS directives about treatment of Jews and the Roma, frames 000026–27; USHMM, RG-49.010M, reel 17, box 19, folder 1, MBS report on situation of Jews, 17 June 1941; Božović, *Stradanje Jevreja*, 19, 233; Božović, *Specjalna* policija, 43.

92. YVA, M29 FR/138, MBS report on situation of Jews, 6 January 1942, 4.

93. L. Ivanović, "Teror," 305; Shelach, "Sajmište," 246–47.

94. USHMM, RG-49.002*1, testimonies of witnesses and survivors, microfiche 14; Löwenthal, *Crimes*, 24–27; Koljanin, *Nemački logor*, 54–55.

95. L. Ivanović, "Teror," 300, 307; Shelach, "Sajmište," 246–27; Božović, *Stradanje Jevreja*, 17, 89.

96. USHMM, RG-49.002*1, microfiche 4, Belgrade Jewish community to city administration, undated letter; Koljanin, *Nemački logor*, 96–97; B. Ivanović, "Uništenje," 387.

97. Koljanin, *Nemački logor*, 77–78, 81–82.

98. Božović, *Stradanje Jevreja*, 81–82, 93.

99. Shelach, "Sajmište," 249–53; L. Ivanović, "Teror," 309–10.

100. B. Ivanović, "Uništenje," 391–92; Dejanović et al., *Niš*, 304–5; Zorkić, "Teror," 482.

101. Janjetović, "Arbeitskräfterekrutierung," 405–6.

102. Koljanin, *Nemački logor*, 236.

103. D. Đorđević, *Ožiljci*, 1:109–11; Stevanović, *Sura grobnica*, 15–16, 21–22.

104. Božović, *Stradanje Jevreja*, 17–18; Begović, *Logor Banjica*, 2:30–31; Löwenthal, *Crimes*, 40.

105. Manoschek, "Vernichtung," 228; Glišić, *Užička republika*, 251–59.

106. YVA, M29 FR/125, MBS report, 6 November 1941, 4; Glišić, *Teror*, 116; Erpenbeck, *Serbien*, 162.

107. YVA, M29 FR/134, MBS situational report, 16 (?) December 1941, 4–5; Shepherd, *Terror*, 147; Browning, "Wehrmacht Reprisal Policy," 42.

108. Božović, *Stradanje Jevreja*, 5, 15–16.

Chapter 7. "Serbia Is Quiet," 1942–1944

1. Schmider, *Partisanenkrieg*, 421.

2. YVA, M29 FR/138, MBS report, 6 January 1942, 4; Janković, *Grupa*, 51–52, 53.

3. Dudić, *Dnevnik*, 233–34; Borković et al., *Komunistička partija*, 1:91–92, 103, 137; Janković, *Grupa*, 68, 117.

4. *Ponedeljak*, no. 23, 5 January 1942, 1.

5. Shimizu, *Die deutsche Okkupation*, 129.

6. Janković, *Grupa*, 108–13, 122–23, 138; Kroener et al., *Organisation*, 2:157.

7. USHMM, RG-49.010M, reel 17, box 20, folder 1, Niš administration report, 14 January 1942; USHMM, RG-49.010M, reel 17, box 20a, folder 2, VNS report on Partisan and Chetnik activities, April 1942; Dejanović et al., *Niš*, 234–35.

8. AVI, file 1128/46, "Presuda" [August Meyszner], trial of August Meyszner, 12–13; Madajczyk, *Faszyzm*, 1:439.

9. Hehn, *German Struggle*, 97; Momčilović-Brkica, *Banat*, 234, 242–46.

10. Glišić, *Teror*, 96–97; Seckendorf and Keber, *Okkupationspolitik*, 51.

11. AVI, file 75/47, "Presuda" [Harald Turner], trial of commandant of Crveny Krst, Karl Freiherr von Bothmer; Glišić, *Teror*, 124; Mirčetić, "Niški koncentracioni logor," 110–11.

12. USHMM, RG-49.010M, reel 21, box 51, folder 4, Ministry of Interior report, 20 March 1942; *Obnova*, no. 230, 4–6 April 1942, 5; *Obnova*, no. 236, 13 April 1942, 5; *Obnova*, no. 244, 22 April 1942, 5; *Novo vreme*, no. 279, 29 March 1942, 4; *Novo vreme*, no. 326, 27 May 1942, 3.

13. M. Marković, *Rat*, 145–46, 149; Hoare, *Genocide*, 233.

14. YVA, M29 FR/124, 9; USHMM, RG-49.008M, reel 21, box 132, folder 2, Special Police interrogation of Dobrosav Simić, 9 March 1942; Mešterović, *Lekarev dnevnik*, 57–58, 76.

15. USHMM, RG-49.010M, reel 18, box 25, folder 1, Ministry of Interior to the SDK, 8 July 1942; M. Marković, *Rat*, 152; I. Gligorijević, *Partizanski odredi*, 244–45, 258.

16. Madajczyk, *Faszyzm*, 1:439.

17. Shepherd, *Terror*, 201; Shepherd, "With the Devil," 84.

18. Petranović, *Srbija*, 447–48; Borković et al., *Komunistička partija*, 30–31, 67, 118, 144.

19. Ž. Jovanović, *Nova vlast*, 100–102.

20. I. Gligorijević, *Partizanski odredi*, 90–91; Momčilović-Brkica, *Banat*, 212, 320.

21. Borković et al., *Komunistička partija*, 114, 116, 131, 144.

22. IAB, UGB collection, file IV-Q-44, 280/6, Special Police report, April 1942, 14; Borković et al., *Komunistička partija*, 205–7; Wheeler, "Pariahs," 143; Slavin, "Yugoslaviia," 146–47, 149.

23. S. Cvetković, *Između srpa*, 162.

24. Božović, "Juraj Špiler," 248–50, 274.

25. Janković, *Grupa*, 224f; Glišić, *Teror*, 117.

26. Drapac, *Constructing Yugoslavia*, 181.

27. M. Marković, *Rat*, 125–27.

28. Glišić, *Beograd*, 1:187–88, 240–43; Begović, *Logor Banjica*, 1:223.

29. Tomasevich, *War: Occupation*, 135; Milazzo, *Chetnik Movement*, 137; Lampe, *Yugoslavia*, 215–16.

30. I. Gligorijević, *Partizanski odredi*, 273.

31. USHMM, RG-49.008, reel 3, box K27, folder 2, MBS situational report, 16 February 1943; USHMM, RG-49.008, Bader's order to commandant of Veliki Bečkerek, 24 February 1943; USHMM, RG-49.008M, reel 14, box 56, folder 1, MBS list of reprisals, 17 March 1943; USHMM, RG-49.008, reel 3, box K27, folder 2, Bader's order, 3 April 1943; Nicolić, "Ravnogorskė hnuti," 266–67.

32. AVI, file 75/47, "Presuda" [Harald Turner], testimonies of Darinka Jovičić, Pers Jovanović, Milka Joksimović, and Zora Mitrović; USHMM, RG-49.005M, testimony of unknown provenace, digital file 779-113, 860; Seckendorf and Keber, *Okkupationspolitik*, 237, document 142.

33. I. Gligorijević, *Partizanski odredi*, 308; *Dokumenti o izdajstvu*, 631.

34. Ž. Jovanović, "Poljoprivreda," 148.

35. Wheeler, "Pariahs," 148–49.

36. USHMM, RG-49.010M, reel 16, box 1, folder 2, and reel 17, box 20, folder 4, Nedić administration reports, February 1942; USHMM, RG-49.010M, reel 17, box 20a, folder 2, Nedić administration report, April 1942; Petranović, *Srbija*, 270–71.

37. Roberts, *Tito*, 38–39.

38. Barker, "Some Factors," 30–33; Bailey, "British Policy," 65.

39. *Dokumenti o izdajstvu*, 474; Karapandžić, *Građjanski rat*, 66–69.

40. Roberts, *Tito*, 38–39.

41. I. Gligorijević, *Partizanski odredi*, 359, 361; Petar Višnjić, "Borbe," 104–5, 108.

42. Slavin, "Yugoslaviia," 149.

43. NARA, T-501, reel 248, Southeast Command situational report, August 1942, frame 000385; USHMM, RG-49.010M, reel 16, box 1, folder 2, Nedić's directive, 16 January 1942, 3; Topalović, *Srbija*, 95–96.

44. Božović, *Beograd*, 278–79; Borković, *Kontrarevolucija*, 1:67, 72–73.

45. Latas, *Saradnja četnika*, 67–72.

46. YVA, M29 FR/138, meeting between Turner and Nedić, 28 March 1942, 17.

47. USHMM, RG-49.005M, reel 86, trial of a collaborationist official (Đorđe?) Čijović; Tomasevich, *War: Chetniks*, 207; Hoare, *Genocide*, 154.

48. Latas, *Saradnja četnika*, 29–30; *Dokumenti o izdajstvu*, 24–25.

49. USHMM, RG-49.005M, reel 86, trial of Milan Cvetković and trial of Vukašin Petković; Filipović, *Logori*, 157–62; *Dokumenti o izdajstvu*, 540–42; Petar Višnjić, "Borbe," 107.

50. Stefanović, *Zbor*, 162; Borković et al., *Komunistička partija*, 205–7; *Dokumenti o izdajstvu*, 554.

51. D. Đorđević, *Ožiljci*, 1:70–74; Kuprešanin, *Banjica*, 54.

52. NARA, T-120, reel 200, Benzler to State Secretary Woermann, 11 March 1942, frames 0153555–58; Milazzo, *Chetnik Movement*, 103; *Dokumenti o izdajstvu*, 474; Karapandžić, *Građjanski rat*, 66–69.

53. Avakumović, *Mihailović*, 179; Tomasevich, *War: Chetniks*, 111; Nicolić, "Ravnogorskė hnuti," 253.

54. NARA, T-501, reel 248, Southeast Command report (November 1942?), frame 1098; Tomasevich, *War: Chetniks*, 201; Schmider, *Partisanenkrieg*, 446; Nicolić, "Ravnogorskė hnuti," 255–56.

55. USHMM, RG-004M, reel 3, Yugoslav Commission for Investigating Axis Crimes report, 3; Mitrovski et al., *Bulgarian Army*, 122–23.

56. IAB, BdS collection, file B-737, "Dušan Bogdanović"; Nicolić, "Ravnogorskė hnuti," 253–54; Karchmar, *Draža Mihailović*, 1:287.

57. Milazzo, *Chetnik Movement*, 105–6.

58. USHMM, RG-49.008, reel 3, box K32, folder 6, MBS report (December?) 1943; Seckendorf and Keber, *Okkupationspolitik*, 274, document 198; Nicolić, "Ravnogorskė hnuti," 256, 260.

59. USHMM, RG-49.010M, reel 18, box 25, folder 1, Chetnik situational report (March 1943?); Tomasevich, *War: Chetniks*, 250; Begović, *Logor Banjica*, 2:13–16.

60. USHMM, RG-49.010M, reel 18, box 25, folder 1, MBS situational report, April 1943, 1; Burgwyn, *Empire*, 211; Begović, *Logor Banjica*, 2:13–14, 16.

61. Schmider, *Partisanenkrieg*, 459; Nicolić, "Ravnogorskė hnuti," 267–68; Begović, *Logor Banjica*, 2:18.

62. USHMM, RG-49.010M, reel 18, box 29, folder 8, Užice district administration report to Ministry of Interior, 1 January 1944, and Kraljevo district administration report to Ministry of Interior, 2 January 1944.

63. USHMM, RG-49.010M, reel 18, box 25, folder 1, deputy chief of Belgrade district report to Ministry of Interior, 31 December 1943; YVA, file M29 FR/138, MBS situational report, undated, 22; D. Đorđević, *Ožiljci*, 1:254–55; Mihailović, *Uspomene*, 88.

64. USHMM, RG-004M, reel 3, "Bugarska okupacija Jugoslavije," 3; Mitrovski et al., *Bulgarian Army*, 122–23.

65. *Obnova*, no. 633, 31 July 1943, 3; *Obnova*, no. 686, 1 October 1943, 3; Vučković, *Balkan Tragedy*, 126–27, 176, 228–29; Parežanin, *Drugi svetski rat*, 426–30; Stefanović, *Zbor*, 229; Topalović, *Srbija*, 91; Karchmar, *Draža Mihailović*, 1:290–91.

66. Hubatsch, *Hitlers Weisungen*, 217, 220, 222.

67. Tomasevich, *War: Chetniks*, 319–27; Marjanović with Stanišić, *Collaboration*, 109–13; *Dokumenti o izdajstvu*, 540.

68. Iampol'skii et al., *Organy*, 272.

69. Pavlowitch, *Hitler's Disorder*, 192; Wuescht, *Jugoslawien*, 65.

70. Pavlowitch, *Hitler's Disorder*, 223–24; Vučković, *Balkan Tragedy*, 258–59; Topalović, *Srbija*, 156–57; Tomasevich, *War: Chetniks*, 399–404.

71. USHMM, RG-49.010M, reel 18, box 36, folder 1, Nedić memorandum to Ministry of Education and Religion, 22 February 1944; Tomasevich, *War: Chetniks*, 335–38.

72. Hoare, *Genocide*, 341.

73. Apostolski, *Februarski pohod*, 181–85, 189–95; Dedijer, *War Diaries*, 3:369, 374; M. Marković, *Rat*, 294–95.

74. USHMM, RG-49.008M, reel 6, Gestapo reports, 3–4 June 1944, and RSHA memo, 12 June 1944; USHMM, RG-49.008M, reel 14, box 50, folder 16, SDK report to German police, 24 May 1944; Mešterović, *Lekarev dnevnik*, 295–97.

75. Glišić, "Proces prestrojavanja," 272.

76. NARA, T-501, reel 256, Southeast Command report, frames 754–55; USHMM, RG-49.010M, reel 18, box 36, folder 1, Nedić to Ministry of Education and Religion, memo 22 February 1944; Tomasevich, *War: Chetniks*, 335–38.

77. D. Đorđević, *Ožiljci*, 1:310–11.

78. Roberts, *Tito*, 225.

79. D. Đorđević, *Ožiljci*, 1: 297; Kazimirović, *Srbija*, 4:1153.

80. Karchmar, *Draža Mihailović*, 2:562–63; Topalović, *Srbija*, 163–64.

81. Karapandžić, *Građjanski rat*, 320–21; Schmider, *Partisanenkrieg*, 495–96; Tomasevich, *War: Chetniks*, 338–41.

82. Apostolski, *Februarski pohod*, 181–85, 189–95; Seckendorf and Keber, *Okkupationspolitik*, 323, document 263, 342, document 290.

83. Glišić, "Proces prestrojavanja," 273–75; Borković, "Osnivacki kongres," 13.

84. Tomasevich, *War: Chetniks*, 392; Pavlowitch, *Hitler's Disorder*, 236.

85. Glišić, *Beograd*, 2:585.

86. Minić, *Oslobodilački ili građanski rat*, 158–59; Karapandžić, *Građjanski rat*, 324–25.

87. USHMM, RG-49.010M, reel 18, box 36, folder 1, Nedić's order, 31 August 1944; Petar Višnjić, *Operacije*, 82–83.

88. Petar Višnjić, *Operacije*, 92; Terzić et al., *Oslobodilački rat*, 2:297–98.

89. USHMM, RG-49.005M, microfiche 512, undated MBS report, frames 548, 552; Mihailović, *Uspomene*, 129–30; Tomasevich, *War: Chetniks*, 412–16.

90. Wuescht, *Jugoslawien*, 69; Pavlović, "Srbija na kraju," 160–61, 176.

91. Schmider, *Partisanenkrieg*, 519.

92. AVI, file 75/47, card 16, "Presuda" [Harald Turner], trial of Field Marshal Maximilian Freiherr von Weichs and Field Commandant of Belgrade Major General, Walter Firow; Tripković, "Izveštaj generala F. Maklejna," 179; Dedijer, *War Diaries*, 3:420.

93. Bosiljčić, *Istočna Srbija*, 46, 179; Petranović, *Srbija*, 659–61; Ž. Jovanović, *Seljaštvo*, 389.

94. USHMM, RG-49.005M, report on investigation of crimes of occupiers and their accomplices, November (1945?), digital file 742/45; Tripković, "Izveštaj generala F. Maklejna," 191–92; S. Cvetković, *Između srpa*, 179–87.

95. Pavlowitch, *Hitler's Disorder*, 267; S. Cvetković, *Između srpa*, 265–66.

Chapter 8. Serbs and Jews

Another version of this chapter, titled "The Role of the Collaborationist Administration in the Holocaust in Serbia," was first presented at the international conference *The Holocaust in Yugoslavia: History, Memory and Culture—A Reappraisal*, 24 June 2013, at the International Institute for Holocaust Research, Yad Vashem.

1. Freidenreich, *Jews*, 38–39; Popović, *Jevreji*, 37–38, 96–97, 114.

2. Freidenreich, *Jews*, 65; Popović, *Jevreji*, 121–22, 153–54.

3. Lebel, "*Final Solution*," 147–50, 159, 184–86; Sekelj, "Anti-Semitism," 161; Freidenreich, *Jews*, 28–33. Signed 28 June 1919 by Poland, Romania, Greece, Czechoslovakia, and the SCS, the Minority Treaty guaranteed these countries' national minorities civil, religious, and political rights, and the right to use native languages in communal life.

4. Lebel, "*Final Solution*," 147–50, 159, 184–86; Freidenreich, *Jews*, 28–33; Popović, *Jevreji*, 23–24, 119–20.

5. Falina, "Between 'Clerical Fascism,'" 253; Slijepčević, *Istorija*, 3:46; IAB, BdS collection, file N-65, "Nikolai Velimirović," 4.

6. USHMM, RG-49.002*01, microfiche 1, Ljotić's pamphlet, October 1940; ibid., microfiche 3, 1–16; Sekelj, "Anti-Semitism," 166–68.

7. Popović, *Jevreji*, 136–37; Koljanin, *Jevreji*, 397.

8. Lebel, "*Final Solution*," 268–70; Popović, *Jevreji*, 142–43; Freidenreich, *Jews*, 180–82, 187–88.

9. Sekelj, "Anti-Semitism," 169; Popović, *Jevreji*, 166–67.

10. USHMM, RG-49.002*1, MBS orders, 22 May 1941, microfiche 2, 49–50; IAB, UGB collection, file 2326, III-8/A, order of Dunava district chief, 26 May 1941, 15; Božović, *Beograd*, 139–40.

11. USHMM, RG-49.010M, reel 17, box 19, folder 2, Morava district office to Ministry of Interior, 28 June 1941; USHMM, RG-49.010M, reel 17, box 19, folder 5, Ministry of Interior report, 15 November 1941; USHMM, RG-49.010M, reel 17, box 20, folder 1, Ministry of Interior report to Nedić, 14 January 1942.

12. USHMM, RG-49.010M, reel 18, box 36, folder 7–8, Belgrade city administration to district chiefs, 17 May 1941 and 25 June 1941.

13. USHMM, RG-49.005M, reel 1, report to Yugoslav government in exile, October 1941, 4; Borković, *Kontrarevolucija*, 1:88–89.

14. Koljanin, *Jevreji*, 397.

15. YVA, M29 FR/126, MBS report, 6 October 1941, 5–6, 11; Kreso, *Nemačka uprava*, 154.

16. IAB, "Suđenje . . . Bećareviću," interrogation of Vujković, 113; Byford, "Collaborationist Administration," 120.

17. *Obnova*, no. 300, 29 June 1942, 3; Cvijić and Vasović, *Milan Đ. Nedić*, 57, 71, 119, 149, 151.

18. Borković, *Kontrarevolucija*, 1:133.

19. YVA, M29 FR/138, meeting between Turner and Nedić, 28 March 1942, 9; Byford, "Willing Bystanders," 306.

20. Božović, *Stradanje Jevreja*, 209–10; Fogel et al., *Righteous*, 270.

21. Ristović, "M. Nedić," 645; Kazimirović, *Srbija*, 1:133, 4:1122.

22. USHMM, RG-49.007M, reel 1, MBS decrees about Jewish property, frame 000191; Schlarp, *Wirtschaft*, 297–98, 301; Löwenthal, *Crimes*, 49.

23. USHMM, RG-49.010M, reel 18, box 30, folder 1, "Stav Zbora u spolnoj politici," 5–8; *Novo vreme*, no. 114, 14 September 1941, 13; Byford, "Willing Bystanders," 298.

24. L. Ivanović, "Teror," 296; *Zločini fašističkih okupatora*, 48.

25. IAB, UGB collection, file 2326, III-8/A, SDK report, 26 December 1941, 2; Božović, *Stradanje Jevreja*, 112–13; Božović, *Specijalna policija*, 129, 178.

26. *Novo vreme*, no. 38, 24 June 1941, 3.

27. Petranović, *Revolucija*, 1:248; Ristović, "M. Nedić," 650–52.

28. *Novo vreme*, no. 369, 16 July 1942, 3.

29. USHMM, RG-49.010M, reel 18, box 30, folder 1, SDK appeal, 9 October 1941; USHMM, RG-49.010M, reel 21, box 48, folder 1, "Komunisti protiv Srba i Srbije," 1–5; *Ponedeljak*, no. 17, 24 November 1941, 4.

30. *Novo vreme*, no. 38, 24 June 1941, 6; USHMM, RG-49.08, reel 16, box K63, folder 2, anti-Semitic pamphlets.

31. Stefanović, *Zbor*, 34–35.

32. USHMM, RG-49.010M, reel 21, box 48, folder 1, Milorad D. Mojić, "Zakoni i dela jevreja," 26–28, 30, 47.

33. *Obnova*, no. 546, 17 April 1943, 3; ibid., no. 547, 18 April 1943, 3.

34. N. Jovanović, "Odnos," 78–79; D. Đorđević, *Ožiljci*, 1:36–37.

35. N. Jovanović, "Odnos," 78–85; Mihailović, *Uspomene*, 52.

36. USHMM, RG-49.010M, reel 16, box 1a, folder 3, Nedić to Council of Ministers, 24 December 1941, 2; USHMM, RG-49.010M, reel 17, box 19, folder 2, Ministry of Interior report, July 1941; N. Jovanović, "Odnos," 87–88.

37. USHMM, RG-49.010M, reel 18, box 34, folder 10, commissar for human resources to Velibor Jonić, 20 October 1941; Božović, *Specijalna policija*, 88.

38. Koljanin, "Antisemitski stereotipi," 110.

39. Božović, *Specijalna policija*, 88; Milosavljević, *Potisnuta istina*, 190–91, 195; Lebel, *"Final Solution,"* 319–20.

40. IAB, UGB collection, file IV-Q-44, 280/6, Lazar Prokić to Belgrade mayor Dragi Jovanović, 18 August 1941, 7; USHMM, reel 17, box 19, folder 2, Ministry of Interior report, July 1941; N. Jovanović, "Odnos," 88.

41. *Novo vreme*, no. 164, 11 November 1941, 3; ibid., no. 175, 23 November 1941, 3; ibid., no. 176, 25 November 1941, 3; ibid., no. 190, 11 December 1941, 3; Božović, *Stradanje Jevreja*, 225.

42. YVA, M29 FR/125, MBS report, 6 November 1941, 31; *Novo vreme*, no. 182, 2 December 1941, 3; ibid., no. 200, 23 December 1941, 3; N. Jovanović, "Odnos," 89, 92, 94, 96–7; Koljanin, "Antisemitski stereotipi," 102–4.

43. *Novo vreme*, no. 208, 1 January 1942, 3; ibid., no. 210, 3 January 1942, 3; ibid., no. 211, 4 January 1942, 3; ibid., no. 215, 14 January 1942, 3.

44. *Ponedeljak*, no. 375, 23 July 1942, 5; *Obnova*, no. 355, 29 August 1942, 7; Koljanin, "Antisemitski stereotipi," 113.

45. Radanovic, *Kazna*, 296.

46. IAB, UGB collection, file 2206/29-H-12, personal file of Jovan P. Nikolić, 1–8, 21–30.

47. Božović, *Beograd*, 174, 259–61.

48. USHMM, RG-49.010M, reel 17, box 20, folder 2, Ministry of Interior arrest warrants, 31 January 1942.

49. IAB, UGB collection, file 2326, III-8/18, police report, undated, 2; Božović, *Stradanje Jevreja*, 213.

50. USHMM, RG-49.008M, reel 21, box 130, folder 4, Special Police to Ministry of Social Policy and National Health, 31 October 1941, and Special Police to "Jewish" department of Ministry of Interior, 31 October 1941; Božović, *Specijalna policija*, 88.

51. Božović, *Stradanje Jevreja*, 216–19.

52. IAB, UGB collection, folder 2326, III-8–8/34, file of Berta Filatović, 11, 15; ibid., III-8/2, file of Elvina Kolb, 1–4; ibid., III-8/3, file of Elsa Kovać, 1.

53. IAB, UGB collection, folder 2326, III-8/31, Gestapo memo to Special Police, 5 October 1942, 2; USHMM, RG-49.010M, reel 17, box 20a, folder 2, Special Police report, 1–2; Božović, *Specjalna policija*, 39, 42, 64, 72, 177; Božović, *Stradanje Jevreja*, 230–32.

54. Ristović, "Persecuted," 219–21.

55. Ristović, "Flüchtlinge," 111.

56. USHMM, RG-49.007M, reel 1, death penalty decree for helping and abetting Jews, frame 000061; L. Ivanović, "Teror," 291, 300; Romano, *Jevreji*, 204–6.

57. Ristović, "Flüchtlinge," 116–19; Koljanin, *Nemački logor*, 63–64.

58. YVA, file 03/3457, testimonies of survivors, 3; *Novo vreme*, no. 210, 3 January 1942, 3.

59. Almuli, *Stradanje*, 144–45.

60. Ristović, "Flüchtlinge," 139–41.

61. Ristović, "Persecuted," 225, 229–30; Ristović, "Flüchtlinge," 135–36.

62. Löwenthal, *Crimes*, 42–43; Ristović, "Persecuted," 222–24; Ristović, "Flüchtlinge," 126.

63. USHMM, RG-49.010M, reel 16, box 1, folder 2, MBS decrees about stolen Jewish property, May 1941, January 1942; *Obnova*, no. 238, 15 April 1942, 5; Perica Višnjić, "Nemački okupacioni system," 87.

64. Schlarp, *Wirtschaft*, 296, 301; Löwenthal, *Crimes*, 46–47.

65. Löwenthal, *Crimes*, 48–49; L. Ivanović, "Teror," 310.

66. IAB, UGB collection, folder 2326, III-8/18, undated informant's report to Special Police, 2; ibid., folder IV-Q-44, 280/1, informant's report to Special Police, 27 July 1941.

67. Ristović, "Persecuted," 221.

68. Rakić, *Teror*, 217–19.

69. Hoare, *Genocide*, 156–62; Löwenthal, *Crimes*, 42–43.

70. USHMM, RG-49.005M, reel 86, trial of Chetnik commander Dobrosav Jevdejević; *Obnova*, no. 237, 14 April 1942, 4; Mirčetić, "Niški koncentracioni logor," 109.

71. Božović, *Stradanje Jevreja*, 225; Ristović, "Flüchtlinge," 129–31; Ratković, "Organizacija," 295.

72. Almuli, *Stradanje*, 357–58.

73. Fogel et al., *Righteous*, 33–35.

74. NARA, T-77, reel 983, Southeast Command Propaganda Department report for 1–31 December 1941, frame 4472875.

75. Almuli, *Stradanje*, 109.

Chapter 9. Living with the Enemy

1. Terzić et al., *Oslobodilački rat*, 1:34–39, 46–53.

2. D. Aleksić, *Privreda*, 140.

3. USHMM, RG-49.010M, reel 17, box 19, folder 2, K. Stanarević, "Doprinos Srbije i Banata," frame 379; Brborić, "Ministarski savet," 172.

4. D. Aleksić, *Privreda*, 165.

5. USHMM, RG-49.010M, reel 17, box 19, folder 2, K. Stanarević, "Doprinos Srbije i Banata," frame 381; Marjanović, "German Occupation," 275–76; Tomasevich, *War: Occupation*, 650–51.

6. USHMM, RG-49.010M, reel 17, box 19, folder 2, K. Stanarević, "Doprinos Srbije i Banata," frames 383 and 386; Glišić, *Teror*, 121.

7. NARA, T-501, reel 248, military commandants' reports, frames 572–75; NARA, T-501, reel 256, frames 1081–85; Ž. Jovanović, "Poljoprivreda," 146.

8. USHMM, RG-49.010M, reel 17, box 21, folder 2, Kraljevo administration to Ministry of Interior, February 1942, 3–4.

9. USHMM, RG-49.010M, reel 16, box 1, folder 2, VNS conference, 4 February 1942, 11, and district chiefs' reports to Nedić, 22 July 1942; D. Aleksić, *Privreda*, 171–72.

10. USHMM, RG-49.010M, reel 18, box 25, folder 1, military commandants' reports, March 1942; USHMM, RG-49.010M, reel 18, box 25, folder 1, Valjevo administration report, December (?) 1941.

11. Kroener et al., *Organisation*, vol. 1:325; Tomasevich, *War: Occupation*, 647–48.

12. USHMM, RG-49.010M, reel 17, box 21, folder 2, Kraljevo administration to Ministry of Interior, February 1942, 3–4; NARA, T-501, reel 248, military commandant offices' reports, frames 572–75; NARA, T-501, reel 256, military commandant offices' reports, frames 1081–85; Ž. Jovanović, "Poljoprivreda," 146.

13. USHMM, RG-49.005M, testimony of Tvrko Mitić, digital file 742/45; Živković, "Kontribucije," 195–99.

14. Glišić, *Teror*, 45.

15. YVA, M29 FR/125, MBS report, 6 November 1941, 7, 18; USHMM, RG-49.010M, reel 18, box 34, folder 3, notes on Serbian laborers sent to Germany; Banović, "Izvoz," 383–84.

16. AVI, file 75/47, "Presuda" [Harald Turner], testimony of Konrad Listemann; Janjetović, "Arbeitskräfterekrutierung," 362, 370–71; Kreso, *Njemačka okupaciona uprava*, 73; Tomasevich, *War: Occupation*, 655.

17. Petranović, *Srbija*, 478; Rutar, "Employment," 48; Tomasevich, *War: Occupation*, 633–34.

18. Živković, *Ratna šteta . . . Nemačka*, 173–74, 177; Rutar, "Employment," 50.

19. Janjetović, "Arbeitskräfterekrutierung," 343–45; Živković, *Ratna šteta . . . Nemačka*, 179–81; Rutar, "Employment," 49–50.

20. USHMM, RG-49.005M, testimony of Nadja Ulić, digital file 742/67; IAB, UGB collection, file 2339, III-157/1, report of unknown provenance, 1–10; Bosiljčić, *Istočna Srbija*, 121–22.

21. Božović, *Beograd*, 147.

22. Ibid., 46–47; Kreso, "Opšti uslovi," 72.

23. D. Marković, *Zabranjeni život*, introduction (unpaginated).

24. Nikolić, *Strah*, 101–2; Pavlowitch, *Hitler's Disorder*, 51–52.

25. USHMM, RG-49.010M, reel 16, box 1, folder 2, VNS conference minutes, 6 February 1942, 9–10; *Nove vreme*, no. 366, 12 July 1942, 5; Kreso, "Opšti uslovi," 72.

26. NARA, T-501, reel 248, Southeast Command reports, frames 572–55, and reel 256, frames 1081–85.

27. USHMM, RG-49.010M, reel 16, box 1, folder 2, VNS conference minutes, 5 February 1942, 32; Nikolić, *Strah*, 103–6; Božović, *Beograd*, 46–48.

28. YVA, M29 FR/125, MBS report, 6 November 1941, 6–7, 17; Kreso, *Njemačka okupaciona uprava*, 59.

29. Kreso, *Njemačka okupaciona uprava*, 117; Živković, "Kontribucije," 185–86.

30. Zorkić, "Teror," 464.

31. USHMM, RG-49.005M, reel 1, note to Ministry of Propaganda, winter 1942, 2–3.

32. NARA, T-501, reel 248, MBS reports, summer–fall 1942, frames 572–53, and reel 256, frames 1081–85; Nikolić, *Strah*, 128; Schlarp, *Wirtschaft*, 181–82, 307–9, 323.

33. Tomasevich, *War: Occupation*, 709; Mihailović, *Uspomene*, 58, 77; D. Marković, *Zabranjeni život*, 138–39.

34. Schlarp, *Wirtschaft*, 197; Dejanović et al., *Niš*, 233.

35. Borković, *Kontrarevolucija*, 2:97–99, 101.

36. RG-49.008M, reel 1, digital file 143/11, testimonies of Žarko Zojić, Stan Rojin, and Galina (?) Strof.

37. Mihailović, *Uspomene*, 81.

38. Bogavac, *Stanovništvo*, 87; Topalović, *Srbija*, 262–67.

39. Tomasevich, *War: Occupation*, 184–85; Ž. Jovanović, *Seljaštvo*, 52–53, 55.

40. Mihailović, *Uspomene*, 9, 12–15, 34, 41.

41. Pintar, "Delusion," 99–100.

42. Ibid., 98–99; Petranović, *Srbija*, 503.

43. *Novo vreme*, no. 253, 27 February 1942, 5; *Novo vreme*, no. 267, 15 March 1942, 7; *Obnova*, no. 541, 11 April 1943, 2; *Obnova*, no. 546, 17 April 1943, 5; *Obnova*, no. 575, 24 May 1943, 4.

44. *Ponedeljak*, no. 91, 19 August 1941, 7; Nikolić, *Strah*, 104–6.

45. NARA, T-77, Southeast Command Propaganda Department report, reel 983, frame 4472787.

46. *Novo vreme*, no. 240, 12 February 1942, 5; *Obnova*, no. 25, 2 February 1942, 9; *Obnova*, no. 236, 13 April 1942, 5; B. Đorđević, *Srpska kultura*, 45, 53–54; S. Cvetković, *Repertoar*, 88, 114.

47. *Novo vreme*, no. 22, 6 June 1941, 5; *Novo vreme*, no. 29, 15 June 1941, 3; *Novo vreme*, no. 372, 19 July 1942, 4; *Novo vreme*, no. 65, 21 July 1941, 3; *Obnova*, no. 192, 18 February 1942, 9.

48. *Ponedeljak*, no. 2, 11 August 1941, 3; *Novo vreme*, no. 88, 15 August 1941, 5; Kreso, *Njemačka okupaciona uprava*, 133–37.

49. NARA, T-77, reel 983, Southeast Command Propaganda Department report, frame 4472767; Kirk, "Film," 249.

50. Savković, *Kinematografija*, 34, 39, 41.

51. *Obnova*, no. 248, 27 April 1942, 13; *Novo vreme*, no. 219, 18 January 1942, 5; *Novo vreme*, no. 537, 7 April 1943, 4.

52. Savković, *Kinematografija*, 49, 57.

53. *Obnova*, no. 717, no. 6, November 1943, 8; *Novo vreme*, no. 198, 7 September 1941, 5; *Novo vreme*, no. 124, 26 September 1941, 5; *Novo vreme*, no. 231, 1 February 1942, 7.

54. *Novo vreme*, no. 231, 1 February 1942, 7; Mihailović, *Uspomene*, 38.

55. NARA, T-77, reel 983, Southeast Command Propaganda Department report, frame 4472767; Kreso, *Njemačka okupaciona uprava*, 133–34; Savković, *Kinematografija*, 43–45.

56. Nikolić, *Strah*, 93.

57. USHMM, RG-49.010M, reel 17, box 20, folder 1, Niš administration report, 14 January 1942; reel 16, box 1, folder 2, VNS conference minutes, 5 February 1942, 32; Mihailović, *Uspomene*, 80.

58. USHMM, RG-49.005M, reel 1, letter of Dr. Sekulić, fall (?) 1941, 2–3.

59. USHMM, RG-49.005M, reel 1, VNS memo, undated.

60. Koljanin, "Antisemitski stereotipi," 97–98.

61. USHMM, RG-49.008M, reel 21, box 130, folder 6, Belgrade administration report, 22 December 1941; IAB, UGB collection, file IV-Q-44, 280/24, collection of anti-German leaflets, 15–16, 18.

62. IAB, UGB collection, file 2339, card 157/9, letter of Dragi Jovanović to Special Police, undated, 2; IAB, UGB collection, file 2339, card 157/1, Ministry of Interior to Special Police, 1–3.

63. Janjetović, "Arbeitskräfterekrutierung," 340–41.

64. Ž. Jovanović, "Poljoprivreda," 146.

65. Ž. Jovanović, *Seljaštvo*, 202–8.

66. Ž. Jovanović, *Nova vlast*, 98–100; Ž. Jovanović, *Seljaštvo*, 177; Glišić, *Užička republika*, 81.

67. USHMM, RG-49.010M, reel 17, box 20, folder 4, Belgrade district chief's report to VNS, 1 February 1942; Nikolić, *Strah*, 288–89.

68. Kazimirović, *Srbija*, 3:773–74; Ž. Jovanović, *Seljaštvo*, 90–91.

69. Mihailović, *Uspomene*, 28–29.

70. Janković, *Grupa*, 135; Gligorijević, *Partizanski odredi*, 260.

71. Vučković, *Balkan tragedy*, 132–33.

72. Djilas, *Wartime*, 93, 104.

73. USHMM, RG-49.010M, reel 17, box 19, folder 5, Ministry of Interior report, 15 November 1941.

74. AVI, file 75/47, "Presuda" [Harald Turner], testimony of Ernst Hauschildt; Nikolić, *Strah*, 200–201, 211, 214–15; Dedijer, *With Tito*, 39. In official Soviet parlance, *kulak* referred to a well-to-do peasant. In practice, it was applied to anybody who did not surrender agricultural products or did not sympathize with the communists.

75. IAB, BdS collection, [Gestapo] file J-345, "Aleksandar Janković," 1–4; [Gestapo] file B-533 "Vukašin Bogdanović," 2, 4, 7; Ž. Jovanović, *Seljaštvo*, 347–49.

76. USHMM, RG-49.010M, reel 20, box 53, folder 2, Leskovac district office report, 24 October 1943; Dejanović et al., *Niš*, 227–28.

77. USHMM, RG-49.010M, reel 16, box 1, folder 2, VNS conference minutes, 5 February 1942, 5, 12; Dudić, *Dnevnik*, 154–57, 211, 225–26; Petrović, "Četništvo," 92.

78. USHMM, RG-49.010M, reel 17, box 21, folder 2, Kraljevo district-administration to Ministry of Interior, February 1942, 3–4; USHMM, RG-49.010M, reel 18, box 21, folder 2, letter of SDK to Užice district administration, 3 July 1942, 1–5.

79. USHMM, RG-49.010M, reel 17, box 19, folder 2, gendarmerie command to Aćimović, 1 July 1941; USHMM, RG-49.010M, letter of Aćimović to Schröder, 4 July 1941; USHMM, RG-49.010M, reel 17, box 20, folder 4, Serbian border guard command to SDS information bureau, 6 March 1942.

80. USHMM, RG-49.010M, reel 17, box 19, folder 1, Serbian police reports, 23 May 1941, 30 May 1941, and 25 June 1941; Ž. Jovanović, *Seljaštvo*, 369–71, 379.

81. USHMM, RG-49.010M, reel 20, box 53, folder 2, Leskovac district office report, 24 October 1943; *Dokumenti o izdajstvu*, 554.

82. USHMM, RG-49.005M, reel 86, Miloš Čijović court case.

83. IAB, UGB collection, IV-Q-44, 280/4, district chiefs' report, 14, 16; USHMM, RG-49.010M, reel 17, box 19, folder 3, Serbian police report, 11 August 1941; USHMM, RG-49.010M, reel 17, box 19, folder 5, Ministry of Interior report, 15 November 1941.

84. Mihailović, *Uspomene*, 9–10, 49.

Conclusion

1. Wuescht, *Jugoslawien*, 208–9.
2. Živković, *Ratna šteta . . . Nemačka*, 493–527.
3. Žerjavić, *Population*, 184, 186.
4. Schmider, *Partisanenkrieg*, 589.
5. Rings, *Life*, 272–73; Judt, introduction, 5.
6. S. Cvetković, *Između srpa*, 150.

Bibliography

Archival Materials

Arhiv Vojnoistorijskog Instituta (AVI), Belgrade, Serbia

BdS Collection: "Der Befehlshaber der Sicherheitspolizei und des SD."

File 75/47, "Presuda grupi ratnih zločinaca" [Harald Turner and the others].

File 1128/46, "Presuda grupi ratnih zločinaca pripadnika nemačke policije" [August Meyszner and the others].

File "Suđenje Božidaru Bošku Bećareviću, Svetozaru Vujkoviću i Nikoli Gubarevu."

Files 03/3457, M29 FR/61, M29 FR/124, M29 FR/125, M29 FR/126 M29 FR/132, M29 FR/134, M29 FR/138, M29 FR/145.

Isorijski arhiv Beograda (IAB), Belgrade, Serbia

Microfilm Series T-77—Records of Headquarters, German Armed Forces High Command (Oberkommando der Wehrmacht/OKW).

Microfilm Series T-120—Records of the German Ministry of Foreign Affairs.

Microfilm Series T-175—Records of the Reichsführer SS and Chief of Police.

Microfilm Series T-312—Records of German Field Commands: Armies.

Microfilm Series T-501—Records of German Field Commands: Rear Areas, Occupied Territories, and Others.

National Archives and Records Administration (NARA), Washington, D.C.

RG-49.002*1—Records relating to the occupation of Yugoslavia during World War II.

RG-49.005M—[Yugoslav] State Commission to Investigate Crimes Committed by the Occupants and Their Collaborators records, 1943–48.

RG-49.007M—Selected Records from the Archives of the Jewish Historical Museum, Belgrade.

RG-49.008M—Selected Records from the Archives of the Military Historical Institute of the General Staff of the Armed Forces of Serbia Relating to the German Zone of Occupation Yugoslavia.
RG-49.010M—Selected Records from the Nedic Archives of the Military Historical Institute of the Ministry of Defense of Serbia.
UGB Collection: "Uprava grada Beograda 1837–1944 [Specijalna policija]."
United States Holocaust Memorial Museum (USHMM), Washington, D.C.
Yad Vashem Archives (YVA), Jerusalem, Israel

Newspapers

Novo vreme (1941–43)
Obnova (1941–43)
Ponedeljak (1941–42)
Službene novine (1941–43)

Other Works

Aleksić, Dragan. *Privreda Srbije u Drugom svetskom ratu.* Belgrade: Institut za noviju istroriju Srbije, 2002.

Aleksić, Mara. "Užičke 'Vesti' 1941. godine o ustanku u Jugoslaviji i prilikami u Evropi." In Kačavenda et al., *Užički kraj u jesen ratne 1941*, 151–60.

Almuli, Jaša. *Stradanje i spasanje srpskih Jevreja.* Belgrade: Zavod za uđbenike, 2010.

Apostolski, Mihajlo. *Februarski pohod: operacjie jedinica NOV i POJ u zimu 1943–1944 u Makedoniji i južnom Pomoravlju.* Belgrade: Vojno delo, 1963.

Avakumović, Ivan. *Mihailović prema nemačkim dokumentima.* Belgrade: Institut za savremenu istoriju, 2004.

Avramovski, Živko, et al., eds. *Jugoslovensko-bugarski odnosi u XX veku: zbornik radova.* 2 vols. Belgrade: Institut za savremenu istoriju—Narodna knjiga, 1980–82.

Bailey, S. W. "British Policy Towards General Draža Mihailović." In *British Policy Towards Wartime Resistance in Yugoslavia and Greece*, ed. Phyllis Auty and Richard Clogg, 59–92. London: Macmillan, 1975.

Bambara, Gino. *La guerra di liberazione nazionale in Jugoslavia (1941–1943).* Milan: U. Mursia editore, 1988.

Banac, Ivo. *The National Question in Yugoslavia: Origins, History, Politics.* Ithaca, N.Y.: Cornell University Press, 1984.

Banović, Branimir. "Izvoz radne strane i deportacije stanovništva s teritorija NDH u toku Drugog svetskog rata." *Putovi revolucje* 1–2 (1963): 375–89.

Barker, Elisabeth. "Some Factors in British Decision-Making over Yugoslavia 1941–4." In *British Policy Towards Wartime Resistance in Yugoslavia and Greece*, ed. Phyllis Auty and Richard Clogg, 22–58. London: Macmillan, 1975.

Begović, Sima. *Logor Banjica 1941–1944.* 2 vols. Belgrade: Institut za Savremenu Istoriju, 1989.

Biondich, Mark. *The Balkans: Revolution, War, and Political Violence since 1878*. New York: Oxford University Press, 2011.

Bjelajać, Mile S. *Generali i admirali Kraljevine Jugoslavije, 1918–1941: studija o vojnoj eliti i biografski leksikon*. Belgrade: Institut za noviju istoriju Srbije, 2004.

Bjelica, Obrad. "NOP odredi u zapadnoj Srbiji kao nezamenljiv oblik vojne organizacije i faktor političke mobilizacije masa 1941. godine." In Jončić et al., *Narodni ustanak i borbe za Kraljevo 1941*, 107–28.

Blood, Philip W. *Hitler's Bandit Hunters: The SS and the Nazi Occupation of Europe*. Washington, D.C.: Potomac Books, 2006.

Bogavac, Tomislav. *Stanovništvo Beograda 1918–1991*. Belgrade: Muzej grada Beograda, 1991.

Bogdanov-Senko, Dušan. *Antifašistički pokret u južnom Banatu 1941–1944*. Pančevo: Istorijski arhiv, 2005.

Bokovoy, Melissa K. *Peasants and Communists: Politics and Ideology in the Yugoslav Countryside, 1941–1953*. Pittsburgh, Pa.: University of Pittsburgh Press, 1998.

Borković, Milan, et al. *Komunistička partija Jugoslavije u Srbiji 1941–1945*. 2 vols. Belgrade: Izdavačko preduzeħe Rad, 1974–75.

———. *Kontrarevolucija u Srbiji: kvislinška uprava 1941–1944*. 2 vols. Belgrade: Sloboda, 1979.

———. *Milan Nedić*. Zagreb: Centar za informacije i publicitet, 1985.

———. "Osnivacki kongres KP Srbije i njegov značaj." *Vojno-istorijski glasnik* 36, no. 1 (1985): 11–26.

Bosiljčić, Slobodan. *Istočna Srbija*. Belgrade: Nolit-Prosveta, 1963.

Bošnjak, Ljubomir. *Diverzantska dejstva u narodnooslobodilačkom ratu 1941–1945*. Belgrade: Vojnoistorijski institut, 1983.

———. "Partizanske diverzije na području Kraljeva u oružanom ustanku 1941." In Jončić et al., *Narodni ustanak i borbe za Kraljevo 1941*, 384–99.

Božović, Branislav. *Podzemna borba (specijalne organizacije Gestapoa za borbu protiv NOP-a)*. Belgrade: Sedma Sila, 1964.

———, and Mladen Stefanović. *Milan Aćimović, Dragi Jovanović, Dimitrije Ljotić*. Zagreb: Centar za informacije i publicitet, 1985.

———. "Juraj Špiler." In *Pavle Đurišić, Lovro Hacin, Juraj Špiler*, ed. Radoje Pajović, Dušan Željeznov, and Branislav Božović, 209–99. Zagreb: Centar za informacije i publicitet, 1987.

———. *Beograd pod komesarskom upravom 1941 godine*. Belgrade: Institut za Savremenu Istoriju, 2001.

———. *Specijalna policija u Beogradu 1941–1944*. Belgrade: Srpska školska knjiga, 2003.

———. *Stradanje Jevreja u okupiranom Beogradu 1941–1944*. Belgrade: Srpska školska knjiga, 2004.

Brborić, Ivan. "Ministarski savet Milana Nedića decembar 1941–novembar 1942." *Istorija 20. veka: časopis Instituta za savremenu istoriju/History of 20. Century: Journal of the Institute of Contemporary History* 28, no. 3 (2010): 169–80.

Browning, Christopher R. "The Final Solution in Serbia: The Semlin Judenlager—A Case Study." *Yad Vashem Studies* 15 (1983): 55–90.

———. "Wehrmacht Reprisal Policy and the Mass Murder of Jews in Serbia." *Militärgeschichtliche Zeitschrift* 1 (1983): 31–47.

———. "Harald Turner und die Militärverwaltung in Serbien 1941–1942." In *Verwaltung contra Menschenführung im Staat Hitlers: Studien zum politisch-administrativen System*, ed. Dieter Rebentisch and Karl Teppe, 351–73. Göttingen: Vandenhoeck & Ruprecht, 1986.

———. *The Origins of the Final Solution: The Evolution of Nazi Jewish Policy, September 1939–March 1942* (with contributions by Jürgen Matthäus). Lincoln: University of Nebraska Press, 2004.

Burgwyn, H. James. *Empire on the Adriatic: Mussolini's Conquest of Yugoslavia, 1941–1943*. New York: Enigma Books, 2005.

Byford, Jovan. "The Collaborationist Administration and the Treatment of the Jews in Nazi-Occupied Serbia." In Ramet and Listhaug, *Serbia and the Serbs in World War Two*, 109–27.

———. "Willing Bystanders: Dimitrije Ljotić, 'Shield Collaboration,' and the Destruction of Serbia's Jews." In *In the Shadow of Hitler: Personalities of the Right in Central and Eastern Europe*, ed. Rebecca Haynes and Martin Rady, 295–312. New York: I. B. Tauris, 2011.

Čirković, Simo C. *Ko je ko u Nedićevoj Srbiji 1941–1944. Leksikon ličnosti: slika jedne zabranjene epohe*. Belgrade: Prosveta, 2009.

Cohen, Philip. *Serbia's Secret War: Propaganda and the Deceit of History*. College Station: Texas A&M University Press, 1996.

Čulinović, Ferdo. *Okupatorska podjela Jugoslavije*. Belgrade: Vojnoizdavački Institut, 1970.

Cvetković, Sava V. *Repertoar Narodnog pozorišta u Beogradu 1868–1965: hronološki pregled i premijera i obnova*. Belgrade: Muzej pozorišne umetnosti, 1966.

Cvetković, Srđan. *Između srpa i čekića: represija u Srbiji 1944–1953*. Belgrade: Institut za Savremenu Istoriju, 2006.

Cvijić, Anđelka, and Milenko Vasović. *Milan Đ. Nedić: Život, govori, saslušanja*. Belgrade: Anđelka Cvijić and Milenko Vasović, 1991.

Dedijer, Vladimir. *With Tito through the War: Partisan Diary, 1941–1944*. London: A. Hamilton, 1951.

———. *Tito*. New York: Simon and Schuster, 1953.

———, and Anton Miletić, eds. *Proterivanje Srba sa ognjišta 1941–1944: svedočanstva*. Belgrade: Prosveta, 1989.

———. *The War Diaries of Vladimir Dedijer*. 3 vols. Ann Arbor: University of Michigan Press, 1990.

Dejanović, Dragoljub, Dragoslav Živković, Miroslav Milovanović, and Đorđe Stamenković. *Niš u vihoru oslobodilačkog rata (1941–1945)*. Novi Sad: Savez udruženja boraca narodnooslobodilačkog rata SR Srbije, 1968.

Deroc, Milan. *British Special Operations Explored: Yugoslavia in Turmoil, 1941–1943 and the British Response.* Boulder, Colo.: East European Monographs, 1988.

Dimitrijević, Bojan. *Vojska Nedićeve Srbije: oružane snage srpske vlade 1941–1945.* Belgrade: Institut za savremenu istoriju, 2011.

Dimitrijević, Bojan, and Kosta Nikolić. *Đeneral Mihailović: biografija.* Belgrade: Srpska reč, 2000.

Djilas, Milovan. *Wartime.* New York: Harcourt Brace Jovanovich, 1977.

Djokić, Dejan. *Elusive Compromise: A History of Interwar Yugoslavia.* New York: Columbia University Press, 2007.

———. "'Leader' or 'Devil'? Milan Stojadinović, Prime Minister of Yugoslavia (1935–39), and His Ideology." In *In the Shadow of Hitler: Personalities of the Right in Central and Eastern Europe*, ed. Rebecca Haynes and Martin Rady, 153–68. New York: I. B. Tauris, 2011.

Documents on German Foreign Policy 1918–1945. 13 vols. Washington, D.C.: Government Printing Press, 1962.

Dokumenti o izdajstvu Draže Mihajlovića. Belgrade: Državna komisija za utvrđivanje zločina okupatora i njihovih pomagača, 1945.

Đorđević, Bojan. *Srpska kultura pod okupacijom.* Belgrade: Službeni glasnik, 2008.

Đorđević, Dimitrije. *Ožiljci i opomene.* 3 vols. Belgrade: Beogradski izdavačko-grafički zavod, 2000.

Dragnich, Alex N. *Serbia through the Ages.* Boulder, Colo.: East European Monographs, 2004.

Drapac, Vesna. *Constructing Yugoslavia: A Transnational History.* New York: Palgrave Macmillan, 2010.

Dudić, Dragojlo. *Dnevnik 1941.* Belgrade: Prosveta, 1981.

Eberhardt, Piotr. *Ethnic Groups and Population Changes in Twentieth-Century Central-Eastern Europe: History, Data, and Analysis.* Armonk, N.Y.: M. E. Sharpe, 2003.

Erpenbeck, Dirk-Gerd. *Serbien 1941: Deutsche Militärverwaltung und Serbischer Widerstand.* Osnabrück: Biblio Verlag, 1976.

Falina, Maria. "Between 'Clerical Fascism' and Political Orthodoxy: Orthodox Christianity and Nationalism in Interwar Serbia." *Totalitarian Movements and Political Religions* 8, no. 2 (2007): 247–58.

Filipović, Stanoje. *Logori u Šapcu.* Novi Sad: Savez udruženjia boraca narodnooslobodilačkog rata NR Srbjie, 1967.

Fogel, Milan, Milan Ristović, and Milan Koljanin, eds. *Righteous among the Nations: Serbia.* Belgrade: Jewish Community in Zemun, 2010.

Freidenreich, Harriet Pass. *The Jews of Yugoslavia: A Quest for Community.* Philadelphia: Jewish Publication Society of America, 1979.

Gligorijević, Branislav. "Politički pokreti i grupe s nacjonalsocijalističkom ideologijom i nihova fuzija u Ljotičevom Zboru." *Vojno-istorijski institut* 4 (1965): 35–83.

Gligorijević, Ivan. *Partizanski odredi istočne Srbije 1941–1944*. Belgrade: Vojnoizdavački zavod, 1969.

Glišić, Venceslav. *Teror i zločini nacističke Nemačke u Srbiji 1941–1944*. Belgrade: Rad, 1970.

———. "Zločini Bugarskog okupatora u Srbiji 1941–1944." In Avramovski et al., *Jugoslovensko-bugarski odnosi u XX veku*, 2:313–30.

———, ed. *Beograd u ratu i revoluciji 1941–1945*. 2 vols. Belgrade: Istorijski arĥiv Beograda, 1984.

———. "Proces prestrojavanja revolucionarnih i kontrarevolucionarnich snaga u Srbiji 1943." *Vojno-istorijski glasnik* 35, no. 1 (1984): 271–77.

———. *Užička republika*. Belgrade: Nolit, 1986.

———. "Nemačka ofansiva na slobodnu teritoriju sa posebnim osvrtom na borbu na Kadinjači." In Kačavenda et al., *Užički kraj u jesen ratne 1941*, 93–98.

Gross, Jan. "Themes for Social History of War Experience and Collaboration." In *The Politics of Retribution in Europe: World War II and Its Aftermath*, ed. István Deák, Jan T. Gross, and Tony Judt, 15–35. Princeton, N.J.: Princeton University Press, 2010.

Gumz, Jonathan. *The Resurrection and Collapse of Empire in Habsburg Serbia, 1914–1918*. New York: Cambridge University Press, 2009.

Hehn, Paul N. *The German Struggle against Yugoslav Guerrillas in World War II: German Counter-Insurgency in Yugoslavia 1941–1943*. Boulder, Colo.: East European Quarterly, 1979.

Herzog, Robert. *Gründzuge der deutschen Besatzungsverwaltung in den ost- und süd-osteuropäischen Ländern während des Zweiten Weltkrieges*. Tübingen: Institut für Besatzungsfragen, 1955.

Hoare, Marko Attila. *Genocide and Resistance in Hitler's Bosnia: The Partisans and the Chetniks 1941–1943*. New York: Oxford University Press, 2006.

———. "The Partisans and the Serbs." In Ramet and Listhaug, *Serbia and the Serbs in World War Two*, 201–21.

Hoptner, Jacob B. *Yugoslavia in Crisis 1934–1941*. New York: Columbia University Press, 1962.

Hubatsch, Walther, ed. *Hitlers Weisungen für die Kriegführung, 1939–1945: Dokumente des Oberkommandos der Wehrmacht*. Koblenz: Bernard & Graefe, 1983.

Iampol'skii, V. P., et al. *Organy gosudarstvennoi bezopasnosti SSSR v Velikoi Otechestvennoi voine: sbornik dokumentov*. 5 vols. Moscow: Izdatel'stvo Rus, 1995–2007.

Istorijski arhiv Komunističke partije Jugoslavije. 7 vols. Belgrade: Istorijsko odelenje Centralnog Komiteta Komunističke partije Jugoslavije, 1949.

Ivanović, Božidar. "Uništenje jevreja i plačka njihove imovine u Banatu 1941–1944." *Tokove revolucijie* 1, no. 1 (1967): 373–403.

Ivanović, Lazar. "Teror nad jevrejima u okupiranom Beogradu 1941–1942." *Godišnjak grada Beograda* 13 (1966): 289–316.

Janjetović, Zoran. "Arbeitskräfterekrutierung und Zwangsarbeit im Militärverwaltungsgebiet Serbien 1941–1944." In *Pflicht, Zwang und Gewalt: Arbeitsver-*

waltungen und Arbeitskräftepolitik im deutsch besetzten Polen und Serbien 1939–1944, ed. Florian Dierl, Zoran Janjetović, and Karsten Linne, 317–440. Essen: Klartext Verlag, 2013.

Janković, Milorad B. *Grupa partizanskih odreda u zapadnoj Srbiji: zimi 1941/42. godine*. Belgrade: Vojnoizdavački Zavod, 1967.

Jareb, Mario. "Allies or Foes? Mihailović's Chetniks during the Second World War." In Ramet and Listhaug, *Serbia and the Serbs in World War Two*, 155–74.

Jelavich, Barbara. *History of the Balkans*. 2 vols. Cambridge: Cambridge University Press, 1983.

Jelić-Butić, Fikreta. *Četnici u Hrvatskoj, 1941–1945*. Zagreb: Globus, 1986.

Jončić, Koča. "Rušenje organa vlasti stare Jugoslavije i razvijanje političkih oblika organizacije NOP-a u zapadnoj Srbiji i Kraljevačkom okrugu 1941. godine." In Jončić et al., *Narodni ustanak i borbe za Kraljevo 1941*, 659–90.

Jončić, Koča, Bogdan Koričanac, and Vladimir Berežnov, eds. *Narodni ustanak i borbe za Kraljevo 1941. godine: zbornik radova naučnog skupa*. Belgrade: Narodna knjiga, 1985.

Jovanović, Batrić. *Crna Gora u narodnooslobodilačkom ratu i socijalističkoj revoluciji*. Belgrade: Vojno delo, 1960.

Jovanović, Nadežda. "Odnos okupatora i kvislinga prema masoneriji u Srbiji 1941–1942." *Godišnjak grada Beograda* 18 (1971): 77–107.

Jovanović, Žarko S. "Poljoprivreda Srbije u ratu 1941–1945." In *Srbija u modernizacijskim procesima XX. veka (naučni skup)*, ed. Latinka Perović, Maria Obradović, and Dubravka Stojanović, 143–50. Belgrade: Institut za noviju istoriju Srbije, 1994.

———. *Seljaštvo u Srbije u Drugom svetskom ratu, 1941–1945*. Belgrade: Institut za noviju istoriju Srbije, 1995.

———. *Nova vlast u Srbiji, 1941–1945*. Belgrade: Institut za noviju istoriju Srbije, 1997.

———. "Seljaštvo okoline Kraljeva u ustanku 1941. godine." In Jončić et al., *Narodni ustanak i borbe za Kraljevo 1941*, 691–703.

J.Š. "Kragujevačka tragedija." In Kalabić, *Ravnogorska istorija*, 145–50.

Judt, Tony. Introduction. In Judt, *Resistance and Revolution in Mediterranean Europe*, 1–28.

———, ed. *Resistance and Revolution in Mediterranean Europe, 1939–1948*. New York: Routledge, 1989.

Kačavenda, Petar. "Parizansko-četnički odnosi u jesen 1941. godine." In Kačavenda et al., *Užički kraj u jesen ratne 1941*, 46–49.

Kačavenda, Petar. Venceslav Glišić, and Petar Marković, eds. *Užički kraj u jesen ratne 1941. godine: zbornik radova sa naučnog skupa*. Užice: Kadinjača, 1996.

Kalabić, Radovan, ed. *Ravnogorska istorija*. Belgrade: Evro, 1992.

Karapandžić, Borivoje M. *Građjanski rat u Srbiji (1941–1945)*. Cleveland, Ohio: Sjedinjene Države Amerike, 1958.

Karchmar, Lucien. *Draža Mihailović and the Rise of the Chetnik Movement, 1941–1942*. 2 vols. New York: Garland, 1987.

Kazimirović, Vasa. *Srbija i Jugoslavija 1914–1945*. 4 vols. Kragujevac: Prizma, 1995.

Kerenji, Emil. "Antisemitism and Corporatism in the Writings of Dimitrije Ljotić." Master's thesis, Central European University (Budapest), 1998.

Kirk, Tim. "Film and Politics in South-East Europe: Germany as 'Leading Cultural Nation,' 1933–1945." In *Cinema and the Swastika: The International Expansion of the Third Reich Cinema*, ed. Roel Vande Winkel, 244–54. Basingstoke, U.K.: Palgrave Macmillan, 2008.

Kolanović, Nada Kisić. *Zagreb-Sofija: prijateljstvo po mjeri ratnog vremena 1941–1945*. Zagreb: Hrvatski državni arhiv; Dom i svijet, 2003.

———. "Nezavisna Država Hrvatska, zemlje Jugoistočne Europe, Turska i Japan 1941–1945." In *Nezavisna država Hrvatska 1941–1945: zbornik radova*, ed. Sabrina P. Ramet, 193–214. Zagreb: Alinea, 2009.

Koljanin, Milan. *Nemački logor na beogradskom Sajmištu 1941–1944*. Belgrade: ISI, 1992.

———. "Antisemitski stereotipi i propaganda u Srbiji 1941–1942." *Istorija 20. veka: časopis Instituta za savremenu istoriju/History of 20. Century: Journal of the Institute of Contemporary History* 21, no. 1 (2003): 83–118.

———. *Jevreji i antisemitizam u Kraljevini Jugoslaviji 1918–1941*. Belgrade: Institut za savremenu istoriju, 2008.

Kostić, Boško M. *Za istoriju naših dana: odlomci iz zapisa za vreme okupacije*. Lille: Jean Lausier, 1949.

Krakov, Stanislav. *General Milan Nedić*. 2 vols. Munich: Iskra, 1963, 1968.

Kreso, Muharem. "Opšti uslovi života i rada u okupiranom Beogradu." *Vojnoistorijski glasnik* 23, no. 3 (1972): 67–83.

———. *Njemačka okupaciona uprava u Beogradu 1941–1944 (sa osvrtom na centralne okupacione komande i ustanove za Srbiju, Jugoslaviju i Balkan)*. Belgrade: Istorijski Arhiv Beograda, 1979.

Kroener, Bernhard R. von, Rolf-Dieter Müller, and Hans Umbreit. *Organisation und Mobilisierung des deutschen Machtbereichs*. 2 vols. Das Deutsche Reich und der Zweite Weltkrieg 5. Stuttgart: Deutsche Verlags-Anstalt, 1988–99.

Krstić, Miloš. *Nepokorena mladost: koncentracioni logor u Smederevskoj Palanci 1942–1944*. Belgrade: Vuk Karadzić, 1981.

Kulić, Dimitrije. *Bugarska okupacija Srbije, 1941–1944*. 2 vols. Belgrade: Justicija, 1992–93.

Kuprešanin, Veljko, ed. *Banjica*. Belgrade: Istorijski arhiv Beograda, 1967.

———, ed. *Revolucionarni likovi Beograda*. Belgrade: Istorijski arhiv grada Beograda, 1967.

Lampe, John R. *Yugoslavia as History: Twice There Was a Country*. New York: Cambridge University Press, 2000.

Lašić-Vasojević, Milija M. *Enemies on All Sides: The Fall of Yugoslavia*. Washington, D.C.: North American International, 1976.

Latas, Branko, ed. *Saradnja četnika Draže Mihailoviča sa okupatorima i ustašama (1941–1945). Dokumenti.* Belgrade: Društvo za istinu o antifašističkoj narodnooslobodilačkoj borbi 1941–1945, 1999.

Laub, Thomas Johnston. *After the Fall: German Policy in Occupied France, 1940–1944.* New York: Oxford University Press, 2013.

Lebel, Jennie. *Until "the Final Solution": The Jews in Belgrade 1521–1942.* Bergenfield, N.J.: Avotaynu, 2007.

Lemkin, Raphael. *Axis Rule in Occupied Europe: Laws of Occupation, Analysis of Government, Proposals for Redress.* Washington, D.C.: Carnegie Endowment for International Peace, 1944.

Ljotić, Dmitrije V. *U revoluciji i ratu.* Munich: Iskra, 1961.

———. *Light of Truth: Selected Philosophical, Moral, and Political Ideas of Dimitrije Ljotić.* Birmingham, U.K.: Lazarica Press, 1986.

Löwenthal, Zdenko, ed. *The Crimes of the Fascist Occupants and Their Collaborators against Jews in Yugoslavia.* Belgrade: Federation of Jewish Communities of the FPRY, 1957.

Lumans, Valdis O. *Himmler's Auxiliaries: The Volksdeutsche Mittelstelle and the German National Minorities of Europe, 1933–1945.* Chapel Hill: University of North Carolina Press, 1993.

Macura, Ljubica. "List 'Borba' o oslobodilačkoj borbi u Jugoslaviji i situacjiji u svetu 1941. godine." In Kačavenda et al., *Užički kraj u jesen ratne 1941*, 161–68.

Madajczyk, Czesław. *Polityka III Rzeszy w okupowanej Polsce 1939–1945.* 2 vols. Warsaw: Państwowe Wydawnictwo Naukowe, 1970.

———. "'Restserbien' unter deutscher Militärverwaltung." In *The Third Reich and Yugoslavia 1939–1945*, ed. Života Anić et al., 458–76. Belgrade: Institute for Contemporary History, 1977.

———. *Faszyzm i okupacje 1938–1945: wykonywanie okupacji przez Państwa Osi w Europie.* 2 vols. Poznań: Wydawnictwo Poznańskie, 1983.

Magaš, Branka. *Croatia through History: The Making of a European State.* London: Saqi Books, 2007.

Manoschek, Walter. *"Serbien ist judenfrei": Militärische Besatzungspolitik und Judenvernichtung in Serbien 1941/42.* Munich: R. Oldenbourg Verlag, 1993.

———. "Die Vernichtung der Juden in Serbien." In *Nationalsozialistische Vernichtungspolitik, 1939–1945: Neue Forschungen und Kontroversen*, ed. Herbert Ulrich, 209–34. Frankfurt am Main: Fischer Taschenbuch Verlag GmbH, 1998.

———. "The Extermination of the Jews in Serbia." In *Nationalist Socialist Extermination Policies: Contemporary German Perspectives and Controversies*, ed. Ulrich Herbert, 163–84. New York: Berghahn Books, 2000.

Marjanović, Jovan. "The German Occupation System in Serbia in 1941." In *Les systèmes d'occupation en Yougoslavie 1941–1945: Rapports au 3e Congrès international sur l'histoire de la résistance européenne à Karlovy Vary, les 2–4 septembre 1963*, ed. Petar Brajović, Jovan Marjanović, and Franjo Tuđman, 263–301. Belgrade: Institut pour l'étude du movement, 1963.

———, with collaboration of Mihailo Stanišić. *The Collaboration of D. Mihailović's Chetniks with the Enemy Forces of Occupation (1941–1944)*. Belgrade: Arhivski pregled, 1976.

———. "The Neubacher Plan and Practical Schemes for the Establishment of a Greater Serbian Federation (1943–1944)." In *The Third Reich and Yugoslavia 1939–1945*, ed. Života Anić et al., 486–501. Belgrade: Institute for Contemporary History, 1977.

Marković, Dragan. *Zabranjeni život (Beograd 1941–1944)*. Belgrade: Nolit, 1956.

Marković, Moma. *Rat i revolucija u Srbiji (Sečanja 1941–1945)*. Belgrade: Beogradski izdavačko-grafički zavod, 1987.

Mazower, Mark. *Hitler's Empire: How the Nazis Ruled Europe*. New York: Penguin Press, 2008.

Mešterović, Julka. *Lekarev dnevnik*. Belgrade: Vojnoizdavački zavod, 1968.

Mihailović, Ariton. *Uspomene iz okupacije*. Belgrade: Narodna knjiga/Alfa, 2004.

Milazzo, Matteo J. *The Chetnik Movement and the Yugoslav Resistance*. Baltimore, Md.: Johns Hopkins University Press, 1975.

Milinčević, Stjepan. *Ħronika moga vremena*. 2 vols. Belgrade: Izdanje autora, 1952–55.

Milosavljević, Olivera. *Potisnuta istina: kolaboracija u Srbiji 1941–1944*. Belgrade: Zagorac, 2006.

Milošević, Slobodan D. *Izbeglice i preseljenici na teritorij okupirane Jugoslavije 1941–1945. godine*. Belgrade: IRO Narodna knjiga-Institut za savremenu istoriju, 1981.

Minić, Milos. *Oslobodilački ili građanski rat u Jugoslaviji 1941–1945*. Novi Sad: Agencija Mir & IP Cvetnik, 1993.

Mirčetić, Dragoljub. "Niški koncentracioni logor i streljanje na Bubnju." *Leskovački zbornik* 12 (1972): 105–16.

Miša, Branislav Popov. *Nemački zatvori i koncentracioni logori u Banatu, 1941–1944*. Belgrade: Institut za savremenu istoriju, 1992.

Mitrović, Dragomir. "Mere nemaca za razbijanje ustaničke opsade Kraljeva 1941. godine sa pravca Kruševca." In Jončić et al., *Narodni ustanak i borbe za Kraljevo 1941*, 629–40.

Mitrović, R. "Sudbina jevreja u krajevima gde su folksdojčeri preuzeli vlast aprila 1941." *Jevrejski istorijski muzej* 2 (1973): 265–72.

Mitrovski, Boro, Venceslav Glišić, and Tomo Ristovski. *The Bulgarian Army in Yugoslavia 1941–1945*. Belgrade: Međunarodna politika, 1971.

Momčilović-Brkica, Đorđe. *Banat u narodnooslobodilačkom ratu*. Belgrade: Vojnoizdavački zavod, 1977.

Neubacher, Hermann. *Sonderauftrag Südost 1940–1945: Bericht eines fliegenden Diplomaten*. Berlin: Musterschmidt Verlag, 1956.

Nikolić, Kosta. *Strah i nada u Srbiji, 1941–1944: svakodnevni život pod okupacijom.* Belgrade: Zavod za udžbenike i nastavna sredstva, 2002.

———. "Ravnogorskė hnuti a nemeckė okupacni sily v Srbsku v letech 1942–1944." *Slovanský Přehled* 90, no. 2 (2004): 249–74.

Parežanin, Ratko. *Drugi svetski rat i Dmitrije V. Ljotić.* Munich: Iskra, 1971.

Pavlović, Momčilo. "Srbija na kraju rata. Izveštaj majora Džona Henikera Mejdžora o Srbiji u periodu april–novembar 1944." *Istorija 20. veka: časopis Instituta za savremenu istoriju/History of 20. Century: Journal of the Institute of Contemporary History* 2, no. 2 (1996): 153–76.

Pavlowitch, Stevan K. *Serbia: The History behind the Name.* London: Hurst, 2002.

———. *Hitler's New Disorder: The Second World War in Yugoslavia.* London: Hurst, 2008.

Petranović, Branko. *Revolucija i kontrarevolucija u Jugoslaviji (1941–1945).* 2 vols. Belgrade: Izdavačka radna organizacija Rad, 1983.

———. *Srbija u drugom svetskom ratu, 1939–1945.* Belgrade: Vojnoizdavački i novinski centar, 1992.

Petrović, Dragoljub S. "Četnička organizacija Koste Pećanca u okupiranoj Srbiji do početka oktobra 1941." *Vojno-istorijski glasnik* 2 (1968): 173–205.

———. "Četnistvo Koste Pacanca u okupiranoj Srbiji 1941/1942 godine." *Istorijski glasnik* 1–2 (1983): 81–98.

Piekalkiewicz, Janusz. *Krieg auf dem Balkan 1940–1945.* Munich: Südwest Verlag, 1984.

Pintar, Olga Manojlović. "Delusion and Amnesia: Ideology and Culture in Nedić's Serbia." In Ramet and Listhaug, *Serbia and the Serbs in World War Two*, 93–108.

Pisarev, Iu. A. "Serbia." In *Za balkanskimi frontami Pervoi mirovoi voiny*, ed. V. N. Vinogradov, 135–41. Moscow: Izdatel'stvo Indrik, 2002.

Popović, Nebojša. *Jevreji u Srbiji 1918–1941.* Belgrade: Institut za Savremenu Istoriju, 1997.

Pospieszalski, K. M. "Nazi Terror in Poland 1939–1945." *Polish Western Affairs* 5, no. 1 (1964): 61–95.

Radanovic, Milan. *Kazna i zločin: Snage kolaboracije u Srbiji: odgovornost za ratne zločine (1941–1944) i vojni gubici (1944–1945).* Belgrade: Rosa Luxemburg Stiftung; Regionalna kancelarija za jugoistočnu Evropu, 2015, in http://www.rosalux.rs/sites/default/files/attachments/current_events/Kazna%20i%20zlocin_1.pdf (accessed May 9, 2016).

Radziwończyk, Kazimierz. "Rola i specyfika terroru fizycznego w hitlerowskim systemie walki z ruchem oporu na okupowanych ziemiach polskich w latach 1939–1945." In *Zbrodnie i sprawcy: ludobójstwo hitlerowskie przed sądem ludzkości i historii*, ed. Czesław Pilichowski, 238–56. Warsaw: Państwowe Wydawnictwo Naukowe, 1980.

Rakić, Hranislav A. *Teror i zločini okupatora i domaćih izdajnika u leskovačkom i vranjskom kraju 1941–1944.* Leskovac: Narodni muzej u Leskovcu, 1986.

Ramet, Sabrina P. *The Three Yugoslavias: State-Building and Legitimation, 1918–2005*. Bloomington: Indiana University Press, 2006.

———. Introduction. In Ramet and Listhaug, *Serbia and the Serbs in World War Two*, 1–16.

Ramet, Sabrina P., and Ola Listhaug, eds. *Serbia and the Serbs in World War Two: Collaboration and Resistance.* New York: Palgrave Macmillan, 2011.

Ramet, Sabrina P., and Sladjana Lazić. "The Collaborationist Regime of Milan Nedić." In Ramet and Listhaug, *Serbia and the Serbs in World War Two*, 17–43.

Ratković, Miodrag. "Organizacija istočne Srbije." In Kalabić, *Ravnogorska istorija*, 291–99.

Reitlinger, Gerald. *The House Built on Sand: The Conflicts of German Policy in Russia 1939–1945*. New York: Viking Press, 1960.

Rings, Werner. *Life with the Enemy: Collaboration and Resistance in Hitler's Europe 1939–1945*. New York: Doubleday, 1982.

Ristanović, Jelena. "Ustanak i revolucionarne tradicije." In Kačavenda et al., *Užički kraj u jesen ratne 1941*, 41–45.

Ristović, Milan. "General M. Nedić—Diktatur, Kollaboration und die patriarchalische Gesselschaft Serbiens 1941–1944." In *Autoritäre Regime in Ostmittel- und Südosteuropa 1919–1944*, ed. Erwin Oberländer et al., 633–88. Padeborn: Ferdinand Schöningh, 2001.

———. "Die Flüchtlinge und ihre Verbündeten: Solidarität und Hilfe in Serbien 1941–1944." In *Solidarität und Hilfe für Juden während der NS-Zeit: Regionalstudien 4 Slowakei, Bulgarien, Serbien, Kroatien mit Bosnien und Herzegowina, Belgien, Italien*, ed. Wolfgang Benz and Juliane Wetzel, 99–155. Berlin: Metropol, 2004.

———. *Niemački novi poredak i jugoistočna Evropa 1940/41–1944/45*. Belgrade: Službeni Glasnik, 2005.

———. "Zwangsmigrationen in den Territorien Jugoslawiens im Zweiten Weltkrieg: Pläne, Realisierung, Improvisation, Folgen." In *Zwangsmigrationen im mittleren und östlichen Europa: Völkerrecht, Konzeptionen, Praxis (1938–1950)*, ed. Ralph Melville, Jiři Pešek, and Claus Scharf, 309–30. Mainz: Von Zabern, 2007.

———. "The Persecuted and Their Abettors: Solidarity and Help for the Jews in Serbia 1941–1944." In *Izraelsko-srpska naučna razmena u proučavanju Holokausta: Zbornik radova s naučnog skupa, Jerusalem—Jad Vashem, 15–20. jun 2006*, ed. Krinka Vidaković Petrov, Jovan Čulibrk, Silvana Haci-Čokić, and Jovan Mirković, 209–55. Belgrade: Muzej žrtava genocida, 2008.

Roberts, Walter R. *Tito, Mihailović and the Allies, 1941–1945*. Durham, N.C.: Duke University Press, 1987.

Romano, Jaša. *Jevreji Jugoslaviji, 1941–1945: žrtve genocida i učesnici NOR*. Belgrade: Savez jevrejskih opština Jugoslavije, 1980.

Roschwald, "Europe's Civil Wars, 1941–1949." In *The Oxford Handbook of European History, 1914–1945*, ed. Nicholas Doumanis, 537–54. Oxford: Oxford University Press, 2016.

Roš, Fran. *Slovenski izgnanci v Srbiji 1941–1945*. Maribor: Založba Obzorja, 1967.

Rothschild, Joseph. *East Central Europe between the Two World Wars*. Seattle: University of Washington Press, 1974.

Rutar, Sabine. "Employment of Labour in Wartime Serbia: Social History and the Politics of Amnesia." In Ramet and Listhaug, *Serbia and the Serbs in World War Two*, 46–69.

Savković, Miroslav. *Kinematografija u Srbiji tokom Drugog svetskog rata 1941–1945*. Belgrade: Fakultet dramskih umetnosti—Institut za pozorište, film, radio i televiziju, 1994.

Schlarp, Karl-Heinz. *Wirtschaft und Besatzung in Serbien, 1941–1944: ein Beitrag zur nationalsozialistischen Wirtschaftspolitik in Südosteuropa*. Stuttgart: F. Steiner Verlag Wiesbaden, 1986.

Schmider, Klaus. *Partisanenkrieg in Jugoslawien 1941–1944*. Hamburg-Berlin-Bonn: Verlag E. S. Mittler & Sohn GmbH, 2002.

———. Foreword. In Shepherd and Pattinson, *War in a Twilight World*, 181–88.

Seckendorf, Martin, and Günter Keber. *Die Okkupationspolitik des deutschen Faschismus in Jugoslawien, Griechenland, Albanien, Italien und Ungarn (1941–1945)*. Berlin: Hüthig, 1992.

Sekelj, Laslo. "Anti-Semitism in Yugoslavia, 1918–1945." *East European Quarterly* 22, no. 2 (1988): 159–72.

Shelach, Menachem. "Sajmište—An Extermination Camp in Serbia." *Holocaust and Genocide Studies* 2, no. 2 (1987): 243–60.

Shepherd, Ben. "With the Devil in Titoland: A Wehrmacht Anti-Partisan Division in Bosnia-Herzegovina, 1943." *War in History* 16, no. 1 (2009): 77–97.

———. "Bloodier than Boehme: The 342nd Infantry Division in Serbia, 1941." In Shepherd and Pattinson, *War in a Twilight World*, 189–209.

———. "Introduction: Illuminating a Twilight World." In Shepherd and Pattinson, *War in a Twilight World*, 1–24.

Shepherd, Ben, and Juliette Pattinson, eds. *War in a Twilight World: Partisan and Anti-Partisan Warfare in Eastern Europe, 1939–45*. New York: Palgrave Macmillan, 2010.

———. *Terror in the Balkans: German Armies and Partisan Warfare*. Cambridge, Mass.: Harvard University Press, 2012.

Shimizu, Akiko. *Die deutsche Okkupation des serbischen Banats 1941–1944 unter besonderer Berücksichtigung der deutschen Volksgruppe in Jugoslawien*. Münster: Lit-verlag, 2003.

Simeunović, Dragan. "Relations between Germany and Serbia (Yugoslavia)." In *Germany and Southeastern Europe—Aspects of Relations in the Twentieth Century/Deutschland und Südosteuropa—Aspekte der Beziehungen im Zwanzigsten Jahrhundert*, ed. Roland Schönfeld, 71–82. Munich: Südosteuropa-Gesellschaft, 1997.

Slavin, G. M. "Yugoslaviia: pobedy i porazheniia povstantsev." In *Dvizhenie soprotivleniia v stranakh central'noi i iugo-vostochnoi Evropy 1939–1945*, ed. V. V. Mar'ina, 128–52. Moscow: Radiks, 1995.

Slijepčević, Đoko. *Istorija Srpske pravoslavne crkve.* 3 vols. Munich: Iskra, 1986.

Stanković, Siniša. "Sećanja iz Banjičkog logora i zatvora u Dušinoj ulici." In *Otpor u žicama: sećanja zatočenika*, ed. Dušan Azanjac, Ivo Frol, and Đorđe Nikolić, 1:95–107. Belgrade: Vojnoizdavacki zavod, 1969.

Stefanović, Mladen. *Zbor Dimitrija Ljotiča 1934–1945.* Belgrade: Narodna knjiga, 1984.

Stevanović, Dragomir S. *Sura grobnica: "Prihvatni logor Zemun," 1942–44.* London: Savez Oslobodjenje, 1967.

Stojiljković, Miroslav. "Bugarska kao saveznica sila Osovine u okupaciji Srbije 1941–1944." In Avramovski et al., *Jugoslovensko-bugarski odnosi u XX veku*, 2:249–311.

Strazhas, A. *Deutsche Ostpolitik im Ersten Weltkrieg: Der Fall Ober Ost 1915–1917.* Wiesbaden, Germany: Harrassowitz Verlag, 1993.

Strugar, Vlado. "Sistem Bugarske okupacjie u Jugoslovenskim oblastima (1941–1944)." In Avramovski et al., *Jugoslovensko-bugarski odnosi u XX veku*, 1:251–93.

———. *Iugoslaviia v ogne voiny, 1941–1945.* Moscow: Nauka, 1985.

Sundhaussen, Holm. "Improvisierte Ausbeutung—der Balkan unter deutscher Okkupation." In *Das organisierte Chaos: "Ämterdarwinismus" und "Gesinnungsethik": Determinanten nationalsozialistischer Besatzungsherrschaft*, ed. Gerhard Otto and Johannes Houwink ten Gate, 55–75. Berlin: Metropol Verlag, 1999.

———. *Geschichte Serbiens 19.–21. Jahrhundert.* Vienna: Böhlau Verlag, 2007.

Swain, Geoffrey. "The Comintern and Southern Europe, 1938–1943." In Judt, *Resistance and Revolution in Mediterranean Europe*, 29–53.

Terzić, Velimir, et al. *Oslobodilački rat naroda Jugoslavije 1941–1945.* 2 vols. Belgrade: Vojni Istoriski Institut Jugoslovenske Narodne Armije, 1957.

Tomasevich, Jozo. *Peasants, Politics, and Economic Change in Yugoslavia.* Stanford, Calif.: Stanford University Press, 1955.

———. *War and Revolution in Yugoslavia, 1941–1945: The Chetniks.* Stanford, Calif.: Stanford University Press, 1975.

———. *War and Revolution in Yugoslavia, 1941–1945: Occupation and Collaboration.* Stanford, Calif.: Stanford University Press, 2001.

Topalović, Živko. *Srbija pod Dražom.* London: Institut za savremenu istoriju, 2004.

Tripković, Đoko. "Izveštaj generala F. Maklejna—'Beograd pod partizanima.'" *Istorija 20. veka: časopis Instituta za savremenu istoriju//History of 20. Century: Journal of the Institute of Contemporary History* 1 (1987): 175–95.

Umbreit, Hans. "Die Rolle der Kollaboration in der deutschen Besatzungspolitik." In *Okkupation und Kollaboration (1938–1945): Beiträge zu Konzepten und Praxis der Kollaboration in der deutschen Okkupationspolitik*, ed. Werner Röhr, 33–44. Berlin: Hüthig Verlagsgemeinschaft, 1994.

———. "Zur Organisation der Besatzungsherrschaft." In *Das organisierte Chaos: "Ämterdarwinismus" und "Gesinnungsethik": Determinanten nationalsozialistischer Besatzungsherrschaft*, ed. Gerhard Otto and Johannes Houwink ten Gate, 35–54. Berlin: Metropol Verlag, 1999.

Vegh, Sandor. "Le système du pouvoir d'occupation Allemand dans le Banat Yougoslave 1941–1944." In *Les systémes d'occupation en Yougoslavie 1941–1945: Rapports au 3e Congrès international sur l'histoire de la résistance européenne à Karlovy Vary, les 2–4 septembre 1963*, ed. Petar Brajović, Jovan Marjanović, and Franjo Tuđman, 495–561. Belgrade: Institut pour l'étude du movement, 1963.

Višnjić, Perica M. "Nemački okupacioni system u Srbiji 1941 godine." *Istorijski glasnik* 3–4 (1956): 84–92.

Višnjić, Petar. "Borbe u Srbiji za vreme bitke na Sutjesci." *Vojno-istorijski glasnik* 9, no. 2/3 (1958): 103–16.

———. *Operacije za oslobođenje istočne Srbije jun–oktobar 1944*. Zaječar: Istorijski arhiv Timočka krajina, 1985.

Vučković, Zvonimir. *A Balkan Tragedy, Yugoslavia, 1941–1946: Memoirs of a Guerilla Fighter*. Boulder, Colo.: East European Monographs, 2004.

Vujošević, Ubavka. *Tito u Beogradu (1926–1944)*. Belgrade: Jugoslovenska kniga, 1977.

Wheeler, Mark. "Pariahs to partisans to power: The Communist Party of Yugoslavia." In Judt, *Resistance and Revolution in Mediterranean Europe*, 110–56.

Wuescht, Johann. *Jugoslawien und das Dritte Reich: Eine dokumentierte Geschichte der deutsch-jugoslawischen Beziehungen von 1933 bis 1945*. Stuttgart: Seewald Verlag, 1969.

Zločini fašističkih okupatora i njihovih pomagača protiv Jevreja u Jugoslaviji. Belgrade: Federation of the Yugoslav Jewish communities, 1952.

Žerjavić, Vladimir. *Population Losses in Yugoslavia 1941–1945*. Zagreb: Dom & Svijet, 1997.

Živković, Nikola. "Kontribucije u Srbiji 1941–1944." *Vojno-istorijski glasnik* 1 (1970): 185–206.

———. *Ratna šteta koju je Nemačka učinila Jugoslaviji u drugom svetskom ratu*. Belgrade: Institut za savremenu istoriju i NIP Export-Press, 1975.

———. *Ratna šteta koju je Bugarska učinila Jugoslaviji 1941–1944*. Belgrade: Institut za savremenu istoriju, 1985.

Zorkić, Sretenije. "Teror u Beogradu za vreme neprijatelske okupacije." *Godišnjak grada Beograda* 6 (1959): 459–97.

Index

ALEXANDER PRUSIN is a professor of history at the New Mexico Institute of Mining and Technology. He is the author of *The Lands Between: Conflict in the Eastern European Borderlands, 1870–1992* and *Nationalizing a Borderland: War, Ethnicity, and Anti-Jewish Violence in East Galicia, 1914–1920*.

The History of Military Occupation

An Imperfect Occupation: Enduring the South African War *John Boje*
Mussolini's Army in the French Riviera: Italy's Occupation of France *Emanuele Sica*
Last Outpost on the Zulu Frontiers: Fort Napier and the British Imperial Garrison *Graham Dominy*
The British Army of the Rhine: Turning Nazi Enemies into Cold War Partners *Peter Speiser*
Serbia under the Swastika: A World War II Occupation *Alexander Prusin*

The University of Illinois Press
is a founding member of the
Association of American University Presses.

Composed in 10.5/13
with Minion Pro display
by Lisa Connery
at the University of Illinois Press
Cover designed by Dustin J. Hubbart
Cover illustration: People of Belgrade demonstrate their support for breaking with the Tripartite Pact, March 27, 1941. Digital Library of Slovenia.
Manufactured by Sheridan Books, Inc.

University of Illinois Press
1325 South Oak Street
Champaign, IL 61820-6903
www.press.uillinois.edu